MOON POWER STARGUIDE 2006

Yearly Edition

****

Dr. Louis Turi, M.D.S.

Startheme Publications Inc.

4411 N. 23Rd St Phoenix, AZ 85016

Prepress by www.Bookwarren.com

Permission to use book cover artwork from Rubberball Productions - Royalty Free 3-D Stock Volume I and composed by Martin Hodgson

ISBN: 0-974520-97-7

Published by Startheme Publications Inc.

MOON POWER STARGUIDE 2006

Special 2006 Issue Limited Edition
Produced June 2005

Printed in the United States of America

Visit our website: www://drturi.com

E-mail: Dr. Turi@cox.net

Table of Contents

UNIVERSAL GUIDANCE AND PREDICTIONS

"He is wise who understands that the stars are luminaries, created as signs. He who will conquer the stars will hold the golden keys to God's mysterious universe."

— Nostradamus

Acknowledgments

Special thanks are given to all my great friends and family, faithful clients, students and readers from all over the world. A special thanks to George Noory Coat To Coast radio Host and the numerous open-minded people I known, friends, journalists and worldwide hosts of radio and television programs. I am grateful to all of those spiritual men and women who have helped me enlighten their lives and audiences with the knowledge of the stars. I appreciate all those souls who have guided and supported my work. In their common efforts to further the truth they all are vital participants in the understanding of the human experience. All of you have been invaluable in furthering the truth, and I am infinitely grateful for allowing me to pass on my celestial message to the world.

My Story

Dreamer, Slacker, Head in the Clouds, Stargazer, I am sure that we have all heard those terms, but none rang so clear in my head as "Stargazer." I am not in the strictest sense of the word a Stargazer but I do read the messages that they have left indelibly across men's souls. Now, I did not start out in life with this intent. No way, I was going to be a big rock-and-roll star. That's right. I went to the Royal School of Music and began the long process of mastering the piano. My teacher said that I would be great but you never believe that kind of thing until it actually happens. I still had to work to pay for my studies and I worked hard as a barman for a prestigious hotel. This job suited me well; I was young and full of life and I got to meet new people all the time and make just enough money to pay for my studies and a pint of lager at the end of the day. But when I wasn't working, I practiced my piano until my fingers bled. All the while wishing I still had my guitar, but a gang that hung out in the Victoria Station metro after dark had stolen it from me. These days in 1974 were very hard and surviving was my full time job then. In my new book "You Are God" all my peripheries and incredible experiences are divulged and I am sure, barely believable for some of my readers. This book is in the process of being turned into a movie. Please join my newsletter to find out all about my life and busy career.

Before I was able to get a job and a piano teacher, I had to survive in a new country I did not speak the language, and being a Frenchman, English was a real twist. So I started out in the tubes singing French songs and making a few pence a day to able to eat. Incidentally, my first English words came to me as I went shopping for my first dinner. I scanned the shelves in the store until I found the cheapest thing that I could. It came out of a can and was cold and crunchy but it filled my belly. After eating, I got out my little French-to-English dictionary and looked up to words, "Dog" and "Food." You can imagine my disgust when I found out what this meant, but I was lucky I got to eat that day. When there was a lull in the metro I would run up the steps and be right at Victoria Station, a huge and busy place with a whole bank of telephones. I would run up and down, listening for someone who spoke my native tongue. I finally found a Swiss man who spoke both English and French who gave me a job in the hotel. I started out as a janitor and moved up to dishwasher and finally to barman after much work. I was to stay in England for almost ten years as I worked and studied my music. Finally, I graduated at the top of my class ahead of four hundreds students earning the prized "Distinction Cup" and commendation from some faraway Royal family members. This led me to a deal, not a good deal but still a deal with Phillips Phonogram records in my own country in France. I produced several records and then went back to home to promote them for a while, glad to leave the harsh English weather behind. Incredible experiences breed incredible people and for many years I was reluctant to even mention the following; not knowing more was to happen to me later on in my life. But I am the truth and all that I promote is the future and why shouldn't I share the incredible with others? In the name of fear, ignorance or jealousy, I also quickly realized that the world was not exactly ready for my incredible experiences and me. After all a magnet will not attract a piece of wood, I deal with the future, promote and explore the future, thus things from the future are a part of my life and my incredible experiences with UFO are very real.

In those days, my older brother Georges owned a discotheque at the time called L'Interdit or The Forbidden. It was quite the hot spot, and he asked me to come and do my songs there. I gladly accepted the invitation and we left his farmhouse about forty-five minutes from his place about 9:00 p.m. While driving through the deserted roads by the vineyards in a cold November night in 1981, I saw lights flashing out in the vineyards and remarked to my brother that there were people in the vineyards harvesting. He looked at like I had lost my mind, "Louis," he said, "its November, all the grapes have been picked a long time ago!" I then watched the lights come closer and closer until our car was bathed in light so bright that we could not see, and my brother's brand-new Mercedes stalled right there in the middle of the road and would not restart. We both had our noses to the windscreen trying to see this thing in the air. It was showering us in light, but it was still too bright. I got out of the car, and then the lights dimmed down in the car, with my brother still in it. This left him scared to death, and me outside swathed in a reddish pink light with a pleasing glow, that came from none other than a Spaceship or UFO suspended about thirty feet above our heads It stayed there for at least five minutes, and it made a slight humming sound. It was beautiful, with multi-colored lights all around it that couldn't be seen, while its two main bright white headlights were on.

It just hung there in the sky for our viewing pleasure just out of reach. We stared in awe, me banging on the car, yelling and cursing for all I was worth for my brother to get out of the car, but he wouldn't. So much for being a big bad guy is he? Big brothers, what do you expect! Finally, it just flew away, careless as you please and we watched as it picked up speed and disappeared. When I got back into the car, my brother swore me to secrecy that "We would never tell anyone about this ever!" When we arrived at the disco that night everything was in full swing. This is very strange because we should have arrived with the crew who was opening; looking back I would say that we had a missing-in-time thing happen, but we didn't know anything about that back then, just that it was really strange.

The next day, my mother called me and asked if my brother was okay. I laughed, remembering the secrecy deal and assured my mom everything was fine. Which it was, but my soul had somehow changed and I began to think that there was more to life than singing and making records. Maybe I could make a greater contribution, I didn't know what yet, but I wanted something. It didn't take me long to get the wanderlust again, and I was off to America. With a dream in my heart just a few short years before, I had written a song about this great land. Now I was going. I didn't know anybody and didn't have any money, because it turns out my contract had my music playing everywhere in Europe except my own country, and I couldn't collect my share.

Oh, the trials of youth! But I had high hopes and a business card from a man I met in London who said, "Come to America, I will help you start a new life!" I arrived in Los Angeles, the City of Angels, smoggy and yucky, caught a Greyhound bus to San Diego, gorgeous and green got out my little wallet with fifty dollars and the business card searching for the business on Garnet Avenue in Pacific Beach, California. I am still looking for this man and his business. Disheartened, I took thirty of my precious dollars and paid for a motel for the night, and then went to a bar up the street. I ordered a drink and then went to the cigarette machine. Weird thing never saw one of those before, I couldn't figure out how to work it. So I asked a man at the end of the bar if he could help me out. He looked at me funny for a minute or two and then showed me how it worked. Later he told me why the odd gaze; he thought I was gay and that this was a come-on! This man's name is John Steward and he became one of my best friends. We got drunk and found two beautiful girls soon after, what a start!

I thought I might as well, didn't know what the future would hold, but I still held a shiny bit of enthusiasm in my soul. Sadly enough, years later after an accident, fate turned him from a very wealthy attorney, into a homeless. I had predicted this for him in Hawaii, upon one of his numerous visits. Life's experiences are dramatic in nature and when the moon resides in a water sign, usually the past, guilt and depression follow. That's why I decided to write this book annually to help those in need to face their challenges.

I had begun to learn the ways of the great Cosmic Clock then and knew that I arrived on American soil during a great trend! When I awoke the next morning, I went up the street with my suitcase in one hand and a purse in the other. In France it is customary for men to carry purses. This may be another reason why John looked at me funny, as that is definitely not the custom here. I smelt the ocean and took off in that direction; the waves crashing against the shore were soothing to my nerves, but seeing the girls wearing tops was more culture shock for me. I spent another dollar or two of my precious money getting a cup of coffee and then grabbed a newspaper, The La Jolla Light. I needed a place to stay and found a section called "Roommates." There was a great ad for a beautiful house on the ocean in La Jolla with a telephone number and an address. I called the lady up and told her that I was on my way. When I arrived with my suitcase, she remarked how fast and eager I was, with a worried look on her face.

She then explained that with two more guys like me, we would all be able to afford a beautiful home on the sea. Wow, new word for me, roommate. I explained my situation and she felt sorry for me, and said I could stay with her and tutor her daughter in French. Housing settled for the moment, I went to find a job. Up the street, I ran into a little restaurant called, "The French Gourmet." Soon I had my first job in America, washing dishes, not glamorous, but a job. Nice guy, my boss then, Michel Malecot. I worked for him for four years, laboring my way to general manager. I also soon moved into my very own apartment and in every spare minute I read and studied my new obsession: Astrology. I inhaled books and knowledge everywhere from the bible to heavy metaphysics.

I even painted the apartment that Michel gave me to oversee his catering department with my own astrological chart, the human body and which sign rules each part, as well as other pictures with UFOs prevalent in the bringing of knowledge. As I read, I continually went back to the books about Nostradamus and his works, as well as the books that the great man himself had written. He had a particular way of interpreting the stars that echoed down the valleys of my soul, totally free of mathematical jargon. His methods made much more sense than the other mathematical processes in every way, especially when the great Prophet did not have the luxury of a computer or even a watch then. I dedicated myself to his method for many years, and learned and learned, and then seemed to channel knowledge from the universe itself. When Michel came to collect his rent the first month and found his beautiful apartment all painted, you can imagine his shock, but I sat him down and said, "I want to give you a reading."

He was my first client! He is still a client today and one of my best friends in the US. I began to tell people about my passion and people began to come for readings. I had stopped working for Michel; I couldn't take the stress any longer. I went back to working in engineering, welding and heavy equipment, skills I had learned as a young boy from my stepfather. I worked on San Diego US base then Pearl Harbor in Hawaii then in 1991 my entire life changed following the ultimate UFO encounter with my ex-wife Brigitte. I painted my entire house with UFO drawings and astrological symbols and I could not stop reading and re-kindly the great Nostradamus' Divine Astrology methodology.

Years later with thousands of satisfied clients in all walks of life and hundreds of successful predictions I am still trying hard to further man's cosmic consciousness and sharpen his intuition by making obvious statements and premonitions in predictive astrology. Some of these were the destruction of the WTC in New York, the fall of Saddam Hussein, SARS break out, the Washington sniper, earthquakes, disasters, NASA failures and the Asia tsunami etc. Note also that the printing process in all my previous books make those premonitions totally unarguable.

Letter From the Author

2006: Happy New Year to all

6/25/2005

Dear Clients and Friends:

One more year has gone and 2006 is already here. The loss of my great friend and student Dave from Las Vegas was a terrible blow but surely it has been an incredibly difficult year for many other people. After a terrible heartache and two years to recuperate love entered my life again but for only a short period of time. Everything was against us in this relationship and while traveling in the UK she simply decided to move on. Well its was her decision to let me go and I collected my shattered heart again as to pay some old karma for the emotional pain I inflicted the many pretty girls of my past.

The war is still raging and as predicted in previous Starguide many young people lost their lives. Most of the world's population is undergoing a reevaluation of its religious, philosophical and spiritual values; especially following the July 7th surprise attack in the London and the September 11th WTC destruction by religious fanatics from the Middle East and Saddam Hussein regime as predicted a two year earlier is now completely dead. The tsunami disaster in Asia also made us aware how powerful Mother Nature really is and how vulnerable we all are. America is a great country but also a very young religious country going through metamorphosis where rules of the past do not apply any longer for the populations of the future.

Back home in France we had our one hundred year religious war where Protestants and Catholics alike in the name of ignorance, made it a full time job killing one another. Blame it all on deadly Pluto ruler of Scorpio (death/terrorism) going through the sign of Sagittarius (foreigners/religions) forcing the world to rise to a higher level of awareness.

> "Only two things are infinite, the universe and human stupidity, and I'm not sure about the former."
>
> — Albert Einstein

Many God fearing people were forced to realize that a bunch of religious lunatics from abroad, in the name of their own respective religion would cross the ocean and blew up trains in Spain, buses in London and fly planes into the twin towers in New York. Many are quick to judge the Muslims and their fanatic religious views but can the gullible Christians of this country auto analyze themselves and finally realize that any and all religions is a cancer to mankind spiritual growth. Allah, Buddha and Jesus are the leaders of the youngest and deadliest religions mankind's folly created by turning centuries of myths into a deceiving reality. None of those deities brought peace and harmony to this unsafe world but differences leading to continuous deadly religious wars. Love and most of all education of man's relationships with the Universal Mind will change this world, not religion.

As long as one is committed to the idea that the stars are something above the head, they will lack the eye of knowledge. (Fredrick Nietzsche)

In some ways, all those dramatic predicaments with religion and terrorism we all suffer are a form of wake up call to humankind, in respect to the promotion of any and all archaic beliefs. But the world is still young and the war is also taking place above in the haven as Uranus (the future, the US, technology, New Age) confronts Neptune (Middle-East, the past, religions, imagination, oil).

More shocking news are ahead of us and are produced by the explosive, surprising planet Uranus (shocking news, nuclear devices, the future) passage into the sign of Pisces (religion, Arabia, deception) and will slowly expose and transform the church from what it is today. Have the people of this country and other parts of the world finally realized that confining God to a multitude of churches, temples, synagogues destructive doctrines and deities is wrong? But how long will it take to disentangle over 2000 years of Neptune's deceiving powers and its religious jurisdiction upon this world?

Ignorance is evil and for all its purposes, positive and negative, religions ignore and avoid the teachings of the true manifestation of the creator through its own creation, the stars! And yes, astrology is against my religion I heard, what about those 3 Kings (astrologers?) following a bright Star? And how did the sailors promoting the good words of the Lord in the "Dark Ages" sail the ocean? By and with the help of the stars I presume. Too many people do not have enough common sense and many of them are simply religiously poisoned with doctrines to the point of spiritual numbness since childhood. Their true spirit sank into fears and ignorance as planned by a politically oriented and the extremely wealthy and well-organized church of your choice.

Back in 1991 on the Art Bell radio show I had made that awful prediction and said the words, "religious war in the US." But he and his audience did not hear me then. He didn't even believe me with a copy of my book sent to him certified with his name and my predictions printed (Art Bell - OFF THE AIR!) and an upcoming US religious war.

It all unfolded as predicted and printed in the book but no acknowledgement of the facts came from this very scared and devout man! Many people have had to endure drastic psychological and physical changes losing a loved one or a position. I must admit that the Dragon passage through any sign and house, or its location at birth, will always bring an incredible positive or negative energy to that area and will induce the badly needed changes. Better be aware of its impact by sign and house and most of all get ready emotionally and financially for the imposed challenges. To learn more about YOUR specific Dragon and for all signs and houses of the Zodiac, you may order or download "The Power Of The Dragon" any of my books from my site at http://drturi.com/. Never forget that ignorance is evil and knowledge is power.

...Perhaps there is a pattern set up in the heavens for one who desires to see it, and having seen it, to find one in himself – (Plato)

The Dragon's Head (Aries) and Tail (Libra) moved on December 26, 2004 and will be in both signs until June 22nd, 2006 and like 2005, the year 2006 will be nothing less than VERY dramatic for many of us and the world at large. The Dragon stays nearly 2 years or so in both sign then after June 2006 The Head of the Dragon will move into the sign of Pisces and the Tail into the sign of Virgo. You may learn more about the dragon by visiting my site at or better read the five hundreds pages book titled "The Power Of The Dragon".

More than ever take a chance on me and order your 90-mn Full Life Reading and learn about this crucial celestial Dragon move. Your very mental or financial survival may well depend on the awareness of how this Dragon's Head and Tail will cause dramatic changes in your own life. Go to www.drturi.com and order it now and most of all be patient as I am extraordinarily busy.

Many of our experiences have brought us more knowledge and much more new strength. The firmament of the new millennium is already upon us and with this New Year, various opportunities and new tasks are ahead of us. Whatever you had to go through last year, learn to promote only positive thoughts. There is no room for the sorrows of the past in your future, and whatever you had to go

"When men realize the church is the Universe and the twelve apostles are a reflection of the twelve signs of the zodiac, Gods commandments written in light will bring true love, respect, and peace to this world." — Dr. Turi

through, the job of building a new life must be done. For every action, positive or negative, physical or spiritual, there will be an equal reaction. So, be aware of your thoughts, as your future starts right there. The reincarnation of your own very thoughts will sooner or later become your reality. No matter what you've been through, you must let go of the past, refine your thoughts, purify your spirit and keep working towards your goals.

Whether you realize it or not, progress was made towards some of your objectives. If, after all the hard work you completed, things got messed up, the universe may be trying to tell you something. Either you did not try hard enough, or the people you are working with do not have the same ethical aims as you. Possibly some of your wishes cannot be granted because of your limited working environment, lack of respect for the Universal Law, a limitation from your Astro-Carto Graphy location, or an inappropriate emotional relationship. Therefore, you were first fired or dismissed, allowing the universe to grant you the freedom and opportunity you needed to go in the right direction. Now, knowing it was a blessing that you've lost your job, someone you loved, etc., you must accept the challenge to start all over again with a positive attitude. It might sound strange at first to accept my theory, but subconsciously you actually did set the stage over the years. Look back with an objective mind; after all, those experiences were needed so that you ultimately could do the right thing for yourself.

You may also need to educate or trust yourself a bit more, or take more chances. Keep in mind the principle "for every action there will be a reaction," and that's called (good or bad) Karma. Are you willing to initiate the changes? If you do, the upcoming year will be a formidable year of accomplishment for you.

Offensive people may have mistreated you emotionally or financially and left you in a distressed situation. No matter what you experienced, you must go on with your life. This world is a teaching ground, and sometimes we learn lessons that may be harsh to deal with where we must feel the result of all our negative words and actions through pain and suffering. Exacting experiences seem to be the only way for humankind to burn karma and gain real knowledge. It is an inferno of passions and stress, well designed by God, to refine us from ignorance and destruction to the purest form of love and knowledge.

Before reincarnating yourself in this dense physical world, you have chosen a specific time in space. You also picked a set of stars (your natal chart), the country and city of your birth, as well as the souls who ultimately became your parents. You may not be aware of it just yet, but your karmic plan on this "hell" plane was chosen by you. Your soul's aim is to free itself from this low dimension and reach perfection to further its eternal purpose. What you are actually doing is furthering your cosmic consciousness, rising above all earthy vices and becoming a CO-creator with God.

Over the years, the experiences you suffered will consume some of that karmic debt and further the awareness of your purpose of immortality. Some precious people whom you loved have left you and moved on while others have been called to the great beyond and are now performing in another reality much closer to God. They will act as Guardian Angels and will always watch over you. By interacting with the Dynamics of our universe and conforming to the dialogue of God's will through the stars, man's karmic journey could be easier. My book, Moon Power Starguide was created for the purpose of assisting you to live your life in harmony with the cosmic will. This book will provide you with a day-to-day celestial guidance and genuine spiritual support.

Its content is healing, informative, entertaining and useful. In times of trouble, this work will touch you directly and give you solid direction and a means of divine support. The daily message of the stars will prepare you for your day and beyond. With patience and investigation, you will notice how much the planets affect you, others and your life in general. In this work, you will find cautionary and specific guidance for certain days. Just be aware of the dates and, most of all, listen and watch those around you. Like robots, your friends, parents, children, loved ones will respond to the tremendous pull of the stars. To the learned man, the daily celestial energy released upon the earth is obvious, and it shapes our thoughts and actions, vices and virtues. Teaching anyone to recognize and respect God's subtle tools is a large task. However, with education, time and observations, those who "ask, shall receive" cosmic knowledge.

The stars do not pick favorites, not you, me or anyone else, but, much as with everything in nature, and they simply do their jobs. As imposed by the Creator in its sublime celestial design, their task is to affect us to make us discover. Learning to interpret the universal mind will be beneficial to us all. Curiosity will bring the golden key to wisdom and further more cosmic consciousness upon the world. This fact changes lives, mostly because knowledge means power. The possibility of achieving the best, in promoting education, peace of mind, faith, love - a chance to experience genuine happiness. Over the years, Starguide's essence will help you to control the outcome of your destiny. Do not hesitate to offer Starguide to a loved one or a friend in need.

You are not just giving a book; you become a contributor of hope and enlightenment. You are empowering someone with a genuine piece of the Divine. You may also help us to set a weeklong crash course in Astropsychology, Kabalistic Healing or Astro-Tarot in your area and benefit from a free course for yourself. (See www.drturi.com for more info).

Lastly my new book "You Are God" will be available soon and dedicated to my good friend and student Dave Cree who passed away on July 7, 2005 in his sleep. This book is a reflection of my dramatic life experiences and will be made into a movie. This book is non-fiction and will make you aware of your direct relationship with the Divine and your utmost connection with your own subconscious creative forces and god himself.

Once more, thank you for your patronage and trust in my work.

Dr. Turi

> "Man is superior to the stars if he lives in the power of superior wisdom. Such a person being the master over heaven and earth by means of his will is a magus and magic is not sorcery but supreme wisdom"
>
> — Paracelsus

Starguide Purpose
2006 — Universal Guidance and Predictions

Starguide Universal Calendar of predictions is the result of thirty years of strenuous research into the architecture of our Universe. My findings will help you triumph over your daily challenges by identifying and obeying the Divine will of the cosmos. Starguide offers genuine guidance, positive growth and vital, daily information. Starguide offers the kind of support and direction you are looking for to achieve knowledge. The easy-to-read suggestions for each day of the year will get you started with the right attitude and expectations. Each period of time is empowering you with the Herculean will of the cosmos, thus, the opportunity to synchronize with the creative forces of the universe. Starguide will encourage and guide you to take positive steps to improve your world, and find love, a great career and financial security. This publication will correctly guide you each day of the year. It will give you the opportunity to avoid costly emotional or financial mishaps. Everything you need to know about any and all people's spiritual make up and forecast is in "Moon Power Starguide" and "Nostradamus Dragon Forecast for all Signs." This work will accurately translate the implacable rules of the universe into daily practical guidance. This physical world could not exist without its spiritual counterpart. Starguide's purpose is to help you to understand and respect God's universal laws.

You have been taught to drive and respect the physical laws of the road to avoid an accident. Moon Power Starguide will teach you the spiritual laws of the universe and will guide you all along the wonderful road of your life. Breaking the physical laws will bring heavy penalty! The same applies for God's celestial laws. Starguide is specifically designed to teach and remind you of those implacable Universal Laws. Finally, this publication will help you to conduct your life safely in both the physical and spiritual planes.

Important note: For years I produced and assembled much of this work by myself alone. Other people took the challenge to fix my grammar and phrasing and did an incredible job by making me look more professional in my writing. Even though it surely would look more professional my decision not to have Moon Power professionally edited for years was to make sure no one has changed the meaning of my work. Realize that my work is not for entertainment only and will accurately translate the ultimate will of the cosmos on a daily base.

— Dr. Turi

"When suffering is on all sides and man hungers for the unmanifested mystery in all phenomena: He seeks the reflection of the divine. God's higher truths are cloaked in his creation and the message is in the stars."

—Nostradamus

Moon Power – The Universal Law

Ancient Greek beliefs on the moon

Our closest satellite has often been linked with spirits of the deceased. The Greek mythology teaches that the moon was the focus point between Earth and Heaven. The ancients believed that spirits going to and from Heaven would stop upon the moon. Before entering the afterlife, the spirits would have their souls purified. On the way back to Mother Earth, through reincarnation, the spirits would go right to the face of the moon to receive their new physical bodies.

The Hindu texts "Upanishads" also states the advanced souls went to the moon after passing away to await reincarnation. Also stated is that the progressive souls who are untied from chain of reincarnation, will go straight to the sun. Many cultures associated the gods and goddesses with the moon and are represented with horns (Moses was a Lunar cult Leader fighting a Sun Stellar group, religious wars started in antiquity.)

Changes and growth is associated with the moon, due to its waxing and waning every 28 days...the moon expire and then is reborn for a new cycle.

The Greek philosopher Plutarch alleged that we have two ends. The first would take place on this world when our physical body expires. The physical body will then turned into dust, while the soul and the mind will journey into the spiritual world. There, the second death takes place, separating the mind and soul. The spirit would then return to the Moon, retaining all of that person life's memories. The mind would then journey to the Sun where it was absorbed into the light and then reborn. Lastly, the mind would return to the Moon, rejoin with the soul and then journey back to Earth for the eternal reincarnation process.

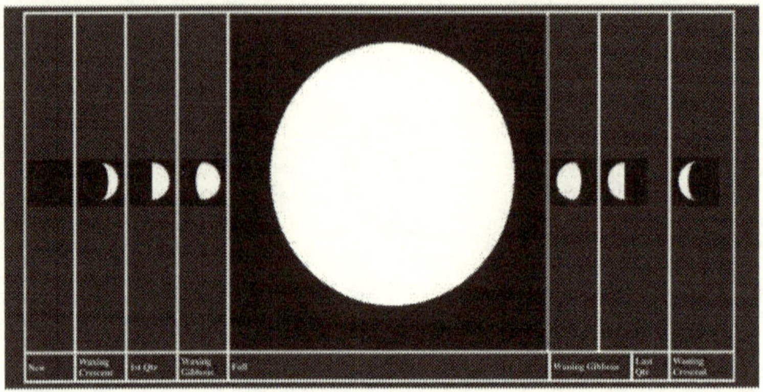

> "There is a tide in the affairs of men which, taken at the flood, leads on to fortune; omitted, all the voyage of their life is bound in shallows and in miseries."
>
> —Julius Caesar, Act IV, Scene iii

Every day that God has created, sees the procession of stars across the vault of the sky. They have followed the same regular path through the heavens, tracing the immutability of the cosmos and its constellations, which have spoken to the wise since the beginning of time. This work will explain in detail the subtle energy produced by the Moon's passage through the twelve houses and signs of the Zodiac. These houses govern the twelve facets of our life, and the rhythms of our life's cycle, our emotions, finances, consciousness, home, children, career, friends, wishes, fears, love, personality and all that goes to make our sorrows and joys. Depending on the mystical rhythm of the Moon and her relationship—-harmonious or discordant—-to the constellation and houses of the sky over which they rule, she will govern our human activity and give birth to our vices and virtues. The infinite and concealed dance of the Moon through the Zodiac is far from affecting only *you*, but all of us. You are a "microcosm" or a child of the Universe and there is reason for *you* to be. You are a part of this incredible physical and spiritual structure called a "macrocosm."

Sir Isaac Newton wrote "for every action there is an equal and opposite reaction". We are what we think, having become what we thought. This statement emphasizes that for every thought or action there will be an effect. This is what I call the "Universal Law," the causes and effects of the *yin* and *yang* recognized as the law of karma. The Moon is by herself quite responsible for some of the world and people's fate. By tracking the Universal Law and using the Moon Power's information, you will be allowed to see this lunar impact and reaction every day of your life. Obviously, the waxing and waning periods of our closest satellite will produce the daily process of tides. Thus, women will have spiritual and physical manifestations (menstruation), and all of us will be responding subconsciously to the word "lunatic." Without a form of opposition such as the Moon's fluctuations, there would be no reaction and thus no life possible on both the spiritual and physical planes.

> "Our so-called "dead" satellite is very much alive; she is the beating heart of the earth. Vigilantly observing her whereabouts will aid understanding of the psychology of man."
>
> — Dr. Turi

The Changing face of the Moon was revered and understood by the ancients as an aspect of the feminine and idolized as the Lady of the Night who ruled over fertility and magic. Your awareness of the Moon's passage through the Zodiac will enable you to discover a basic structure of energy patterns that underlies the changes and circumstances of your life. This is, indeed, the purpose of a good astrologer, and his main objective is to reveal an order or meaning beneath or within what often appears to be a random or chaotic situation. The Moon's passage through the housing system is one expression of the archetypal structure we call a cycle.

While many of the formally educated scientists have lost their cosmic consciousness, it has remained hidden within astrological values and basic astrological foundations. All of the signs of the Zodiac, the twelve houses, and the numerous astrological aspects are based upon God's higher order in the established, interstellar cycle. Their subtle meanings are derived from a particular place or negative affliction or function to each other's, and all operate within the ordered cycle as a whole. Our lives unfold according to our specific cyclic pattern, interacting with the Universal cycle. Discerning the Universal Mind at work is difficult; those gifted at birth will naturally understand the cosmic mind, using their inborn, intuitional and objective mental tools. However, when properly educated, anyone can learn to further his cosmic consciousness and realize his close relationship with God and the Universe. It often starts with a willingness to expand the consciousness and the simple realization: that which may be invisible to our senses nevertheless still exists. That's what makes a real scientist, investigation! Sadly enough, the majority of these souls fear ridicule or abandonment by their peers or churches.

The obvious structure of the Moon's cycle is derived from the fact that it consists of a beginning, middle and an end. Thus, the monthly lunar cycle suggests by observation that it is divided into two halves. During the first half, the movement is outward, as our close satellite travels away from the area of space occupied by the Sun. As this happens, the powerful light of the Sun increases, "waxing" (positive) on the white face of the Moon. The Full Moon symbolizes the turning point in it reverses motion. The Moon begins to approach the Sun as the reflected light on its surface "wanes" (negative), until they meet again at the New Moon (new start). Halfway between the New Moon and the Full Moon, we notice another important division point where light and darkness are equal on the moon's surface. At the first waxing quarter, the light is increasing, while at the last waning quarter, it is decreasing. These simple astronomical observations can only provide the scientist's mind with knowledge for interpreting the physical lunar cycle's phase. Now if the positive cannot be with the negative, and knowing that it takes "Two to Tango" for anything to be, then the scientist should be able to "investigate" the intuitional domain of this work. There was hidden truth beyond to this "lunar manifestation," and I then began to nurture my own critical observations. Later in life I realized that there was so much more beyond traditional star study (Astronomy).

As a child, I always thought of the moon to be something more than a dead satellite orbiting the earth. Many times in the darkness of the night, I found myself staring at her, wondering about her hidden power. She is the swiftest of the planets, passing through the 12 signs of the zodiac in about 28 days. I knew that eventually, I was to uncover her subtle ways and find the answers. To me, all those stars in the sky, shining above my head, were more than bright dead rocks in the darkest night. It does however; take more than our five senses to tap into her subtle manifestation upon our psyches and life in general. Nothing happens randomly in the universe, and the timely return in full each month surely indicates an ultimate order. Month after month, I patiently watched her becoming New and Full, and I learned my first, and one of the most important lesson in metaphysics, "The undiluted truth is not to be found inside man's limited world, but in other worlds and the Universal mind."

Being so close to the earth, the Moon's magnetic pull is so great, that she is solely responsible for the daily process of the tides. Curiosity, observation and comparison become the essential elements to promote anyone's cosmic consciousness. As I met her, becoming full and new, month after month, I slowly began to understand her powers. By constantly watching my environment, friends and family members, she began to speak about her clearly visible impact and control over man's psyche. As the years went by, I realized her uncompromising pull over the sea, and I became more aware of her powerful impact on our daily affairs. I made notes day after day, week after week and month after month, realizing the heavy consequences of either ignoring or adapting to her passage through the twelve signs of the Zodiac. I learned that the farmers of the past followed her fluctuations for the betterment of their crops. Then I carefully put my observations to test in my life and the lives of those around me. I did not take long to realize that by respecting the Universal Law, my life became much more productive. Her positive and negative affect on man's emotions, actions and reactions became so obvious to me that I decided to make it my full time job to tell others about her. As I watched the news in times of a full Moon, I understood why people became destructive, "lunatic," eccentric, moody and psychopathic. I then named it the Uncompromising Universal Law. Since then, as a professional Divine Astrologer, wherever I am needed, I am teaching the value of this simple and valuable knowledge.

When you first learned how to drive a car, you were carefully introduced to the rules of the road. You learned that you must stop at a red light or follow a road sign, as your very life depends on your doing so. These are the codes that you have learned, and they must be respected anywhere you happen to be in the world. Following established rules will take you safely wherever you have to go. Sadly enough, too many people do not respect these rules, and innocent people have died accidentally. Awareness, knowledge and respect of these rules are desperately needed. However, the spiritual rules established by God, written in the constellations, have been misplaced. Only a minority is aware of the impact produced by the moon, and the rest, the majority of us are completely ignorant of God's Divine rules. The result is seen during a Full Moon and each time the moon is crossing a destructive sign. This lack of awareness turns into formidable chaos, which produces despair, psychopaths, drug addicts, depression, violence, criminals ... and the list goes on. Know that by ignoring either the physical or spiritual rules leads to a very heavy penalty.

So-called "holy wars" have plagued man all through the ages. Ignorance and fear cast aside God's true Universal message. To my mind, the millions of deaths produced by continuous religious wars all around the world were a good example of the destructive power of fanaticism. I realized that everyone's relationship to God or many gods was deeply personal and that no two people feel the same way about it. My great mother taught me that God is love, beauty, education, responsibility and knowledge, beliefs I have steadfastly clung to. I have noticed the dualistic nature of life, man/woman, front/back, up/down, black/white, yin/yang, positive/negative, the ultimate law of opposition. I soon began to realize that nothing would exist without its counterpart, and this Law of opposition was much too obvious to be challenged or ignored. I began to wonder if God would exist without the Devil. One month is made up of two 2-week cycles, one year of two 6-month periods. From the New Moon (black dot on your calendar) to the Full moon (a circle on your calendar), the light is green

Those two weeks are called "the waxing time." Then when you see her full, white and round, the light is red. Those two weeks are called "the waning time." As she starts her positive waxing time, you should plant your seeds for life. Go out, meet new people, socialize, get engaged, get married, buy a new car, go shopping, sign important contracts, travel, visit family members and generally promote all you can during this positive trend. My Starguide has all the New and full moons available for entire year. Also, Starguide tells you when and in which sign the New Moon or the Full Moon will mature. You can use this knowledge to master the outcomes of all your endeavors. Initiate ideas or projects as she climbs happily through the heavens. When she finally becomes full, beware of the approaching "yellow light," as this signals a time to slow down and reflect. During the day you must work hard and perform your tasks, while nature requires you to rest and sleep during the night. The same rules apply with the Moon. As she is ascending (waxes) you must dwell with the future, the dense physical world and, as the ancients did, put your seeds in the ground. Again, after the full Moon (and for two weeks) as the Moon descends (wanes), you will deal better with metaphysical endeavors, feel like cleaning up, and possibly suffer psychically, as the moon is the regulator of your inner emotions.

Use your will to fight depression, clean your house, prepare your next move, and write letters but don't send them just yet. Observe and listen to all the people around you. Many will suffer the waning Moon's power and will become negative, moody and lunatic. Watch the news and see for yourself the dramatic differences in the two periods. However, good things can happen then. This means, officially, that somehow you started "that" situation during her waxing, positive time, and you are now being paid-off. Bad things can also happen to you when the Moon is supposedly positive. It might only be a tap on your hand, compared to what could have happened. Keep in mind you have been going through your life not knowing nor using the Universal Law. You did not interact with the Moon's fluctuations (the gearbox of our solar system), and many gears (your experiences) have broken down. Apply your knowledge immediately, and take the time to invest in your understanding of Astrology (the dynamics of our Universe). I often use this sample in reference to the respects of the physical and spiritual laws. If you were to travel in China and you could not read, understand or follow the road signs, chances are that you would get hurt. Those laws, even if you are not aware of them, are solid and practical. There is no room for ignorance in this dense physical world, and a heavy penalty awaits those ignorant and skeptical souls.

The Moon also commands women's menstrual periods, and both the Moon and women share the same twenty-eight-day time period. Work non-stop around the Moon's passage, every sign of the Zodiac, and then her deepest secret will by yours. As she travels through the belt of the Zodiac, she will be residing between two to three days in one sign; she will melt your emotions with the energies (positive or negative) found in that specific astrological sign. Never forget that an ultimate higher order has been established, and the essence of our emotional life is within. Learning and adapting to the Moon's power will help you understand what it really means to be human. This cosmic consciousness will lead you towards the understanding of your own strengths, and the ability to use them to further your life, while minimizing your weakness day by day!

> "All great spirits have encountered opposition from mediocre minds; a human being is part of a whole, called by us the 'Universe,' a part limited in time and space. He experiences himself, his thoughts and feelings, as something separated from the rest—a kind of optical delusion of his consciousness. The stars are the elixir of life"
>
> — A. Einstein

> The reality is that; 99% of the people walking this earth do not possess cosmic consciousness and Presidents, religious leaders and a myriad of powerful people in this world are UNAWARE of the power of the stars upon their psyche and destiny. Hiding oneself behind a PHD or a doctorate or any religious or academic accomplishment does not means justice to ignorance.
>
> There is a gigantic difference between intelligence and education…I favor the former.
>
> — Dr. Turi

I can say that I am not a Stargazer as this is just one who gazes at the stars. You would be, too, if you understood the celestial messages as I do. I believe that everyone, and I mean everyone, should be educated in this discipline. The mystery of life would be solved.

When will the school principals realize this deadly Pluto-in-Scorpio student generation (see my book (The Power of the Dragon ~ Death Wish Generation) and make Astropsychology a part of their curriculum and accepted as a solid discipline in all our Universities. The entire educational system is miserably failing to recognize the power of the stars over some children's destructive behavior inherited at birth and stimulated by the moon (regulator of our emotions). How many more children and teachers must die in the name of archaic beliefs or ignorance before they realize the power of the stars producing all those shocking news? Right there, right in schools, colleges and Universities: students killing teachers, students killing students and schoolmasters then finally committing suicide. What more obvious attestation anyone needs to realize that something drastic is missing in the curriculum.

But again the children must be taught algebra, geography, history, science etc. but who is there to teach them WHO THEY ARE as to regenerate their fragile spirits? The generation of Pluto in Scorpio can only regenerate with spiritual matters and will reject naturally any form of religious doctrines. But does the teachers of your children knows about this fact? Chances are that the teacher does not possess cosmic consciousness and needs to go back to my Astropsychology schools to raise their own spiritual vibrations. A dead end for the children, a confusing deceiving religious jargon breeding future rapists, killers and schizo- phrenics abusing drugs prescribed by a bunch of educated imbeciles.

"A human being is part of a whole, called by us the 'Universe,' a part limited in time and space. He experiences himself, his thoughts and feelings, as something separated from the rest—a kind of optical delusion of his consciousness. This delusion is a kind of prison for us, restricting us to our personal desires and to affection for a few persons nearest us. Our task must be to free ourselves from this prison by widening our circles of compassion to embrace all living creatures and the whole of nature in its beauty."

—Albert Einstein)

Pluto's Impact on Generations: Past — Present — Future

Pluto in Gemini: "The hypnotized Generation" Indeed, Pluto is a dramatic planet and its impact on generations is obvious for those blessed with the knowledge of the stars. For good or for worse, the people and leaders of this Era were born with this affliction. Hitler was born on April 20, 1889 and Pluto (power) was located in the sign of Gemini (communication) from 1883 until 1913. Wherever the planet Pluto is located by sign and house in your chart, a sense of power and regeneration will be offered to you. Thus, using his well-known, inborn "hypnotic sound power," it was easy for Hitler, in his numerous "Plutonic" speeches, to persuade the wise German population to go to war against the rest of the world.

Pluto in Cancer: "The Wasted Baby Generation" the immediate generations to suffer Hitler's manipulation were the young German soldiers and everybody else around the world born between 1913 and 1937 with Pluto (death) in Cancer (family). Thus, the "invaders" and all of the war's victims were the result of an awful Pluto disturbing the basic security principle, homes, families and indeed can be associated with the First and Second World Wars, into the sad historically "Wasted Baby Generation." The entire world and its security (Cancer) were shattered between both deadly (Pluto) World Wars, and millions of children from many different ethnic groups met with their fate.

Pluto in Leo: "The Baby Boom Generation" When Pluto moved from Cancer (security/home) to Leo (love/life) from 1938 to 1957, the world experienced a re-birth of its population. Responding subconsciously to the power of the stars, the unaware masses called the phenomenon "The Baby Boom Generation." Leo (Sun) rules love, the arts, freedom, and the 50's and 60's were good examples of the love and freedom-oriented attitudes with hippie music and drugs (Wood stock) that plagued this generation. Pluto rules sex, and Leo children became a free, sexually oriented generation. Jimmy Hendrix's fate (sex, drugs, rock-and-roll), is a good example of a personal Pluto in Leo that ultimately got the best of him.

Pluto in Virgo: "The Baby Buster Generation" Pluto then moved to the puritanical sign of Virgo (health) from 1957 to 1976, and this generation is next to take governmental power. This generation is fanatic about nature, perfection, work and health. Smokers have already suffered the impact of this "Baby Buster Generation," as this generation must upgrade health and perfection in our society.

Unlike Leo (life) Virgo is dry and sterile, thus fewer babies were produced during this era. Since Pluto entered the sign of Virgo, facilities for health programs and exercising boomed to satisfy a generation that craves fitness. The health businesses (body/ mind/tools) have started and are still booming with Pluto in Virgo. This generation is banning smokers from restaurants and public places (and they voted the 40-cent tobacco tax increase), and more rigid health oriented regulations are ahead of us. Note-This section and its predictions were written and published in the 1995 Moon Power edition. On a more positive note, this age group will fight hard to preserve nature, animals and the remainder of the rain forest. Many powerful computers and microchips developed by this generation as experienced in Operation Desert Storm, are deadly accurate. Their ideal is very pure in thought and action, but this generation must guard against Pluto's (fanaticism) subtle power for "perfection." If the power of Pluto in Virgo is exaggerated, it becomes as deadly as the poison they try so hard to avoid.

Many of these souls will lose their lives by being too concerned with health (anorexia, hypochondria), turning rapidly to vegetarian diets, thus upsetting their naturally weak digestive tracts. They must understand that cats and dogs were born with strong claws and long, sharp teeth to tear apart raw flesh as intended by nature, while cows, horses, lambs, etc. are herbivores and were designed by God with flat teeth and three stomachs to eat only "salad." They are none of those. They are omnivorous and must eat meat as a vigilant balance for their sensitive metabolism. Some souls who are overwhelmed by Pluto are overly crazy for carbohydrates. They are also protein paranoid. Some starve themselves after 6:00 p.m. Others take their heart rates much too seriously, some have a penchant for pain, and more are victims of the fat-burning syndrome. Worst of all for women is the weight lifting dilemma. It is, genetically speaking, impossible for a woman to take on a man's physical power, and no matter how hard they try; they will never look like Arnold Schwarzenegger. Because of the inborn critical attitude and a strong desire for health and perfection, those natural "puritans" will not find someone good enough for them and many will end up alone in the game of love.

Note: Insurance Companies DO NOT have your best interest at heart! When Pluto (investigation/insurance) went thought the sign of Virgo (health) more of our private information went to powerful organizations.

From Dr. Williams licensed practicing medical doctor. In the practice of medicine today, insurance companies don't pay your doctor to spend much time with you and give you all the information you need about your disease. As shocking as it sounds, your insurance company may even forbid your doctor from telling you all there is to know about your condition and all of the available treatment options. Information about you health is priceless, and the less you know about the treatment of your condition, the better the insurance companies like it, because it saves them money for treatments and newer, more expensive medications.

Note: Do you know that, for insurance purposes, if you apply for a credit card, not only your driving record, tax record but also your entire private health record is divulged to those organizations? Please take the time to visit my site and read "SOS To The World"

Pluto in Libra: "The Gang Generation." From October 5, 1971 until November 6, 1983, dramatic Pluto (death) moved into the sign of Libra (partnerships). Traditionally Libra rules the 7th house, associations, open enemies, partners and the day-to-day people entering your life. This nefarious combination created a form of regular open-death manifestations as shown by the infamous, daily drive-by shootings. Born with Pluto (death) in Libra (others), those children are willing to die for their inner Plutonic sense of justice (scales) imposed by their partners (gang members). Constantly influenced (bullied) by Pluto or more ferocious souls, they must give in to their high sense of justice for the group. This righteous "die for you/die for me" attitude is now in full operation in our present society and has created "The unbalanced Aggressive Gang Generation." If not for survival or money, then respect, power and justice belong to the group (no matter what), and Pluto is the subtle force behind gang activity. The Plutonic rough initiation principle (beating) is a form of love/hate/submission, a participation and respect found within the sign of Libra in the declaration of peace or war. Then, the ruthless test for security, love, hate, respect and deadly commitment to others (Libra) in the group (gang) has been established. Contrary to what is commonly believed, and to the amazement of psychologists, many children of the gang generation have had perfect upbringings and many are from middle and upper class families.

Early environment plays an important part in how these souls will react to others. If the upbringing happens to be rough and difficult, these Plutonic souls may become the imposing bullies. Negative members of this generation are in constant need of a dramatic regeneration principle-taking place within a group constantly involved in war with others. To those born with Pluto in Libra, it is also a sure indication of a strong inner sense of justice owed to the group for good or for bad. This Pluto (death) generation in Libra (the law) will savagely fight their enemy (authority figures) and other gangs without any fear or regard for the deadly consequences. This problem with the police force has already started and will keep dangerously growing, making some parts of the cities unsafe for the common citizen. This sad situation will continue swelling to a dangerous size and will force the government to take drastic measures. The year 1998 will be a memorable year, as strong efforts will be made to avoid the breaking down of our society. In the process, many youths and numerous police officers' lives will be wasted.

Pluto in Scorpio: "The Death Wish Generation" Pluto then inhabited, from 1983 until 1995, his own daredevil sign of Scorpio. Those very young and wild children have already made dramatic news by executing each other and murdering adults for any reason. Such as in Rachula, Missouri on December 28, 1994, an off-duty police officer had been shot to death by his girlfriend's 9-year-old grandson. The child was born with Pluto in Scorpio on his Dragon's Tail (negative). Many of those "kids" have been reported killing adults for money to buy drugs and guns at the tender age of 10 years. Again in May 1997 a brutal slaying follows a beer drinking in Central Park, New York. Two teenagers stabbed a real estate agent at least 30 times and tried to chop off his hands so police couldn't use fingerprints to identify him before dumping him in a lake in Central Park. Perpetrators, Daphne Abdela, 15, and her boyfriend, 15-year-old Christopher Vasquez, "gutted the body so it would sink." Both of those young souls are from the dramatic Pluto generation, "The Death Wish Generation." More than previous degrading generations, these children need constant spiritual regeneration and a good reason to be alive.

Note - So far this drugged US generation produced over 800 murderers age 15 or younger in 1995, many of them raised in environments that included abuse, neglect and violence. However, youth violence is neither new nor confined to the United States.

Well, governor. Mike Huckabee you can offer all the sympathy of the world for the victims of the school shooting, and like millions of others lament on a culture that would breed such a tragedy. That is NOT the answer, as you already know that it will happen over again. You, including the educational, psychological, police and governmental system are loosing the battle and will soon watch the breaking down of our young society. Scientists from all levels out there are mesmerized and baffled by the awful events that took place on March 25th, 1998 in JONESBORO, Arkansas. Unless you cast aside your fear of the ridicule fueling your academically oriented ignorance and your mental snobiness, you will not be able to even get closer to the golden key of true knowledge. You might have to challenge your precious books, pass the limitation of your rational mind and realize that the higher truths were never been printed by your kind. It's time to look above your head; into the Universal Mind, with a different attitude. If you have any hope what so ever, to provide serious help to this "Death Wish Generation."

Thus, our society is already witnessing "The Dramatic Death Wish Generation" in action. They are strong-willed, unwavering in thought and action, immensely emotional and totally fearless in front of death. Pluto (sex) is making them very active sexually at an early age, and they will look for a mixture of sex, crime and drugs to survive their harsh young lives. At the tender age of 12 years many of those children have already experienced the use of drugs and sex and some others have committed repellent murders. They are already imposing and displaying their powerful, destructive will on many televised talk shows, where helpless parents complain about their awful behavior. Other much older generations are at bay and baffled, unable to relate to this Plutonic generation.

The passion for self-discovery is extreme and if left without legitimate spiritual food, the worst can only happen to many of these children. They will not react to dogma and common religious teachings as they parents do. Those kids subconsciously understand the principle of life and death and the motivation behind all manifestation. They simply lack the regenerative forces produced by the mystical knowledge to deal with their passionate and rebellious nature. The miserably failing psychological field won't be any help understanding the plutonic motivation behind this upcoming killer generation. Unless the old science of Astrology is reinstated, (Astropsychology) in our colleges and universities, there will be either no understanding or therapeutic healing measures available for these children. A few years from now once in power this unyielding generation has the awful potential to destroy the world with the use of irreversible atomic weapons. Let's just hope that the worst elements of this "Death Wish" generation get spiritual guidance quickly, or imperatively auto-destroy themselves, for the sake of all of us. If God's implacable Universal Rules have been broken and ignored for too long, a serious penalty is awaiting mankind. There is no room for ignorance at any level of consciousness or any other worlds above or below us.

Slowly but surely, mankind is witnessing the slow and painful suffocating end of another young generation. Hopefully, our scientists will cast the "ridicule" aside and a solid investigation of "Divine Astrology" will bring it back into the traditional educational system. Only then, the real therapeutic deeds involving Astrology will begin to heal and regenerate the psyches of all of these unquiet spirits. We, the people, in the name of knowledge, love and happiness, still have time to make the change. That's why I am working fervently to produce this work, for the children of this specific generation. For if they get the right spiritual help, and do rebirth from their own ashes, the incredible potential of this Eagle generation can uplift humanity and the world to its highest and most glorious potential.

To all my readers, I need your help to educate the parents first, as the numbers of requests from the concerned parents will make the badly needed changes and save future lives. Start by sending my newsletters all over, to all that you know, even the skeptics or religious lost lambs waiting for their deities to fix the problem. Their ignorance doesn't give them the right to be blind, but denotes warm hearts for children and your gesture may help them to grow and perceive my work. My wish is to open my own Astropsychology schools if the system is reluctant to make those crucial changes and I need all the help I can get. Any suggestions? Is someone listening?

If you can do anything to help me to help the children of tomorrow PLEASE DO SO and invest in my Astropsychology schools. Your gesture and donations will make a serious difference in the lives of the children of the future. If you have any form of knowledge that can be used to help support me my cause PLEASE DO SO by calling me at 602-265-7667. Invest in the future not the past don't be a promoter of ignorance or any religious institutions, invest in the FUTURE and for the CHILDREN!

> "Insanity: doing the same thing over and over again and expecting different results."
>
> — Albert Einstein

Supernova Windows

2006 A.W.S. P. — ASTRO WEATHER SERVICE PREDICTIONS

There will be three major negative SUPERNOVA windows in the year 2006. Each destructive "window" is operational for three to four weeks, thus caution is strongly advised during this period. Heavy loss of lives due to nature's devastating forces, aeronautical disasters and structural damage is to be expected. Once more realize that I do not use traditional dates found in popular ephemera. Years of practical observation lead me to extend the Mercury retrograde motion and period of time.

January / March: First SUPERNOVA window - From Saturday January 25th 2006, through Thursday March 30th, 2006.

July / August: Second SUPERNOVA window - From Saturday July 1st through Wednesday August 2nd 2006.

October / November: Third SUPERNOVA window - From Saturday October 21st through Tuesday October 21st 2006.

EXPLANATION OF A SUPERNOVA WINDOW

Concentration of negative celestial energy approaching Be extremely prudent in driving, and expect chain-reaction accidents. Be prepared for delays, strikes, and nature producing awful weather, including hurricanes and tornadoes. The same energy that produced the Titanic disaster, the Northridge, Los Angeles, and Kobe, Japan, earthquakes is approaching again. Double-check all your appointments, and if you can, postpone traveling and flying during this Supernova "window".

Communication and electricity will be cut off, and a general loss of power is to be expected. Appliances, computers, telephones, planes, trains, cars, all of these "tools" will be affected by this energy. They will be stopped in one way or another. The people of the past will make the news and will reenter your life. Expect trouble with the post office, education, students, strikes, prisoners' escape, newspapers, broadcasting industries and computer viruses may bother us again.

Many a failed mission and expensive electronic equipment (Mars probe etc.) and our tax dollars have been wasted because of the scientist's lack of knowledge of the stars. As usual NASA, which is not aware of the science of astrology, will waste our tax money with failed missions due to bad weather and electronic malfunctions. In the name of ignorance a few years ago, in the Challenger explosion seven astronauts lost their lives when NASA launched the shuttle under a "Supernova Window".

Note: Regardless of Dr. Turi's expectations posted on his website for the second time and his desperate attempts over the years to make NASA officials aware of dangerous Super Nova Windows, the Columbia was also launched during this window and re-entered the last night of it producing the death of all courageous astronauts.

Marine life sharks, whales etc may also beach themselves due to Mercury retrograde affecting their natural inborn navigational systems. All these malevolent predictions and waste of lives and equipment do not have to occur. Those predictions do not have to affect you directly as they unfold. Instead, they are printed to prepare you for setbacks and frustrations, thus advising you to be patient and prudent during this trend. There is no room for ignorance, and those who are not aware of the celestial order, including the NASA space-program management team, will continue to pay a heavy price. In all mankind's affairs, ignorance is true evil. Why any scientists who are against my research do not honor the word science, which is based upon solid investigation, is solid proof of mental snobbery. By omitting any physical or spiritual laws can only bring penalty; for science's purpose is to explore all possibilities, even those laws written in light via the stars.

Earthquake predictions

Earthquakes tend to occur when diurnal tidal forces are able to release the accumulated strain on a fault. Hard planetary aspects appear able to increase the strain on a fault. Perhaps the computer-aided Astrogeologists of the future will be able to do the kind of micro-mapping and analysis needed to predict which faults are most susceptible to increased strain. As for the timing, my technique to predict earthquakes seems to be more accurate than all the latest computerized electronic equipment combined together!

Earthquakes tend to occur when diurnal tidal forces are able to release the accumulated strain on a fault. Hard planetary aspects appear able to increase the strain upon a fault. Perhaps the computer-aided Astrogeologists of the future will be able to do the kind of micro-mapping and analysis needed to predict which faults are most susceptible to increased strain. As for the timing, my technique to predict earthquakes seems to be more accurate than all the latest computerized electronic equipment combined!

Sample of Proofs

POSTED (Oct, 6th. 1995)
From Dr. Turi -
SUBJECT: RE: Weekly USGS Quake Report

Dear Sirs: - On Oct.8th and Oct.9th a very unusual seismic activity will be noticeable and will produce many quakes above 6.1. More information is available pertaining to my method if requested. Respectfully

— Dr. Turi

Results - Full proofs of predictions:

Oct. 8th a 7.0 EARTHQUAKE HIT SUMATRA (INDONESIAN ISLANDS)

Oct. 9th a 7.6 EARTHQUAKE HIT MEXICO.

More Proof:

Kudos to you Dr. Turi!

I surf the Internet periodically for predictions on forthcoming events, specifically all relating to earthquake activities. You hit the 11/22/95 Egypt/Israel/Saudi Arabia 7.2 quake smack dab on the head, per your earlier prediction. Congratulations again!
E-mail < private @ccmail.jpl.nasa.com> Keep up the good work.

Appreciatively,

— Name withheld

More Proof:

From: /////@mindspring.com
To: Louis a Turi <dr.turi@juno.com>
Date: Fri, 24 Sep 1999 22:31:10 -0400 (EDT)
Subject: Re: Show

I gave you full credit on the show just after the massive Taiwan earthquake and the Turkey aftershock on Sept 20.... I got a lot of email from people who were watching the date prediction as well. This is marvelous my friend. The nice thing about it is how you understate these things and never gloat about them when you hit. I had another fine program with John Hogue last night. Be well, my friend.

"All I have asked for is a fair scientific investigation of my work for the sole purpose of promoting mans cosmic consciousness, saving time, money and the lives of many people."

— Dr. Turi

Predictions For The Century

Approximately every two thousand years, our planet comes under the influence of a new zodiacal sign. January twelve, 1996 marks the entrance of Uranus (the future) into his own sign of Aquarius (new age). We slowly begin to explore the possibility of a new consciousness and uncover both the strength and danger of this incredible upcoming age. This liberal sign follows nebulous Pisces. Over the last twenty years, Uranus (the awakener) has advocated more discoveries than have been made during the last 2000 years spent under the illusive power of Neptune (ruler of Pisces). Pisces is the last sign of the Zodiac, and traditionally, it rules the twelfth house. This area governs restriction, sorrow, imprisonment, psychological trouble and secret enemies as well as creativity, dance, high forms of music and works of art. Enclosed and confined places such as asylums, hospitals, churches, prisons, movie theaters, concert halls and theme parks are Neptune's legacy. It is also a mute energy; it has no voice of its own. Submissive by nature, Neptune tends to make those born under its heavy influence pessimists and fatalists prone to addictions and fanaticism.

It is a deceiving energy prone to suffering and acceptance. Nuns, evangelists, drug addicts are particularly loaded, for good or for bad, with Neptune's illusive power. Interestingly, the two thousand years that has elapsed during the rule of Pisces started around the time of the beginning of Christianity. For nearly 2000 years, the world has been largely under the influence of Judeo-Christian theology, whose first early chosen symbol was the sign of the fish. Oriental and near-Oriental minds delight in fairy stories, and they are continually spinning such beautiful myths about the lives of religious and political heroes. In the absence of printing, when most human knowledge was passed by word of mouth, from one generation to the next, the illusive power of Pisces opened the doors for myths to become tradition and those traditions to eventually be accepted as fact.

Unmistakably, under the sign of Pisces, Jesus Christ suffered sorrow, imprisonment, restrictions and tortures at the hands of secret political enemies. Also, Christianity has been preaching the blind acceptance of suffering, repentance and sacrifice, if you are to proceed to the paradise of God. According to astrology, Neptune's energy (Pisces) forces the soul towards its opposite sign (Virgo) or the Virgin Mary and its purity principle. This indicates why Christians have subconsciously chosen the symbol of the fish to represent their religion and beliefs. The last 2000 years of Neptunian influence have produced over 875 different religions worldwide, and in the process, millions of people have died and still die in devastating holy wars.

It is well documented that many former civilizations simply worshipped God or gods with the stars, the moon and the sun. The Creator's Divine Manifestation throughout the Universe (Astrology) was well used and understood by the ancients. Whereas Pisces is mute and accepting, Aquarius has a voice. Aquarius rules curiosity, invention, electronics, the UFO phenomena and astrological investigation. Uranus rules the future, electronics, electricity, radio, television, airships and aeronautics. Among its metals are uranium, radium and all the other radioactive elements.

Thus, we can look upon the Aquarian age as a bringer of hope, universal love, and as a promoter of great technological advances and vast increases in man's mental exploration. Uranus rules cosmic consciousness, psychic awareness and the genius quality of man. Uranus is also classified as the "sudden release of energy" and is responsible for nature's devastating forces such as earthquakes, tornadoes, hurricanes and typhoons. Wrongly used, Uranus can be the potential destroyer of the human race through the use of atomic weaponry and as yet undiscovered powers.

We must learn to understand the true message of Aquarius and the awesome power of Uranus. We must overcome the negative forces of this planet, for that is the lesson of the age of Aquarius, to enjoy an age of great spiritual awakening. We must learn to accept the values and workings of Uranus upon our thought processes, thus creating our own amazing future reality complete with ETs and UFOs. We must create a universal brotherhood, where love, progress and responsibility become the ultimate goals. If we fail to recognize the awesome power of Uranus, the Aquarius age may be the last age man will live on this planet.

We have twelve months, 12 hours, 12 apostles. The twelve apostles are a hidden representation of the 12 gods of the zodiac. Symbols have survived to this day from very ancient times. In the Catholic church today, the staff the bishops carry is a carry-over of the staff held by the Egyptian God Osiris. The symbol of the Christian cross was taken from the Egyptian ankh which represented life and fertility. The high pointed hat worn by the Pope, was derived from Osiris' tall crown. And even the traditional birthday of Jesus, celebrated on the 25th of December, is taken from the birthday of the Egyptian God, Horus.

2006 Slow-Moving Planets Predictions

The great planet Jupiter entered the sign of Scorpio on October 26th, 2005 and will enter Sagittarius on December 24th 2006.

Jupiter in Scorpio will bring serious improvement in all affairs related to corporate endeavors, insurance companies, secret services (FBI/CIA) and the police where all foreign countries will work in harmony with the US to combat terrorism. Russia (a Scorpio country) will benefit from tourism, as more and more foreigners will visit this great country. A Russian figure will make international news because of a secret coming to light involving nuclear undercover endeavor. A surge with a new form of spirituality will challenge the dying age of Pisces and all its religious doctrines. Wherever Scorpio and Pluto reside by house and sign in your chart expect a serious amount of luck, protection and growth. In 2006 Jupiter in Scorpio will support all sorts of funding for medical pursuit where homeopathic and rare healing philosophies will merge to help society. A surge for the creation of medical means and international investments will be offered to underdeveloped countries. Monuments and funds will be raised for all the children who lost their lives in the Iraq and Afghanistan war.

Saturn in Leo: Saturn, "the teacher" has been going through the sign of Leo since Sunday July 17th, 2005. Then Saturn will enter Virgo on September 3rd, 2007. Karmic Saturn is also called, the "Great Malefic" and its gloomy power brings fears, depression by sign and house he resides. In any case, if you are feeling Saturn's gloomy energy you are probably not using this planet structuring power accordingly and feel inadequate or lost in your career accomplishment. Do not give in to Saturn depressive power and use your will: the part of God in you is much stronger than any planet.

In the sign of Leo expect a complete and serious restructure of the arts industry where much work will be dedicated to the children. Saturn in Leo propagates a subconscious fear of death and diseases or expanding the mind into more advanced topics such as the study of electronic or New Age matters. Saturn is cold and calculated; Leo is hot and fixed. Make solid plans, stick to them and respect the Universal Law in all your endeavors. On a more positive note, the structural power of Saturn will provide Leo's enterprising spirit, objectivity, discipline and a reasonable approach to any business or writing venture. Many people will feel the urge to "assert" the competitive side of Leo and children involved in the arts will accomplish much progress.

Some scientists will bring about incredible inventions that will benefit heart surgery while karmic souls born with an afflicted Saturn (caution) in Leo (the heart) may experience surgery. Expect the US taxpayer's money to be used for the building of better schools and healthy programs. With the passage of Saturn (re-structure) in Leo (fame) many famous people may lose their position or children. Nature devastating forces may affect France, Japan or Italy (see Supernova windows). In the long run, safer and more solid structures will be erected for the benefit of our youngest members of our society. Avoid the insecurity feeling produced by Saturn in your life and work diligently towards a better health and take care of yourself, as the numbers of heart surgery will rise drastically. A 90 MN taped Full Life Reading will tell you more about the location and impact of Saturn in your celestial make up and how to combat fears.

September 15, 2003 - Uranus entered Aquarius: Uranus is the future, be ready to experience a taste of the unbelievable. Uranus in Aquarius has forced the masses to open up to the New Agers' messages. What is now considered eccentric leanings such as: astrology, UFOs, reincarnation, psychic powers, etc., will be approached with an open mind, explored, and in time, finally accepted by the majority. All this will take place within the next few years. Some of the old sciences will be brought back to our colleges and universities and accepted as true and useful disciplines. Soon after this new consciousness, the human race will be prepared for the possibility of exploring the universe with friendly extraterrestrials. Uranus rules the sudden release of energy (earthquakes) and after entering his own sign; the worst of nature's forces will be experienced by mankind and especially in Hawaii, Japan and California. This does not mean the end of the world, but a reminder that old mother earth is still alive and needs to reshape her entrails. Tremendous electronic tools and new discoveries will be brought to the human race. Children born during the passage of Uranus in Aquarius will have sparkling genius qualities and a strong sense of independence. Many will feel the urge to undergo computer studies while others will have to travel far and enjoy their new and exciting careers. Expect more and more electronic breakthrough and a general interest in the new age matters. Many new age schools (Astropsychology) will get attention and more will be accredited and recognized as a valuable discipline in our colleges and Universities. Perfect time to apply your will and decide to start a spiritual Astropsychology, Kabalistic Healing or Astro-Tarot course (Get a super deal - see www.drturi.com or call the office to help us to set a few days crash course in your area).

Important note: This section was written years before the deadly Asia Tsunami.

2003 Uranus in Pisces: Uranus (Age of Aquarius) is the future while Neptune (religion) rules the past. Pisces rules the Middle East and all its destructive outdated religions, while Uranus means explosive news and the use of advanced electronic equipments. Thus the war in the heavens translated into the war in Iraq and with it explosions and changes of regimes where unification means peace with the neighboring countries and more trade. The entire region is still under the jurisdiction of Uranus forcing the past to be replaced by the future. Thus be ready to experience a taste of the unbelievable as far as the entire Middle East and its rulership are concerned. On a negative note Uranus rules the sudden release of energy (quakes in Morocco and explosions (suicides attacks). All happenings pertaining to nature devastative forces at work and war is still unfolding responding to the higher order imposed by the energy of Uranus (changes) in Pisces (religions of the past). The planet of the future meets the artistic and religious sign of Pisces. On a positive note many young souls will benefit from this advanced celestial energy and explore the incredible world of astrology without any religious limitations. The cinematography industry will experience incredible growth, due to use of new technological tools and increases of man's imaginative creativity. Titanic and the Matrix movies are a little sample of the things to come with Uranus (technology) in Pisces (movies). On a negative note, Pisces rules the Middle East and Uranus nuclear devices. Some terrorist groups will try to get their criminals hands on those kinds of weapons in order to impose their personal religious doctrines to the world. The Middle East (Pisces/religion) is undergoing a Uranian (unification/future) changes. Amazing how President Bush "picked" the first day of the New Moon (and a solar eclipse on his Dragon's Head in Gemini) to launch his trip to the Middle East! The FBI or CIA must be watching my site closely too.

Under Uranus jurisdiction what is considered eccentric practices by conventional scientific standards such as: astrology, UFOs, reincarnation, psychic powers, etc., will be approached with an open mind, explored, and in time, finally accepted by the majority as this planet get strength within the next few years. Some of those old sciences will be brought back to our colleges and universities and accepted as true and useful disciplines by the children of tomorrow. Soon after this new consciousness, the human race will be prepared for the possibility of exploring the universe with friendly extraterrestrials. Uranus rules the sudden release of energy (earthquakes) and mankind all over the world will experience the worst of nature's forces. (Note this section was written before the deadly Asia tsunami) This does not mean the end of it all but serves, as a reminder that old mother earth is still alive and now and then she need to reshape her entrails. Expect tremendous electronic tools and new discoveries will be brought to the human race. All the children that were born during the passage of Uranus in Aquarius will have sparkling genius qualities and a strong sense of independence. Many will feel the urge to undergo computer studies while others will have to travel far and enjoy their new and exciting careers. Expect more and more electronic breakthrough and a general interest in the new age matters. Many new age schools (Astropsychology) will get attention and more will be accredited and recognized as a valuable discipline in our colleges and Universities.

Neptune in Aquarius: Neptune will reside in the futuristic sign of Aquarius until April 5th, 2011. When badly asserted, Neptune is known to be the planet of illusion. However, all planets are both positive and negative. Neptune's creative energy was subconsciously used by a wave of evangelists and their bullhorns, using the "last days" of the Apocalypse, to make fortunes in deceiving the uninformed, God-fearing religious masses with their uncontrolled archaic imagination. Upon entering the futuristic sign of Aquarius (new age) Neptune (dogmas) will undergo a full spiritual restructure in the advancement of God's will trough the stars. Either a new crowd of totally psychotic religious fanatics, or highly advanced spiritual lecturers will then roam the world with their teachings. When Neptune, "Poseidon" enters the electronic sign of Aquarius, artists of all orders will invest in incredible imaginative resources, and produce incredible stories. Those Neptunian (sea) and Uranian (UFOs) tales will transform into incredible movies. Again my premonition for such a development was written in your 1996 "Moon power" and took place in 1997 with the "Mars invasion" and "Titanic" and the latest "Matrix" movies busters. Both the actors and the electronic genius of movie producers in Hollywood performed the incredible works. With Neptune's imagination and the electronic sign of Aquarius since 1999 expect more incredible mixture of the future and creativity leading to a solid growth within the cinematography industry.

Important note: This section was written years before September 11th 2001. The full impact has been felt with the 911 WTC dramatic terrorist attacks on the US and the July 7, 2005 London bombing. See predictions at www.drturi.com

Pluto in Sagittarius: Pluto moved from Scorpio to Sagittarius on November 11th, 1995 and will stay in this sign until January 26, 2008. Constrained to face the horrible consequences of his own destructive power, and pay the heavy consequences of mass destruction, man turns to religion for comfort. In Sagittarius (religion) Pluto (regeneration) will promote a disturbing wave of religious fanaticism that will plague the world. In the US, the impact of Pluto in Sagittarius has already spoken with some religious fanatics, committing serious crimes and many will have to pay the ultimate price for their destructive behavior. Some Middle Eastern residents have also shocked the world, and will keep spawning suicidal bomb attacks, on major European and US cities. The "contract" they sign with their manipulators, before blowing themselves up surrounded by the highest possible number of innocent victims, promises "the martyrs" twenty or more virgins after an immediate entrance to paradise! After the painful passage of Pluto (expiration) in Sagittarius (codification of thoughts), the world will be ready for wiser, new age and religious leaders. Those well-adjusted souls will teach all the higher expressions of all the religions of the past. They will introduce a new image of a God free of fear, full of love and attention. Those futuristic religious leaders will combine their teachings with a more comprehensive scientific understanding of the manifestation of the Creator throughout the Universe.

> Ignorance is evil; when you control someone's source of information or education, chances are that you will control that person's entire life.
>
> — Dr. Turi

Do not worry about anything you may hear on CNN and most of all do not fall for the "Apocalyptic" times promised by religious lunatics and/or your own religious poisoning. The dragon Head in Pisces (oceans) has his own way to RE-structure sea life and the oceans and mother nature is much more powerful than humans and its technology.

The same applies for the year 2012 predictions and earth changes lunatics, DO NOT FALL for fear and have faith. God did not put us on earth to die of a terrible death, there is much more behind your comprehension and those of those baffled ignorant scientists would they be from the psychiatric, psychology well known institution or NASA' scientists, the FBI and Oceanography study departments to name a few. Sad enough your tax dollars is going to those well-established governmental institutions while my valuable research and my obvious findings (and predictions) are not taken seriously or even endorsed. Well I am well ahead of those scientists and that is the price I have to pay.

Once more HELP me to pass those predictions to all the people and websites you know. Please help me in my pledge to educate the world and bring hopes to mankind.

Love and light

—Dr. Turi

2006 Dragon's Head and Tail Predictions (Date of prediction 7/15/05)

The Dragon stay about two years in one sign and forces the soul towards his future by imposing world wide karmic work.

The Dragon's Head in Aries

The Dragon's Head entered the sign of Aries on Sunday December 26, 2004 and will stay in the Aries/Libra axis until Thursday June 22nd, 2006. Again knowledge is power and ignorance is evil. Raise your cosmic consciousness and lead a more productive life, this is why God gave us the stars." To be used as signs and lead us to a more productive life". A progressive or full life 90 MN taped reading would give you all very important information as how the Dragon's Head or Tail will affect your entire life in 2006. Call me at 602-265-7667 for more information.

Thursday June 22nd, 2006 The Dragon's Head will enter the sign of Pisces

Important Change of the guard! True New Year for the world.

The news Dragon in Pisces will force a total restructure of the pharmaceutical companies the FDA and the oil industry. Pisces rules the Middle East and will bring more attacks by terrorists worldwide. Neptune (ruler of Pisces) rules also chemicals and poison and could bring about disaster at sea and on the American and allied soils. Serious decision pertaining to the war in the Middle East will have to be taken by the US and British government. The entire region will ally against the west and will force the US into a much-needed adjustment. Expect more devastating attacks in both the US and the UK and parts of Asia that could lead to a secret nuclear debate in due time. This general threat will bring more fears into god-fearing people and will increase the churches humongous wealth and its leaders in the last breath of the dying Pisces age. Certain laws will be passed to stop the proliferations of religious buildings disfiguring Indian lands and cities blocks zonings while many protestors from different holy background will set them on fire. New laws will be established for the shipping industry to avoid a way for terrorists to bring deadly weaponry and chemicals to the US. A full restructure of the shipping industry will also be imposed by the US Homeland security to avoid such possible disasters. Secret business sale of gas masks will be uncovered and coastline cities public dancing places, Sea world and US exotic islands including Australia will become new targets for the terrorists.

Neptune rules also the oceans and the Dragon's Head in Pisces will start its restructuring power as to fight man's pollution and adapt to its destructive habits. Many "educated" scientist will scratch their empty head wondering why the ocean is "dying". Expect also negative news from exotic places with drugs activity and disappearing people such a Natalee Holloway dilemma will become public. The cinematographic industry will also see a serious restructure while activists will work very hard to save the remaining of the rain forest and stop oil companies to ruin our coastlines. A new infectious disease and a very high suicide numbers of people because of abuse and nefarious addictive medical prescriptions will reach the media. Expect some serious legal battle against drugs companies that will be forces a full restructure of the FDA. New pharmaceutical companies will merge under new corporate names to avoid legal battles and future bankruptcy. Accident/terrorism/oil at sea is to be expected while the hurricane / tornadoes season will bring devastating flooding. Neptune rules also oil companies and will impose a serious re-structures and merging of oil giants. Gas price will be skyrocketing forcing the population to ask lawmakers to stop the constant rise of oil price. Expect a wet year with serious floorings and a series of super hurricanes and tornadoes that will destroy costliness and some islands worldwide. The fishing and boating industry will also be restructured while nerve gas and warfare chemical agents will become a serious threat against many countries allied with the US.

Expect disturbing news coming from natural reservoirs, lakes and rivers. Expect also naval accidents involving ships and nuclear submarines during 2006 Supernova windows. The dragon head and tail in Pisces Virgo axis will also bring the highest numbers of incarcerations including serious unrest and riots in jails leading to many death and suicides. Expect many prison riots where deadly force will be used forcing a re-structure of the correctional system. A new drug ring will be uncovered and lead many people to die and to jail. Expect food or water poisoning on cruise lines. The fishing industry will suffer drastically due to over fishing and poisoned oceans. DO NOT TRAVEL AFTER THE FULL MOON especially during a supernova window. Save your life, educate yourself.

Pisces (religions) is ruled by Neptune (deception/illusion) and this planet control the entire Middle East (a region totally poisoned with the three deadliest and youngest religions (Christianity/Muslims/Judaism) created by mankind's folly and manipulative governments of the past. Over the centuries myths became accepted as reality by the uneducated fearful working class and sprayed like a cancer to the masses worldwide. Expect the entire region to ally and support the hidden terrorist (religious) war. Expect the worse of the dragon Head and Tail to impact the world in March and/or September 2006 especially during the 2006 Super Nova Windows. Expect difficult or re-structure disturbing news involving Elizabeth Taylor, Michael Jackson " Neverland", Ex-President Bush and Clinton,

Governor Arnold Schwarzenegger, actors and singers born under the sign of Pisces and Virgo.

> Man is superior to the stars if he lives in the power of superior wisdom. Such a person being the master over heaven and earth by means of his will is a magus and magic is not sorcery but supreme wisdom
>
> — Paracelsus-

Your Personal Horoscope for 2006

Welcome to Each Sign of the Zodiac

Important Note from Dr. Turi: Born and raised in Provence, France, I rekindled and exercise only Nostradamus' 16th-century Divine Astrology method. This formula does not reflect the modern astrology disciplines you may use, study or practice. Realize that over 500 years ago the famous Prophet did not use a watch or any sophisticated computers. Thus like the great Seer, I investigate outer space and the Universal mind with my inborn spiritual telescope. A "microscopic attitude" will not help anyone gain the Golden key to spiritual knowledge. This limited exploitive attitude is for "astronomers" who have long lost their cosmic consciousness with their rigid mathematics and scientifically oriented minds. We have all heard of missing the forest looking at a tree. Every one of them is aware of the twelve constellations of the Zodiac; somehow it is still impossible for them to pass the limitation of their five rational senses. To penetrate the intuitive domain of those stars is the only way for them to enter the archetypal realm of consciousness and decode the subtle meaning behind each symbol. Realize that Divine Astrology is an extremely old celestial art and a very complex science and must be practiced as such. Not everyone is blessed with the "gift" needed to assimilate, understand and translate correctly the heavenly dexterity of the Creator. That's why a section of the bible clearly mentions, "I will talk to you; but you won't hear me! I will present myself to you; but you won't see me!" God speaks to us within his own manifestation and through his Divine light. Only those willing to expand their cosmic consciousness will be able to "perceive and receive" the real manifestation of God. For those born on the cusp of any zodiacal sign, simply refer to the month of your birth, which reflects the exact constellation of your nativity. Divine Astrology, as practiced by Nostradamus, is the creation of Dr. Turi and a more accurate and simplistic way of looking at the stars. All students have found it to be incredibly accurate.

> Ignorance is evil; when you control someone's source of information or education, chances are that you will control that person's entire life.
>
> — Dr. Turi

Saturn Governs the Power-Oriented, Structural Constellation of Capricorn

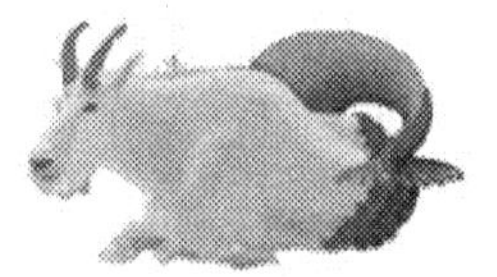

Builder of the greatest towers
Holding all the social powers
Striving to climb to the highest peak
For honor has no place for the weak
I am CAPRICORN, child of Saturn.

Characteristics For Those Born In January

Saturn rules the practical sign of Capricorn and controls the month of January. You are strongly motivated to succeed and gain a position of power during the course of your life. You are gifted with computers and you possess strong organizational principles. More than any other sign of the Zodiac you strive for respect and accomplishment in your career. Saturn is a karmic planet and rules your life, thus you must avoid nurturing depressing thoughts. The part of God in you is much stronger than the stars you inherited and you do have power over the universal mind. You were born in the middle of the winter when nature was asleep. You must have realized early on, that nothing would come easily to you. Like the goat slowly but surely and against all odds (cold/wind/snow) you must climb towards the top of the mountain.

The first part of your life has been a long and painful struggle but Saturn will reward you by giving you a long life and a well-deserved position. You will appreciate old age and solid financial security. You may also marry a much younger or older partner. The fluctuations of the Moon strongly affect your mood and your career success. The wise Capricorn soul will use his fish tail accordingly and synchronize his life and business with the tides. Steadiness, organization, patience, and charm belong to you. You have a strong architectural or mathematical ability and your keen sense of observation will help you succeed in life. Karmic Saturn will exact payment for manipulating others for selfish ends and will throw the soul back to a painful start. You are attracted to power and successful people and you may marry into wealth. Emotional and sensitive, you are very responsible and protective of the family circle. However you must learn to openly communicate your deep feelings.

Your real gifts are Astropsychology, electronics, and any career supported by Uncle Sam. Your natal Dragon can propel you to the highest position and supreme power. But your challenge is to open up to the intangible world of the spirit and it's accompanying Universal rules. Your natural tendency to organize people and business at all times could hinder your sensitivity to others. Capricorns are good homemakers and adept with investments. As a rule you favor a successful business environment where you can apply your tremendous organizational gifts. A word of caution for Capricorn: Be aware of those wild acquaintances willing to help you to climb the ladder of success. Remember to respect the Universal Law (see Moon Power), as your awareness of Moon planning will become a major contribution for happiness and success. The location of your natal Dragon's Head or Tail will seriously alter the strength or weakness of Saturn in your chart. You can learn much more about yourself or anyone else by ordering my new book entitled "I Know All About You", "The Power Of The Dragon" or "And God Created The Stars".

2006 — Forecast For Those Born In January

Personal: The Dragon's Head entered the sign of Aries on Sunday December 26, 2004 and will stay in the Aries/Libra axis until Thursday June 22nd, 2006. Then the Dragon will enter Pisces Virgo axis until December 18, 2007. The Dragon's Head in Pisces can be a blessing if you use your personal Yearly Dragon windows and the Moon fluctuations to further all your wishes, this is a new service and it is strongly recommended for you to do so.

A new way of thinking about the way you perceive your reality will be induced by the Dragon's Head. Many souls born in January operating in the art and creativity will also be promoted to a higher place and gain a position of responsibility. The passage of the Dragon in both the sign of Pisces and Virgo will open exciting new doors in both houses and all affairs related to those houses within the spiritual and physical worlds. This promises many new business endeavors leading you to rewarding contacts. The Dragon's Tail location in your house of education, religion and traveling will induce a general restructure of your spiritual views where much work and studies will force you to travels to far away places.

This could induce quite a lot of activity and social interaction during the waxing moon periods. Some lucky Capricorn will invest in new electronic gadgets and think of moving to a far away place. As a rule Capricorn are career oriented and dedicated parents. Note that this sign (head of the goat) was subconsciously chosen by the Christians as a representation of the devil or as what young souls perceive as evil or the practice of magic/rituals, astrology or the occult. The Christians themselves are under the jurisdiction of deceiving Neptune and subconsciously picked the symbols of the fishes to represent their own religious doctrines.

During the new and Full Moons of January and July 2006 (see Moon Power publication for dates), serious positive or difficult happenings based upon your personal karma will take place. Again, you are strongly advised to use your will and avoid depressing thoughts. Regenerative spiritual endeavors combined with studies, exercise and social interaction could prove to be beneficial at those moments. Do not let the nasty pull of the Dragon's Tail affecting your mental process, traveling and higher education get the best of your body mind and spirit. The positive Dragon's Head in Pisces has much to offer and will induce a variety of opportunities to improve your creativity and perception of life. Promoting a spiritual advanced new Age group or some kind of artistic endeavors can only be beneficial in the long run. Within the next few months or so, the fruits of new studies will open a new perception to your position in life perceive spirituality on a much higher level.

The new Dragon's Head in Pisces will offer luck but could also induce depressions, guilt especially after the Full Moon or when the moon rides your natal Tail of the Dragon. Knowing and using your lucky window dates for the next twelve months will also add more success in all your endeavors, see for information on this new service.

Providing you keep away from antidepressants and avoid nurturing pessimistic thoughts about your spiritual life a very progressive time is ahead of you. As a rule, those born in January strive for success, education and a place of respect that often brings lots of responsibilities and challenges. Saturn is particularly slow to bring any project to fruition or rewards but when he does they last forever. Remember to respect the Universal Law (see Moon Power) and use your natal fish tail in accordance to the Universal rules as this wisdom becomes a major contribution to your success or failure in life.

This celestial process will bring you much luck if you take on the new challenge and invest in education, metaphysical pursuits, traveling, and if you associate with new partners. Those shining stars above your head are on your side and you can make the most of them. Be ready for a new romance or great business deals with those born in May, July, or September.

In the year 2006 the great Jupiter (luck) will cruise through the sign of Scorpio in your 11th house of wishes and friends and will bring about lucky breaks to your life. Much progress is to be expected in this area also, especially where groups, wishes and friends is concerned. Shortly after his entrance into this house you can expect serious changes or advancement with your goals and your financial endeavors in general. Be ready for new associations and great business deals with those born in September, May and July. You may order your taped 90mn Full Life Reading or your Progressive reading to find out more about the upcoming changes in your life. Visit www.drturi.com and use our system or call our office for more information. Knowing and using your lucky window dates for the next twelve months will also add more success in all your endeavors, see for information on this new service. Good luck to all of those born in January.

You may order your taped 90mn Full Life Reading or your Progressive reading to find out more about the upcoming changes in your life. Call 602-265-7667 or visit my site and fill out the order form or call our office for more information. Those born in November will bring you great luck; look for them in your social circle. Good luck to all of those born in January.

Uranus Governs The Ingenious, Freedom-Oriented Constellation Of Aquarius

Holder of knowledge of the dimensions
The spark of all the inventions
Lover of all things in simplicity
Charged with the power of electricity
I am AQUARIUS, child of Uranus.

Characteristics For Those Born In February

The planet Uranus rules the sign of Aquarius and governs those born in February. You are one of the most original people walking this earth. Aquarius has produced many eccentric people and great inventors. Uranus rules originality and the incredible UFO phenomenon. It commands the future of mankind and all celestial knowledge particularly the old science of astrology. You are blessed with curious stars and you are attracted to science, research, electronics, psychology, the police force and Astropsychology to name a few. Aquarius rules aeronautics, avionics, television, the Internet and advanced computers. The option to reach fame and fortune is a high probability during the course of your life if you service the world in an advanced and original way. The motion picture Back to the Future is one of the best ways to illustrate Uranus' ingenuity in terms of creative art. Strong and fixed, you have inherited from the stars, accurate intuition, tremendous common sense, ingeniousness, and a powerful will. Yet, you must learn to listen to others and participate in conversations with equality. Even when the ideas being presented are not of your own making, much knowledge can still be learned. Lend your full ear and do not race ahead with only thoughts of what you need to say.

Those born in February must also learn to positively direct Uranus' innovative mental power for the improvement and well being of the world. Acting eccentric and without forethought is a sure downfall for you. Your idealistic views are legendary and your mission is to promote Universal knowledge and Universal Brotherhood. You will benefit from the opportunity to use the latest technological arsenals to fulfill your unselfish wishes for mankind. You can handle the difficulties of life with a smile and transcend setbacks by using celestial knowledge to your benefit. The women of this sign are original, independent, beautiful, intellectual, and make good use of their incredible magnetic sexuality to reach their purposes. As a rule, women born in February produce extraordinarily intelligent children or twins. You are strongly advised not to eat when upset. The medical aspect of Divine Astrology predisposes those born in February to over-sensitive stomachs. A word of caution for those advanced souls born in February: Many young religious or rational souls will not understand your genius and your advanced message to the world. Many will try hard to stop and hurt you. Remember to respect the Universal Law (see Moon Power), as your awareness and Moon planning will become a major contribution to your happiness and success. The location of your natal Dragons Head or Tail will seriously alter the strength or weakness of Uranus in your chart. You can learn much more about yourself or anyone else by ordering my new book entitled "I Know All About You", "The Power Of The Dragon" or "And God Created The Stars".

2006 — Forecast For Those Born In February

Personal: The Dragon's Head entered the sign of Aries on Sunday December 26, 2004 and will stay in the Aries/Libra axis until Thursday June 22nd, 2006. Then the Dragon will enter Pisces Virgo axis until December 18, 2007. The Dragon's Head in Pisces can be a blessing if you use your personal Yearly Dragon windows and the Moon fluctuations to further all your wishes, this is a new service and it is strongly recommended for you to do so.

The new Dragon's Head in Pisces will affect positively your 2nd house of money and self esteem. The Dragon's Head will reinforce your mental creativity and may lead you to take chance with money and face the world with a more definite attitude for success. This house rules all forms of finances and your self esteem as matters involving creativity and financial security will become newfound interests.

The Dragon's Tail in Virgo in your 8th house will induce great opportunities to gain new business partners and their financial support. The Dragon's Tail may force you to restructure much of the way you handle corporate endeavors and investments and could lead you to studies of some financial real estate endeavors. This house deals also with the mysteries of live and friends will also stimulate your desire to investigate the unknown and contribute to your advanced intellectual and spiritual gifts. The Dragon's Head in Taurus in your metaphysical area will also help to learn, study, or teach deep matters and sharpen your intuition and grow out of archaic inserted religious limitations.

On your corporate money and spiritual house, the Dragon's Tail will induce financial changes and will stimulate your travel both physically and spiritually. A new desire for mental exploration will become a way to explore your capabilities in servicing the world. Be ready, and accept those up- coming changes with confidence. Matters involving finances, traveling, health, insurance, health, metaphysics, education and the arts, including writing and publishing will become a powerful driving force.

Some lucky souls born in February will enjoy a new spiritual study and gather pure cosmic consciousness. A new way of dealing with your own self worth and spirituality will be induced by the Dragon's Head. Many hard-working Aquarius will receive opportunities to improve their knowledge of finance and computers and initiate good and rewarding businesses. Following an investment in a study, many of you will be traveling and enjoying new positions in servicing the world. This will open exciting doors to pass on your knowledge to others and attract very spiritual friends. In the long run, this impact will also bring about rewarding financial contracts.

The Dragon's Tail's location in the sign of Virgo in your 8th house will impose a total re-structure of your finances, and this may bring serious stress involving wrong investments. The Dragon will also remove unworthy business or emotional partners. This turmoil will induce physical and mental stress even depression during the waning moons, (see Moon Power publication for dates). During the new and full moons of March and September 2006 serious happenings based upon your karma with some people will be forced upon you. Be prepared to use your will and avoid disheartening thoughts when dealing with all the weight of legacy death of a close person and insurance matters.

You may not know it just yet, but many of your wishes will be granted after the painful restructure. Keep in mind that Aquarius soul purpose is to investigate the divine and free the body mind and spirit and reach harmony with the universe. Thus the Dragon can only promote your purpose to establish yourself and run your own show. Much of the trouble may also come from emotional stress due to serious losses or new laws established by Uncle Sam. Challenging regenerative spiritual endeavors, combined with spiritual studies or more social interactions could prove to be beneficial then. Do not let the nasty pull of the Dragon's Tail in your area of finance and spiritual death get the best of your body and mind. The positive Dragon's Head in Pisces will induce a variety of circumstances to meet new and interesting people, especially after the New Moons. Within the next two years or so, the fruits of many years of hard work will begin to pay off for all of those born in February.

You must learn to face the world with a higher awareness of your self-worth and work steadily towards your wishes. New friends, some born in December and June including foreigners will also offer you great opportunities and the chance to find love and your true purpose in life. Foreign business connections, partnerships, traveling, and luck in general will be offered by some of those new friends. Providing you avoid nurturing pessimistic thoughts about money or the past a very progressive time is ahead of you. As a rule, those born in February strive to learn and teach universal laws and this year you can do miracles. The

Dragon's Tail might induce stress but it is needed to free you from your own self deceiving attitude. Those who do not deserve your love or your intelligence will have to go. Uranus your ruler can be magical in his rewards to you especially if you deal with foreigners and swim away from dogma and chemicals. And when he does bestow, it usually lasts forever. Your awareness of the Universal Law and planning accordingly will become a major contribution towards reaching your true potential and fulfill many of your dreams. This celestial process will bring you much luck if you take on the challenge and invest in the metaphysical world and spiritual rules instead of religious doctrines. The Dragon smiles at you and all of those shining stars above your head are on your side. The Dragon will establish many of your financial wishes this year but you must let go of your past and put all your heart into your attitude.

In the year 2006 the great Jupiter (luck) will cruise through the sign of Scorpio in your 10th house of career and will bring about serious lucky wind to your life. Much progress is to be expected in this area also, especially where traveling, teaching and publishing is concerned. Shortly after his entrance into this house you can expect serious changes or advancement with work, travel, partnerships and your financial endeavors in general. Be ready for new associations and great business deals with those born in June, October and August. You may order your taped 90mn Full Life Reading or your Progressive reading to find out more about the upcoming changes in your life. Visit www.drturi.com and use our system or call our office for more information. Knowing and using your lucky window dates for the next twelve months will also add more success in all your endeavors, see for information on this new service. Good luck to all of those born in February.

Neptune Governs the Soft, Dreamy, Intuitive, And Artistic Constellation Of Pisces

Mystical and magical
Nebulous and changeable
I work my way up life's rivers and seas
To my place at God's own feet
I am PISCES, child of Neptune.

Characteristics For Those Born In March

The planet Neptune and the sign of Pisces govern souls born in March. You are a natural teacher, a philosopher and a perfectionist. You inherited phenomenal intuition and in general, will exercise more perception than logic in dealing with life. You are a gifted artist and you enjoy holistic endeavors. Many advanced Pisces are also involved in the medical profession. The young Pisces soul may also work in the construction fields. However Pisces must understand the importance of education if he is to use his full potential and teaching gifts. You are noted for your sensitivity, creativity, and artistic values. Michelangelo and George Washington and Einstein were Pisces and used their creativity to the fullest. Your downfall is an over preoccupation with others, guilt feelings and a blind acceptance of religious dogmas. Nevertheless, your good heart is not surpassed by any other sign of the zodiac and the advanced ones possess spiritual healing powers.

Highly evolved people born in March will lead many lost souls out of the deep clouds of deception towards the true colors of love and cosmic consciousness. Your soul's purpose is to swim upstream towards the ethereal light of oneness to find God. A young March spirit is deceiving, complaining and addicted to religious dogmas, cult endeavors, chemicals, drugs, and alcohol. Pisces is a karmic sign and has within itself the potential to reach immortality, fame and fortune through artistic or spiritual work. In the medical aspect of Divine Astrology, Pisces rules the feet. It is important for you to walk barefoot on the grass to regenerate the body through the magnetic fields of the earth itself. Your intuition is remarkable and should be well heeded when confronted with serious decisions. A word of caution for Pisces: Do not swim downstream as your induced faith could take you to Neptune's deepest quicksand with no option for return. David Koresh and the Rev. Jim Jones are good examples of Neptune's deceiving religious Captains. Remember to swim with the tides and respect the Universal Law (see Moon Power), as your awareness and Moon planning will become a major contribution to happiness and success. The location of your natal Dragons Head or Tail will seriously alter the strengths or weakness of Neptune in your chart. You can learn much more about yourself or anyone else by ordering any of my books or order a 90 minutes taped Full Life Reading.

2006 — Forecast For Those Born In March

Personal: The Dragon's Head entered the sign of Aries on Sunday December 26, 2004 and will stay in the Aries/Libra axis until Thursday June 22nd, 2006. Then the Dragon will enter Pisces Virgo axis until December 18, 2007. The Dragon's Head in Pisces can be a blessing if you use your personal Yearly Dragon windows and the Moon fluctuations to further all your wishes, this is a new service and it is strongly recommended for you to do so.

The Dragon's Head on yourself will induce a great opportunity to establish a new you and a fresh way of looking at the world. The Dragon may force you to restructure your body, your thoughts and improve your attitude for success. The Dragon's Head on yourself will also help you to re-create a new image to the world. The Dragon will induce serious change and will not accept anything or anybody that might try to limit your progress.

Be ready, and accept those changes with confidence. Matters involving partnerships will become powerful driving forces. The lucky ones will find a new relationship while other March souls may have to let go of a long but stressful association. A new way of dealing with the world and your new self will be induced by the Dragon's Head in your fist house. Many hard-working Pisces will get the opportunity to improve their knowledge with computers, and initiate good home businesses. Following a study, many of those born in March might also be promoted to a new position in servicing the world. This will open exciting doors to pass on your knowledge to others and enjoy new business partnerships. This impact will also bring about rewarding financial contracts. The Dragon's Tail location in the sign of Virgo in your 7th house (others) will impose a total re-structure and attract new worthwhile associations. The Dragon will remove unworthy business or emotional partners. This turmoil will induce physical and mental stress even depression during the waning moons, (see Moon Power publication for dates).

During the new and full moons of March and September 2005/06, serious happenings based upon your karma with some people will occur forcing either you or in or out of business. Be prepared to use your will and avoid disheartening thoughts when dealing with your past. You may not know it just yet, but many of your wishes can only be granted after the painful emotional restructure. Much of the trouble may also come from a new position and your desire to compete adequately. Challenging regenerative spiritual endeavors combined with studies and social interaction could prove to be beneficial then. Do not let the nasty pull of the Dragon's Tail in your marriage area get the best of your body and mind. The positive Dragon's Head in Pisces "right on you" will induce a variety of circumstances to meet interesting people, especially after the New Moons. Within the next two years or so, the fruits of many years of hard work will begin to pay off, as you might have to relocate and start over again. You must learn to face the world with a new positive attitude and the expectation of a much better partner. New friends, some born in January and July will also offer you great opportunities to meet new people, thus the potential to find your soul mate and your true purpose in life. Foreign business association contracts, partnerships, traveling, and luck in general will be offered by some of those new friends.

Providing you avoid nurturing pessimistic thoughts about a wrong relationship, a very progressive time is ahead of you. As a rule, those born in March strive for security and this year you can do miracles. The Dragon's Tail might induce stress but it is needed, and those who do not deserve you will have to go. Neptune your ruler can be surprising in his rewards to you, especially if you are aware of the moon's fluctuattions. Your awareness of this law and planning accordingly will become a major contribution to reach many of your dreams. This celestial process will bring you much luck if you take on the challenges of letting go of the past and investing in computerized education, metaphysical pursuits, traveling, and accepting new interests with foreign partners. The Dragon smiles at you and all of those shining stars above your head are on your side.

Again, during the new and Full Moons of March and September 2005/06 serious happenings may occur based upon your karma. This could induce physical or mental stress, even depression. Be prepared to use your will and avoid destructive thoughts at all costs when dealing with those losses. This impact will bring about opportunities to deal with the spiritual world and will induce great study and with it spiritual growth. The Tail of the Dragon will still be affecting your 7th house of marriage and will force you to readjust your life in dealing with others.

In the year 2006, the great Jupiter (luck) will cruise through the sign of Scorpio in your 9th house of education and will bring about serious lucky wind to your life. Much progress is to be expected especially where traveling, teaching and publishing is concerned. Shortly after his entrance into this house you can expect serious changes or advancement with work, travel, partnerships and your financial endeavors in general. Be ready for new associations and great business deals with those born in July, November and September. You may order your taped 90mn Full Life Reading or your Progressive reading to find out more about the upcoming changes in your life. Visit www.drturi.com and use our system or call our office for more information. Good luck to all of those born in February. Knowing and using your lucky window dates for the next twelve months will also add more success in all your endeavors, see for information on this new service.

Mars Governs the Aggressive - Warlike and Impatient Constellation Of Aries

All will hear my views and voice
Trial and error is my school of choice
Like a dragon, dashing and daring I appear
Fighting for those that I hold dear
I am ARIES, child of Mars.

Characteristics For Those Born In April

Assertive Mars controls the month of April. In Greek Mythology, this planet is called "The Lord of War," and rules the impatient sign of Aries. You were born a leader. However, because of your inborn impatience you will learn by your mistakes. Your strong and impatient desire to succeed must be controlled and hasty decisions avoided. Others perceive you as a competitive and motivated person. More than any other sign of the zodiac, souls born in April must learn steadiness, organization and most of all, diplomacy. When confronted, grace and charm does not really belong to you. Martian souls possess strong leadership and engineering abilities and April men are attracted to dangerous sports, speed, engineering, and the military. Due to your "turbo charged" personality, you are also accident-prone to the head, and should protect it. Both male and females born in April tend to talk too much and must learn to listen to others and control impatience. You must focus on your needs steadily and finish what you have started. Inadvertently the "red" uncontrolled Martian personality will hurt sensitive souls; thus damaging the chances for respect and promotion. Your explosive temper is generated by an inborn fear of rejection and an inferiority complex.

Do not take rejection or opposition personally. The "childlike" attitude could attract manipulative spirits wishing to structure or use the immense creativity and energy of the Mars competitive spirit. You do love your home and you are responsible with your family. Nevertheless you prefer to be where the action is, as you get bored easily. If you practice patience, tolerance and diplomacy, there is no limit to where Mars will take you: all the way to the highest level of accomplishment. Your main lesson is to learn all the diplomatic and loving traits of the opposite Venus-ruled sign Libra. Once you find yourself and confidence, the option to become a leader in any chosen field will be given to you. Souls born in the month of April must assume a diplomatic attitude when dealing with others and when dealing with corporate money. The location of your natal Dragon's Head or Tail will seriously alter the strengths or weaknesses of Mars in your chart. See Nostradamus Dragon Forecast for more information. You can learn much more about yourself or anyone else by ordering my new book entitled "I Know All About You", "The Power Of The Dragon" or "And God Created The Stars".

2006— Forecast For Those Born In April

Personal: The Dragon's Head entered the sign of Aries on Sunday December 26, 2004 and will stay in the Aries/Libra axis until Thursday June 22nd, 2006. Then the Dragon will enter Pisces Virgo axis until December 18, 2007. The Dragon's Head in Pisces can be a blessing if you use your personal Yearly Dragon windows and the Moon fluctuations to further all your wishes, this is a new service and it is strongly recommended for you to do so.

The Dragon may force you to restructure your body, mind and spirit as to improve your chances for success. The Dragon's Head in your subconscious 12th house can be heavy and will induce serious psychological changes inducing a need for spirituality. You are advised to stay clear from any form drugs and doctor's prescriptions. The Dragon may force you to restructure your own awareness, your inner thoughts and improve your desire to investigate the unknown. The Dragon's Head in Pisces will also help both the studies of metaphysics and astrology, and will sharpen your intuition. The Dragon's Head will induce great opportunities to establish a new way at looking at the world of mystery. This spiritual investment will also bring money and stability to your life. In your subconscious, the Dragon's Head will induce serious fundamental changes and will stimulate your desire for deep mental exploration, but could also bring depression. Stay clear of chemicals, and nurture a positive attitude at all costs. Be ready, and accept those upcoming spiritual changes with confidence. Matters involving the subconscious, your past, mental health, spiritual growth, writing and the arts will become a powerful driving force.

The lucky Aries will enjoy a new and rewarding health endeavor while others will take pleasure in a new job. A new way of dealing with your own self worth and creativity will be induced by the Dragon. Many a hard-working souls born in April will get the opportunity to improve their spiritual knowledge and initiate good rewarding service to the world. Following a spiritual or medical home study, many of you will be promoted to a new position. This will open exciting doors to pass on your knowledge to others and attract very spiritual business partners. In the long run, this impact will also bring about rewarding financial contracts. The Dragon's Tail location in the sign of Virgo in your 6th house (health and work) will impose a total re-structure and may bring serious stress at work and the re-building of your physical appearance. The Dragon will also remove unworthy business or emotional partners. This turmoil will induce physical and mental stress even depression during the waning moons, (see Moon Power publication for dates).

During the new and full moons of March and September serious happenings will force you to aim for a different way to service the world. Be prepared to use your will and avoid disheartening thoughts when dealing with all the stress that the Tail of the Dragon will bring. You may not know it just yet, but many of your wishes will be granted after the painful restructure. Aries does well in communication and healing others, thus the Dragon can only help you to further your soul's purpose and run your own show. Much of the trouble may also come from your past and guilt. Challenging regenerative spiritual endeavors, combined with spiritual studies or more social interaction could prove to be beneficial then. Do not let the nasty pull of the Dragon's Tail in your health and work area get the best of your body and mind.

Be aware and stay clear from any form of deceiving established religions or guru messages. Within the next two years or so, the fruits of many years of hard work will begin to pay off, as you might have to relocate and start fresh again. You must learn to face the world with a higher awareness of your self worth. New friends, some born in August, December and October will also offer you great opportunities to find true love and true meaning in life. Foreign business association contracts, partnerships, traveling, and luck in general will be offered by some of those new friends.

Providing you avoid nurturing pessimistic thoughts about previous failures, a very progressive time is ahead of you. As a rule, those born in April strive for action and money and this can come your way this year. The Dragon's Tail might induce stress at work and on your body but it is needed.. Mars, your ruler, can be surprising in his rewards to you, especially if you are aware of the Universal Law. Your awareness of the Moon law and planning accordingly with her fluctuations will become a major contribution to reach many of your dreams. This celestial process will bring you much luck if you take on the challenge of investing in subconscious and health study and if you accept new challenges with foreign partners. The Dragon smiles at you and all of those shining stars above your head are on your side. Serious changes are ahead. Have faith in yourself and the future.

In the year 2006, the great Jupiter (luck) will cruise through the sign of Scorpio in your 8th house of corportate endeavor and death. This dragon will bring dramatic news your ways but also legacy and good financial partners. Much progress is to be expected in this area especially where mobey and business is concerned. Be ready for new associations and great business deals with those born in August, October and December.

If you never experienced Dr. Turi's gifts you must do it now as this new Dragon will impose incredible challenges and knowing about it in great details can only bring more power to you and avoid depressions. You may order your taped 90mn Full Life Reading or your Progressive reading to find out more about the upcoming changes in your life. Visit www.drturi.com and use our system or call our office for more information. Knowing and using your lucky window dates for the next twelve months will also add more success in all your endeavors, see for information on this new service. Good luck to all of those born in April.

Venus Governs the Beautiful and Financially Oriented Constellation Of Taurus

Luxurious and elegant
I have the memory of an elephant
Loving all of life's finer pleasures
Gifted am I at acquiring more coffers and treasures
I am TAURUS, child of Venus.

Characteristics For Those Born In May

The month of May is governed by the planet Venus and by the reliable sign of Taurus. Others perceive you as beautiful, somehow stubborn and practical. You are the moneymaking sign of the Zodiac and you have stability and true love to offer to others. You need to control your jealousy, insecurity, and your authoritarian attitudes. You are a gifted artist and strive for organization. You are also attracted to the professions of banking, real estate, the arts, computers, radio, television, Astropsychology, aeronautics and investigation, to name a few. Many "Bulls" will reach fame and fortune and enjoy the security of a beautiful and big house. Strong and dominant, you have inherited a deep intuition, a tremendous common sense, and a powerful will. Venus rules love and possession; you must avoid destructive thoughts pertaining to jealousy, stubbornness and insecurity. Learn to channel Venus' constructive powers towards creativity, diplomacy and love. If you behave in an insecure stubborn and unattractive manner you will lose it all in the end. Your down-to-earth approach to life must not interfere with your spiritual growth. Part of your lesson in this lifetime is to keep an open mind to the world of the spirit and use the metaphysical information to ensure financial growth by adapting to the moons fluctuations (see Moon Power). Your desire for practicality and riches is legendary but you will always regenerate with New Age and metaphysical matters. You will courageously handle the difficulties of life with a solid attitude, and you inherited a beautiful nobility of purpose. Girls born in May are beautiful, classic, intellectual, magnetic, and sensitive, and will always combine Venus' beauty and sensual magnetism to attain their goals. You are meticulous and critical about your mate and it is important for you to marry someone well groomed and well respected. With you, love must last forever. Food is often on your mind; do not eat when you are upset Remember to respect the Universal Law (see Moon Power), as your awareness and moon planning will become a major contribution towards reaching many of your dreams. The location of your natal Dragons Head or Tail will seriously alter the strengths or weakness of Venus in your chart. You can learn much more about yourself or anyone else by ordering my new book entitled "I Know All About You", "The Power Of The Dragon" or "And God Created The Stars".

2006 — Forecast For Those Born In May

Personal: The Dragon's Head entered the sign of Aries on Sunday December 26, 2004 and will stay in the Aries/Libra axis until Thursday June 22nd, 2006. Then the Dragon will enter Pisces Virgo axis until December 18, 2007. The Dragon's Head in Pisces can be a blessing if you use your personal Yearly Dragon windows and the Moon fluctuations to further all your wishes, this is a new service and it is strongly recommended for you to do so.

The Dragon Head may force you to reevaluate of your deep wishes and open door for friends. Those new friends will stimulate your desire to investigate the unknown or further your wishes for great success. The Dragon's Head in Pisces will induce serious traveling, studies and a deep thirst for spirituality. You are advised to stay clear from religious groups limiting your cosmic consciousness and spirituality. The Dragon may force you to restructure your own awareness, your inner thoughts and improve your desire to investigate other more advanced groups and new friends. The Dragon's Head in Pisces will also help both the studies of metaphysics and astrology and in the process sharpen your intuition. The Dragon's Head will induce great opportunities to establish a new way at looking at the world of mystery. These investments will force unworthy friends to move away and bring money and stability to your life.

The Dragon's Head in Pisces will also induce new study involving the art, computers and metaphysics. A new desire for mental exploration will become a way to explore your capabilities in servicing the world electronically. Many of you will also consider buying or selling houses, and will land on great opportunities to do so because of new acquaintances. On your wishes area, the Dragon's Head will induce serious fundamental changes to reach your inner desires and will stimulate traveling both physically and spiritually. Be ready, and accept those upcoming changes with confidence. Matters involving friends, wishes, traveling, health, education, electronics and the arts, including writing and publishing will become powerful driving forces.

The lucky Gemini will enjoy a new home and or a new child while older Gemini will enjoy their children's children. A new way of dealing with your own self worth and creativity will be induced by the Dragon's Head. Many hard-working June souls will get the opportunity to improve their knowledge with computers and initiate good home businesses. Following home study, many of you will be prone to travel and enjoy a new and stronger position in servicing the world. This will open exciting doors to pass on your knowledge to others, attract very spiritual groups, and make numerous friends. In the end, this impact will also bring about rewarding financial contracts. The Dragon's Tail's location in the sign of Virgo in your 5th house (love and romance) will impose a total re-structure of your love area and may bring serious stress with a strenuous endeavor, a demanding partner, or with a child. The Dragon will remove unworthy business or emotional partners. This turmoil will induce physical and mental stress even depression during the waning moons, (see Moon Power publication for dates).

Some June souls will rebirth themselves with an old lover where all dramatic lessons were painfully learned. Those karmic lovers will undergo a full and total re-structure and with it the possibility for an incredible happiness forever after. During the new and full moons of June and December 2006 serious happenings based upon your karma with some people will take place and force you or them to readjust your views and feelings for them, while others will aim for more personal wishes. Be prepared to use your will and avoid disheartening thoughts when dealing with all the stress that the Tail of the Dragon has or may bring to you. You may not know it just yet, but many of your wishes will be granted after the painful restructure. Keep in mind that Gemini's soul purpose is to explore the duality of life and to further security to the world. Thus the Dragon can only promote your wishes to establish and run your own show. Challenging regenerative spiritual endeavors, combined with spiritual studies or more social interaction could prove to be beneficial then. Do not let the nasty pull of the Dragon's Tail in your love and speculation area get the best of your body and mind. Instead realize the total rebirth-taking place on both sides, and how much both you and your loved one have grown in the process. The potential for true love, respect and long lasting happiness will become a possibility then.

The positive Dragon's Head in Pisces will induce a variety of circumstances to meet new and interesting people, especially after all the New Moons. The fruits of many months of hard work will begin to pay off, as you might have to relocate to a new house and start fresh again. You must learn to face the world with a higher awareness of your self-worth and work steadily towards your wishes. New friends, some born in February, October and December will also offer you great opportunities to meet different people, thus the potential to find your true purpose in life. Foreign business association contracts, partnerships, traveling, and luck in general will be offered by some of those new friends.

Providing you avoid nurturing pessimistic thoughts about failure, a very progressive time is ahead of you. As a rule, those born in June strive for changes and the art and this year you can do miracles. The Dragon's Tail might induce trouble but it is needed. Those who do not deserve you will have to go. Watch and use the Moon especially if you know how to use the Universal Laws and your

Dragon dates. Your awareness of these laws and planning accordingly will become a major contribution towards reaching many of your dreams. This celestial process will bring you much luck if you take on the challenge of investing in computerized education, metaphysical pursuits, traveling, and if you accept interests with your new friends. The Dragon smiles at you and all of those shining stars above your head are on your side. Gemini will establish many wishes this year, go for them and let go of your past.

In the year 2006, the great Jupiter (luck) will cruise through the sign of Scorpio in your 7th house of marriage and partners. This dragon will bring new emotional experiences to your life and may force you to travel and deal with foreigners. Much progress is to be expected in this area especially where business is concerned. Shortly after his entrance into Scorpio you can expect serious changes or advancement with travel, partnerships and your financial endeavors in general. If you never experienced Dr. Turi's gifts you must do it now as this new Dragon will impose incredible challenges and knowing about it in great details can only bring more power to you and avoid depressions. You may order your taped 90mn Full Life Reading or your Progressive reading to find out more about the upcoming changes in your life. Visit www.drturi.com and use our system or call our office for more information. Good luck to all of those born in May.

Mercury Governs the Nervous and Witty Dual Constellation Of Gemini

Free-thinking and intelligent
You will not find me under rigorous management
You may think you know me well
Then my other half over you casts a spell
I am GEMINI, child of Mercury.

Characteristics For Those Born In June

The planet Mercury rules the sign of Gemini. You are intellectual, nervous and adaptable. Because of your strong desire to communicate, you are classified in Greek mythology as "The Messengers of the Gods." You inherited a gift of youth, a double personality and a quicksilver mind enabling you to adapt easily to any situation. On a negative note, Mercury, the "Lord of the Thieves" breeds volatile and unreliable people due to their dual characteristics. You are a gifted communicator and radio, language, photography, sales, movies and any type of public relations work appeals to you. Your natural speed for life's experiences makes you impatient and nervous. You must learn to focus and crystallize your powerful mind. You have the potential to become an efficient speaker and produce interesting books. Due to your strong desire for security, many of you will be attracted to the real estate and food industries. Your financial potential is unlimited if you learn and make a good use of the Universal Law in charge of your Second House of income. A strong Mercury will produce an incredible amount of physical and spiritual energy that must be dissipated.

Those children are classified by science and unaware psychologists as A.D.D. (Attention Deficit Disorder). Contrary to what scientists assume and perceive as an indisposition, it is actually a potent gift from God. The researchers (scientist's nerds) have created another name AADD or (Aduld Attention Deficit Disorder) but this time the giant poisoning drugs industry target ignorant adults and as always only the doctors, insurance companies and the pharmaceutical Industry benefit for killing ignorant people in the long run. What they do not know is that the soul is simply programmed to naturally reject traditional education (because of a surplus amount of nervous energy produced by a strong Mercury they can not stay still for long or listen) thus opening the rare door to genius and with it the potential for new discovery. Incidentally, President

Clinton, Einstein, and I were born with "ADD." Thus if a teacher is mistaken about some information, the Mercurial soul's inborn sense of curiosity and discovery will bring about potential information leading to the truth. Impatience, nervousness, mental curiosity, and a short attention span are your characteristics. You will never follow long established dogmas. Your Mercurial spirit will open new doors to mental exploration. You are curious by nature and are always questioning. Boredom is your worse enemy and you must associate with intellectual people who can stimulate your incredible mind.

Telling jokes is also a part of your mental agility. A word of caution for you: Always be alert when the Moon crosses the deadly sign of Scorpio at work, especially after the Full Moon. Remember to respect the Universal Law (see Moon Power) as your awareness and moon planning will be a major contribution of avoiding dramatic experiences, and will help you reach many of your dreams. The location of your natal Dragon's Head or Tail will seriously alter the strength or weakness of Mercury in your chart. You can learn much more about yourself or anyone else by ordering my new book entitled "I Know All About You", "The Power Of The Dragon" or "And God Created The Stars".

2006 — Forecast For Those Born in June

Personal: The Dragon's Head entered the sign of Aries on Sunday December 26, 2004 and will stay in the Aries/Libra axis until Thursday June 22nd, 2006. Then the Dragon will enter Pisces Virgo axis until December 18, 2007. The Dragon's Head in Pisces can be a blessing if you use your personal Yearly Dragon windows and the Moon fluctuations to further all your wishes, this is a new service and it is strongly recommended for you to do so.

The Dragon's Head will induce great opportunities to establish or promote a new career for you and a new way to administer to your world. The Dragon may force you to restructure your education and improve your attitude for success. The Dragon's Head in Pisces will help you to re-create a new image to the world and further your desire to stand high in the eyes of others. Right on your professional life, the Dragon will induce serious change and will not accept anything or anybody trying to stop your progress. Be ready, and accept those changes with confidence. Matters involving your status and position in the world will become powerful driving forces.

The lucky Gemini will also enjoy new hobbies while older Gemini will enjoy serious promotions. A new way of dealing with your home, security and your family will be induced by the Dragon's Tail affecting your real estate arena. Following education many of those born in June will be promoted to a new position and travel far and fast. This will open exciting doors to pass on your knowledge to others and may bring new business partners. This impact will also bring about rewarding financial contracts. Location of the Dragon's Tail in the sign of Virgo in your 4th house (home) will impose a total re-structure of your base of operation. The Dragon will also remove unworthy business deals or wrong emotional partners. This turmoil will induce physical and mental stress even depression during the waning moons, (see Moon Power publication for dates).

During the new and full moons of January and July 2006 serious happenings based upon your karma with some people will take place and force you or them to be in or out of your home and/or business. Be prepared to use your will and avoid disheartening thoughts when dealing with the failures of your past. You may not know it just yet, but many of your wishes can only be granted after the painful restructure. Much of the trouble may also come from new laws established by your governing superiors or Uncle Sam. Challenging regenerative spiritual endeavors, combined with studies and social interaction, could prove to be beneficial then. Do not let the nasty pull of the Dragon's Tail in your security area get the best of your body and your mind. You may be forced to lose a house or experience serious stress with family members. The positive Dragon's Head in Pisces right on your career area will induce a variety of circumstances in meeting interesting people and may induce relocation, especially after the New Moons. Within the next two years or so, the fruits of many years of hard work will begin to pay off, as you might have to move and start fresh again. You must learn to face the world with a new positive attitude. New friends, some born in May/November/March will also offer you great opportunities to meet different people, thus the potential to find love and your true purpose in life. Foreign business association contracts, partnerships, traveling, and luck in general will be offered by some of those new friends.

Providing you avoid nurturing pessimistic thoughts about your upbringing or the family circle, a very progressive time is ahead of you. As a rule, those born in June strive for variety in all aspects of their lives, and this year you can do miracles. The Dragon's Tail might induce stress at home but it is needed. Those who do not deserve you will have to go. The Moon is your ruler and she can be surprisingly great in her rewards to you, especially if you are aware of the Universal Laws based upon the moon's fluctuations and your dragon lucky windows. Your awareness of these laws and planning accordingly will become a major contribution in reaching many of your dreams. This celestial process will bring you much luck if you take on the challenge of investing in any form of education and if you accept new challenges with foreign partners. The Dragon smiles at you and all of those shining stars above your head are supporting your career.

In the year 2006, the great Jupiter (luck) will cruise through the sign of Scorpio in your 6th house of work and service to the world. Jupiter will bring new emotional or business partners to your life and may force you to travel and deal with foreigners. Much progress is to be expected in this area especially where work and investment is concerned. Shortly after his entrance into Scorpio you can expect serious changes or advancement at work and your health. Be ready for new associations and great business deals with foreigners. If you never experienced Dr. Turi's gifts you must do it now as this new Dragon will impose incredible challenges and knowing about it in great details can only bring more power to you and avoid depressions. You may order your taped 90mn Full Life Reading or your Progressive reading to find out more about the upcoming changes in your life. Visit www.drturi.com and use our system or call our office for more information. Good luck to all of those born in June.

The Moon Governs the Nurturing and Caring Constellation Of Cancer

I am mother I nurture and provide
In my soul the physical and spiritual collide
I say, "ask and you shall receive."
But also "as you sow, so shall you reap"
I am CANCER, child of the Moon.

Characteristics For Those Born In July

The moon rules the emotional sign of Cancer. You are a moonchild and you are strongly affected by the Moon's fluctuations. Family matters will always play an important role in your life. You are classified as the "caretakers" of the Zodiac. Much of your success depends on the awareness and ability to respect and use the moon's passage through the belt of the Zodiac. You are distinctively gifted with real estate and food (cooking or eating it). Lunar children have a solid sense of organization and have inherited strong managerial gifts. You are a perfectionist and are quite critical. Plants, and green appeals to you, and you tend to worry too much about health to the point of becoming a vegetarian. You will perform very well in a position of power or management. Financial security is important to you and you will shine through your inner ability to amass riches and possessions. You have a gift with children and you have a natural zest to teach them. You must avoid depressing thoughts of the past and keep control over your powerful imagination. Steadiness, organization, warmth, love, and charm belong to you. Your powerful emotions can be channeled positively with music, singing, and the arts in general (country music is a Cancer/July vibration.). You are attracted to successful people (older or younger mates) and many Cancers marry rich. Your natural tendency to smother family members and friends at all times makes you admired and deeply loved. You must learn to control your overwhelming sensitivity and participate with life outside of your home a little more. As a rule, all Moonchildren are great homemakers unless the soul selected a non-domestic masculine Moon before reincarnating on this dense physical world. Like all other water signs you regenerate in research, science, and metaphysics. You tend to worry too much about your and others health and you should adopt a more positive spiritual attitude. Learn to let go of the wrong people and move on with life. It is a must for you to respect the Universal Law (see Moon Power), as your awareness and moon planning will become a major contribution toward avoiding dramatic experiences and reaching many of your dreams. The location of your natal Dragon's Head or Tail will seriously alter the strengths or weakness of the Moon in your chart. You can learn much more about yourself or anyone else by ordering my new book entitled "I Know All About You", "The Power Of The Dragon" or "And God Created The Stars".

2005 — Forecast For Those Born in July

Personal: The Dragon's Head entered the sign of Aries on Sunday December 26, 2004 and will stay in the Aries/Libra axis until Thursday June 22nd, 2006. Then the Dragon will enter Pisces Virgo axis until December 18, 2007. The Dragon's Head in Pisces can be a blessing if you use your personal Yearly Dragon windows and the Moon fluctuations to further all your wishes, this is a new service and it is strongly recommended for you to do so.

The Dragon's Head will induce a great opportunity for education and establish an improved way at looking positively at the world. After a serious study you may gain serious opportunities to improve or gain recognition if you decide to crystallize your thoughts, write and publish your work. A computer course is a must if you have any chance to enjoy this new Dragon's blessing. These studies will help you to structure your thoughts and improve your creativity and prospects for success. The Dragon's Head in Pisces will also seriously improve your desire to travel, physically and mentally. Your potential for a better or improved career will flourish as long as you are willing to expand your education and accept mental challenges with confidence. Matters involving traveling, education, the arts and publishing will become a powerful driving force.

The lucky ones will travel far and fast, while others will spend more time shaping up knowledge. A new way of thinking about your education and the world at large will be induced by the Dragon's Head. Many hard-working Cancer will also get the opportunity to improve their knowledge of computers, television and settle upon a good working position with it. Following a study, many of souls born in July will also be promoted to a higher position while others will publish their work worldwide. This restructure will open exciting doors to promising new businesses and careers in foreign lands and dealings with foreigners. This will also bring about rewarding financial contracts. The Dragon's Tail location in the sign of Virgo in your 3rd house (the mind), will impose legality, contracts or a total re-vamping of your critical thinking, and may even induce cosmic consciousness to the advanced spiritual Cancer.

Avoid unworthy or destructive thoughts, as old ideas or unworthy partners will have to be removed. The new challenges could induce physical or mental stress even depression during the waning moons, (see Moon Power publication for dates). During the new and full moons of March and September 2006 serious happenings based upon your karma will take place, and force you or unworthy partners in or out of business. Be prepared to use your will to avoid depths of despair when the Dragon's Tail will bother your consciousness. You may not know it just yet, but many of your wishes can only be granted after the painful mental or legal restructure. Stay clear of antidepressants, drugs and alcohol at all costs, as your mental sanity will be challenged to the extreme.

Much of the trouble may also come from your own self-destructive thoughts. Challenging regenerative spiritual endeavors combined with studies and social interaction could prove to be beneficial then. Do not let the nasty pull of the Dragon's Tail in your communication area get the best of your body and mind. Avoid depressive thoughts at all times, and relax with the art or spiritual study. The positive Dragon's Head in Pisces will induce a variety of circumstances to study, travel and meet interesting foreign people, especially after the New Moons. Within the next two years or so, the fruits of many years of hard work will begin to pay off as you might have to relocate to a far away place.

You must learn to face the world with a new positive attitude. New friends, some born in November, March and January will also offer you great opportunities to further your wishes, thus the potential to find love and solid purpose with a good reason to be alive. Foreign business connections, partnerships, traveling, and luck in general will be offered by some of those new friends. Providing you avoid nurturing pessimistic thoughts about despair or your past, a very progressive time is ahead of you. As a rule, those born in July strive for security and a good family life, and this year you can do miracles. The Dragon's Head will induce many opportunities for traveling, speaking, writing and teaching. The Sun your ruler can be quite magical in his rewards to you and when he does it is usually very progressive. Remember to respect the Universal Law (Moon's fluctuations) and your dragon window dates as your awareness and planning will become a major contribution towards reaching many of your dreams.

In the year 2006, the great Jupiter (luck) will cruise through the sign of Scorpio in your 5th house of love, romance, children and creativity. Jupiter will bring new emotional or business partners to your life and may force you to travel far and fast. Much progress is to be expected in this area especially where creativity and children are concerned. Shortly after Jupiter's entrance into Scorpio you can expect serious changes or advancement with your love life and financial endeavors in general. Be ready for new birth and great business deals with foreigners. If you never experienced Dr. Turi's gifts you must do it now as this new Dragon will impose incredible challenges and knowing about it in great details can only bring more power to you and avoid depressions. You may order your taped 90mn Full Life Reading or your Progressive reading to find out more about the upcoming changes in your life. Visit www.drturi.com and use our system or call our office for more information. Good luck to all of those born in July.

The Sun Governs the Flamboyant and Majestic Constellation of Leo

Powerful and Charming
All things living find me disarming
I step to the center of God's stage
In the books of history I have always a page
I am LEO, child of the Sun.

Characteristics For Those Born In August

The month of August is governed by the all-powerful Sun and by the magnanimous sign of Leo. Your solar sign reflects the dignified Sun's life force energy and classifies you as "The Life Giver". During the day the Sun outshines all the other planets giving you the option to reach fame, fortune and power during the course of your life. Naturally gifted, you are attracted to professions involving the arts, public life, medicine, research, management, and any endeavors that could offer you a chance to shine. Just as the Sun's rays penetrate the depths of the rainforest, you were born with the potential to bring and promote life to all that you touch. You have a lot to offer others and the world, providing you exercise control over your ego and authoritative nature. The untamed King of the Jungle must positively direct and control the Sun's creative force without burning himself or others in the process. You are fixed and strongly motivated by the will to succeed. Strong and dominant, you nurture a formidable desire to organize and rule others. If you become too overbearing, others will then teach you the lesson of humility, where you will be forced back to start from scratch. Destructive outbursts of emotions and unfettered pride are enemies of success. Your challenge is to recognize the powerful Sun's energy and diligently work towards a better understanding and respect of others. Acting eccentrically or with pride and without forethought is your weakness. However you will courageously handle all the difficulties of life. The advanced Leo possesses nobility of purpose and great spiritual values. Women born in August are stunning, intellectual, magnetic, and attract others with their enthusiastic solar power. Women born in August are protective and dedicated mothers. The desire for fame could also make them overbearing and try to live through their children's accomplishments. The Sun rules life and you may nurture a subconscious fear of death and decay. But nature gives you a strong mind and a robust body. You love animals, especially horses. You tend to be weak and accident prone in the back, knees and joint areas. (President Clinton was born in August and, busted his knee in Florida!) A word of caution for those born in August: use precaution and moderation when running or jogging. Remember to respect the Universal Law (see Moon Power), as your awareness of Sun/Moon planning will become a major contribution towards reaching love and happiness. The location of your natal Dragon's Head or Tail will seriously alter the strengths or weakness of the Sun in your chart. You can learn much more about yourself or anyone else by ordering my new book entitled "I Know All About You", "The Power Of The Dragon" or "And God Created The Stars".

20056 — Forecast For Those Born in August

Personal: The Dragon's Head entered the sign of Aries on Sunday December 26, 2004 and will stay in the Aries/Libra axis until Thursday June 22nd, 2006. Then the Dragon will enter Pisces Virgo axis until December 18, 2007. The Dragon's Head in Pisces can be a blessing if you use your personal Yearly Dragon windows and the Moon fluctuations to further all your wishes, this is a new service and it is strongly recommended for you to do so.

The Dragon's Head will reinforce your desire to establish financial security and may force you to face the world with a more definite attitude for success. This house involves possession and spiritual studies thus the Dragon's Head will induce great opportunities to invest or deal with the affairs of death. Matters involving other people resources, metaphysics and investment will become powerful interests. The lucky ones will benefit from real estate endeavors or take on courses involving financial speculations and investments. A new way of making money will be induced by the Dragon's Head and many hard-working Leos will get a windfall of creative energy to make more money. Many of them will also be promoted, especially if they decide to write or look for investors. Many souls born in August will work hard to get better financial help and positions where business partners are concerned, while others will be able to publish their works. This will open exciting doors to promising new business endeavors and rewarding financial contacts. The Dragon's Tail's location in the sign of Virgo will cruise through your 2nd house of finances and death thus some souls close to Leo will leave this world, and through a legacy, offer them financial due and the fruit of many years of hard labor.

Some unworthy business partners will be removed by the Dragon's Tail and cost you money too. These experiences could induce legal battles and mental stress even depression during the waning moon, (see Moon Power publication for dates). During the New and Full Moon March and September 2006, serious happenings based upon your personal karma will take place. You are strongly advised to use your will and avoid depressing thoughts when dealing with old partners or dear friends that may be called by God or forced to move away. Challenging regenerative spiritual endeavors combined with studies and social interaction could prove to be beneficial then. Do not let the nasty pull of the Dragon's Tail get the best of your body and mind. The positive Dragon's Head in Pisces will induce a form of death and rebirth and a variety of circumstances to promote worthwhile business deals with productive partners. Within the next two years or so, the fruits of many years of hard work will begin to pay off. You may be forced to face the world with a better business attitude and a new profound knowledge.

Foreign business association contracts, partnerships, traveling, and luck in general will be offered by some of those business partners. Providing you keep busy and avoid nurturing pessimistic thoughts about your past, a very progressive time is ahead of you. As a rule, those born in August strive for fame and wealth. This may lead you to travel, deal, or teach in foreign lands. The Sun is quite fast in his rewards and when he does it usually lasts for a long time. Keep in mind to respect the laws of the moon. Your awareness and respect of the Universal Law and your personal dragon dates will become a major contribution to establish emotional, financial and spiritual stability. The opportunity to make serious financial progress is offered to you this year. This celestial process will bring you much luck if you take on any challenges of investing in computerized education, metaphysical, medical, financial pursuits, traveling, or if you accept challenges with new partners. The Dragon smiles at you and those shining stars above your head are on your side.

In the year 2006, the great Jupiter (luck) will cruise through the sign of Scorpio in your 4th house of home, real estate and familly and may induce changes. Jupiter will bring new options for investing in foreign land and may force you to deal with foreigners. Much progress is to be expected in this area especially where finances and business is concerned. Shortly after Jupiter's entrance into Scorpio you can expect serious changes or advancement with travel, partnerships and your financial endeavors in general. Be ready for new associations and great business deals. If you never experienced Dr. Turi's gifts you must do it now as this new Dragon will impose incredible challenges and knowing about it in great details can only bring more power to you and avoid depressions. You may order your taped 90mn Full Life Reading or your Progressive reading to find out more about the upcoming changes in your life. Visit www.drturi.com and use our system or call our office for more information. Good luck to all of those born in August.

Mercury Governs the Precise and Critical Constellation Of Virgo

Cleansing impurities large and small
Don't think yourself immune, for I see all
Attending to every chore and task
Perfection being all that I ask
I am VIRGO, child of Mercury.

Characteristics For Those Born In September

The month of September is governed by the planet Mercury and by the critical sign of Virgo. You are an intellectual, very critical and picky and you tend to work too hard. You are a master of communication and the option to become a speaker or a great writer is offered to you. You may also misuse this power and become sarcastic to others. You will always combine logic and intuition in dealing with life in general. Astrologically, you have been classified as the "perfectionists". You can do well in the fields of medicine, law, teaching, writing, designing, and office work and you are in some areas a refined artist. Your downfall is sarcasm and an overly concerned attitude with trivial matters. Some young Mercurial souls are overwhelmed with health matters and turn themselves into health lunatics. Others simply refuse to work and succumb to chemical drug and alcohol abuse. Letting the rational mind scrutinize everything can hinder your spiritual gifts and neutralize your cosmic consciousness.

You have inherited a powerful investigative mind that could lead you to science, chemicals, research, radio, television, newspaper reporting, computer programming and the law. Advanced souls are great mental leaders and masters in communication. Robert Shapiro and Marcia Clark (O.J. Simpson trial attorneys) are Virgos and indicative of your intellectual potential pertaining to investigation and the law. You may be prone to headaches or head injury, eye and sinus problems. Be aware of your environment in public places. You are prone to poisoning and are strongly advised to keep away from alcohol and narcotics. Also, be aware, diets that are too restrictive may cause just as many problems as over-indulgence. Your body and metabolism are both well equipped to deal with all types of food, including red meat. If your natural desire for perfection prevails and you eliminate this "red" source of food, you must then substitute it with different red foods such as red wine, hot peppers or other thermogenic foods.

If you happen to suffer headaches or migraines, you may find relief by walking barefoot on the grass (or close to a body of water) to regenerate from the earth's magnetic field. As a rule all souls born in September are accident prone to head trauma and violent death. Therefore, if you were born in September, do not take chances, especially during or after the Full Moon. Keep in mind to respect the Universal Law (see Moon Power), as your awareness of the Mercury/Moon planning will become a major contribution for happiness. The location of your natal Dragon's Head or Tail will seriously alter the strengths or weakness of Mercury in your chart. You can learn much more about yourself or anyone else by ordering my new book entitled "I Know All About You", "The Power Of The Dragon" or "And God Created The Stars".

2006 — Forecast For Those Born in September

Personal: The Dragon's Head entered the sign of Aries on Sunday December 26, 2004 and will stay in the Aries/Libra axis until Thursday June 22nd, 2006. Then the Dragon will enter Pisces Virgo axis until December 18, 2007. The Dragon's Head in Pisces can be a blessing if you use your personal Yearly Dragon windows and the Moon fluctuations to further all your wishes, this is a new service and it is strongly recommended for you to do so.

The Dragon's Head will force you to face the world with a different attitude, as the Dragon's powerful rays will make you very magnetic to others. Matters involving marriage, contracts and partners will become newfound interests. The lucky souls born in September will find new partners and great financial support while others may be forced to end long unworthy relationships. A new way of thinking about the way you project yourself to the world will be induced by the Dragon, and many hard-working Virgo will get the opportunity to shine with beautiful partners. Many souls born in September will also be promoted to higher positions or be able to establish new and more powerful personas. This will open exciting doors to promising new business endeavors and rewarding financial contacts. The Dragon's Tail location in your own sign of Virgo in your 1st house (personality) will still force you into a general restructure of your physical and spiritual selves. This could also induce both physical and mental stress including depression. During the new and Full Moons of March and September 2006, serious happenings based upon your personal karma and dealings with others will take place. You are strongly advised to use your will and avoid depressing or destructive thoughts.

Challenging regenerative spiritual endeavors combined with studies and social interaction could prove to be beneficial then. Do not let the nasty pull of the Dragon's Tail get the best of your body and mind. The positive Dragon's Head in Pisces will induce a variety of circumstances to meet interesting, either much younger, or older people in your life. Within the next few months or so, the fruits of many years of hard work will begin to pay off as you may be forced to face the world with a new partner and a new attitude.

Those new partners will offer great opportunities to travel and learn where foreigners will play an important part in your life. The new Dragon's Head in general, will offer foreign business interests, partnerships, traveling, and luck. Providing you keep busy and avoid nurturing pessimistic thoughts about previous unworthy partners or cultivating deep guilt feelings from your past a very progressive time is ahead of you. As a rule, those born in September strive for perfection health and ard work. Mercury the "Messenger of the Gods" will reward you its own ways that will last forever. Remember to respect the Universal Law of the ,oom and use your personal Dragon windows, as your awareness will become a major contribution for your success. The opportunity to make serious progress with others is available to you. This celestial process will bring you much luck if you take on the challenge of investing and trusting others and if you associate with new partners. Those shining stars above your head are on your side.

In the year 2006, the great Jupiter (luck) will cruise through the sign of Scorpio in your 3rd house (mind) and will bring about new studies and new emotional or business partners to your life and may force you to travel and deal with foreigners. Much progress is to be expected in this area especially where contracts and legality is concerned. Jupiter may also bring a lot of good time and with it unwanted pounds, don't drink and keep busy. Shortly after Jupiter's entrance into Scorpio you can expect serious changes or advancement with travel, partnerships and your financial endeavors in general. Be ready for new associations and great business deals with foreigners. If you never experienced Dr. Turi's gifts you must do it now as this new Dragon will impose incredible challenges and knowing about it in great details can only bring more power to you and avoid depressions. You may order your taped 90mn Full Life Reading or your Progressive reading to find out more about the upcoming changes in your life. Visit www.drturi.com and use our system or call our office for more information. Good luck to all of those born in September.

Venus Governs the Diplomatic and Peaceful Constellation Of Libra

Lover of grace and harmony
Seeking the balance of matrimony
Though there are those that hold to opinions tight
I will see it in all the different lights
I am LIBRA, child of Venus.

Characteristics For Those Born In October

The month of October is ruled by the planet Venus and by the charming sign of Libra. You are strongly motivated by a desire for justice and you must create harmony in all areas of life. You are classified as the "Peacemaker" in Astropsychology. You will succeed in your career because of your gentle personality, your sense of diplomacy and your natural "savoir faire." You rarely learn by mistake, but you must avoid prolonged indecision. Those born in October must establish Libra's soul's purpose of achieving balance, emotional, financial, and spiritual stability during the course of their lifetimes. You must stand for yourself and learn decision making by following not only your rational mind but also your accurate intuitions. You possess a strong psychological aptitude and do well in the real estate and the food industries, the stock market, interior design, marriage counseling and the arts in general. You must focus on what you need first by using inner stamina and both your practical and intuitive minds.

These gentle personalities will be attracted to competitive people and one can expect many challenges from them. Rough behavior or the abrupt and assertive manner of a business partner easily offends Libras. The same desire for diplomacy is expected from a friend or a lover. You should also avoid taking remarks too personally. You love a good home and you enjoy the company of business-oriented partners. Your downfall comes from traditional scientific or religious teachings and your inability to challenge your way of life. Casting aside self-discovery and real spirituality will slow down or eliminate your chances to develop your cosmic consciousness. This produces mental snobs, librarians, ministers and religious leaders. As indicated by Libra's scale, you must look at both sides of the dilemma. Using both traditional and untraditional means of education will bring about a better awareness of the laws. The limitation of conventional education (psychology or religion) is overridden by a more progressive spiritual attitude (New Age and Astropsychology) and will bring about all the answers you seek.

You are a philosopher and a great teacher; likewise, you will travel far in search of the truth. The truth you are aiming for is right above your heads in the stars and not in man made religious doctrines. A word of caution to you: stay clear of all chemicals, such as pot, drugs, or alcohol, as these destructive habits could lead you to a hospital or worse to jail. Remember to respect the Universal Law (see Moon Power), as your awareness of Moon planning will become a major contribution for your happiness and success. The location of your natal Dragon's Head or Tail will seriously alter the strengths or weaknesses of Venus in your chart. You can learn much more about yourself or anyone else by ordering my new book entitled "I Know All About You", "The Power Of The Dragon" or "And God Created The Stars".

2006 — Forecast For Those Born in October

Personal: The Dragon's Head entered the sign of Aries on Sunday December 26, 2004 and will stay in the Aries/Libra axis until Thursday June 22nd, 2006. Then the Dragon will enter Pisces Virgo axis until December 18, 2007. The Dragon's Head in Pisces can be a blessing if you use your personal Yearly Dragon windows and the Moon fluctuations to further all your wishes, this is a new service and it is strongly recommended for you to do so.

The Dragon's Head will force you to face the world with a different attitude as far as work or your body is concerned and you will be in serious demand by others. Matters involving work, health, and security will become profound interests. Some lucky Libra will find great real estate deals and will be able to service the world from a new and beautiful base of operation. Other souls born in October may benefit from a study and improve their service to the world. The Dragon Tail located in your 12th house regulating your subconscious will induce a new way of self-perception relating to the world you live in or where you are at in your present incarnation. Many Libras will become extraordinarily sensitive and spiritual and in the process will aim towards higher learning and gain more spirituality. Those who worked hard the last two years will be able to travel, teach or publish their artistic or spiritual works. The passage of the Dragon in both the physical and spiritual houses will open exciting new doors in both the spiritual and physical worlds. This promises many new business endeavors and rewarding financial contacts. The Dragon's Tail's location in your subconscious 12th house will induce a general restructure of your subconscious and your spiritual self. This impact will induce deep psychological changes and will induce deep depression during the waning moon periods. Invest in celestial spiritual study (astrology) and avoid any form of conventional religious or guru type of endeavors. Stay clear of alcohol, drugs and the use of antidepressants. Most of all let g o of your past and the wrong people in your life and seek my help if you need to regenerate your spirit. .

During the New and Full Moons of March and September 2006 (see Moon Power publication for dates) serious happenings based upon your personal karma will take place. Again, you are strongly advised to use your will and avoid depressing or guilty thoughts. Regenerative spiritual endeavors and metaphysical studies, combined with exercise and social interaction, could prove to be beneficial then. Do not let the nasty pull of the Dragon's Tail get the best of your subconscious and your body and stay clear of any prescriptions, drugs or alcohol. The positive Dragon's Head in Pisces will induce a variety of opportunities to improve your spiritual knowledge and your working life and to take care of your body. Joining a health club or doing a Cabalistic healing with me can only prove beneficial in the long run. Within the next few months or so, the fruits of many years of hard work will begin to pay off as you may be forced to service the world with a more advanced attitude.

The Dragon will also offer great opportunities where foreigners will play an important part of your working life. Foreign business interests, partnerships, traveling, and luck in general will be offered by the new Dragon's Head. Providing you keep busy and avoid nurturing pessimistic thoughts about your physical or mental health, a very progressive time is ahead of you. As a rule, those born in October strive for financial power and investigations through traveling and mental exploration. Venus, your ruler is magical in her rewards, and when she does bestow they usually last forever. Remember to respect the Universal Law (see Moon Power) an duse your personal; Dragon windows as this is a major contribution to your success in life. The opportunity to make serious progress this year is available to you. This celestial process will bring you much luck if you take on the challenge of investing in your health, astrology, computerized education, metaphysical pursuits, traveling, and if you associate with foreign partners. Those shining stars above your head are on your side and you can make the most of them.

In the year 2006, the great Jupiter (luck) will cruise through the sign of Scorpio in your 2nd house of money and will bring changes in the way your perceive wealth and power. Jupiter will bring new depths, new study to your life and may force you to travel and deal with foreigners. Much progress is to be expected in this area especially where study and growth is concerned. Jupiter may also bring a lot of study and traveling, take the time to relax. Shortly after Jupiter's entrance into Scorpio you can expect serious changes or advancement with travel, partnerships and your financial endeavors in general. Be ready for new associations and great business deals with foreigners. If you never experienced Dr. Turi's gifts you must do it now as this new Dragon will impose incredible challenges and knowing about it in great details can only bring more power to you and avoid depressions. You may also be forced by the dragon to suffer a serious loss, just be strong when it does happen. You may order your taped 90mn Full Life Reading or your Progressive reading to find out more about the upcoming changes in your life. Visit www.drturi.com and use our system or call our office for more information. Good luck to all of those born in October.

Pluto Governs the Mighty Constellation of Scorpio "The Eagle or Lizard."

Holder of all the secrets deep
Never speaking for they are mine to keep
For those who plunder without care
Tread carefully for I see you there
I am SCORPIO, child of Pluto.

Characteristics For Those Born In November

The planet Pluto and the intense sign of Scorpio govern the month of November. You inherited a powerful will and you are attracted to the unknown; the medical professions, the police force, metaphysics, politics and general investigations. You are classified as the "Eagle" (positive) or the "Lizard" (negative) in Divine Astrology. You are quite private, secretive even mystic and like all other water signs you excel in the study of metaphysics. Unless you are aware of your innate powers you are well advised not to sting yourself with your own dart. You carry in your soul the element of life and death, reincarnation and pure sensuality. On a negative note, your magnetic thoughts can reach anyone anywhere for good or for worse, bringing its accompanying karma into your life. The young Scorpio soul will experience drama, despair and imprisonment during the course of its life. However, the destructive energies of Pluto can be channeled positively to accomplish tremendous results. Your sign rules the Mafia, the police force and the absolute power of creation or destruction, including sex. The message is quite clear when representing anyone born in November. No one should take chances under Pluto's command. Realize the Eagle in you is your challenge and your own birthright for creation or destruction. These souls have no known fears in the face of death. Many advanced Pluto children will "fly" like an eagle above the destructive Lizard emotions and legendary jealousy. You can use your inborn mystical gifts to succeed where others would fail. Strong, private and dominant, you were born with a practical mind and an acute intuition. Your lesson is to control and direct constructively your deep emotions and use Pluto's ultimate power for the well being of society. You regenerate with investigation and spiritual growth, and must uncover your unique mission in life. You are interested and aspire only for the undiluted truth. The women of this sign are seen in Divine Astrology as "la femme fatale." You are sensual, classic, intellectual, reserved, and super magnetic. You tend to use your inner sexual power and physical beauty to reach your goals. However, even as a powerful Scorpio, you are very weak with affairs of the heart and tend to be in love with love. A word of caution for you: Do not use your poisonous stinger against yourself or society. Remember to respect the Universal Law (see Moon Power), as your awareness and Moon planning will become a major contribution to your happiness and success. The location of your natal Dragon's Head or Tail will seriously alter the strength or weakness of Pluto in your chart. You can learn much more about yourself or anyone else by ordering my books entitled "I Know All About You", "The Power of the Dragon" or "And God Created The Stars".

2005 — Forecast For Those Born In November

Personal: The Dragon's Head entered the sign of Aries on Sunday December 26, 2004 and will stay in the Aries/Libra axis until Thursday June 22nd, 2006. Then the Dragon will enter Pisces Virgo axis until December 18, 2007. The Dragon's Head in Pisces can be a blessing if you use your personal Yearly Dragon windows and the Moon fluctuations to further all your wishes, this is a new service and it is strongly recommended for you to do so.

The Dragon's Head will force you to face the world with a different attitude towards love and all that you have accepted as true. The Dragon's powerful energy will make you very magnetic to others. Matters involving speculation, money, security, love and children will or may become a newfound interest. The lucky ones will find new partners and great financial opportunity while others may be forced to end a long lasting relationship with a lover or a child. A new way of thinking about the way you project yourself, and your love to others and to the world will be induced by the Dragon, and many hard-working souls born in November will get the opportunity to create a business or a child, and shine in the process. Many of them will also be promoted to a higher position or able to publish their light work and endeavors. This will open exciting doors to promising new business endeavors and rewarding financial contacts. The Dragon's Tail's location in Virgo your 11th house (friends/wishes) will still force you into a general restructure of all affairs ruled by this house. Wrong friends or impractical wishes will produce physical and mental stress or legal battles during the waning moon periods of the current year. During the New and Full Moons of March and September 2006 serious happenings based upon love, romance and speculations will take place. You are strongly advised to stay clear from drugs, alcohol and relaxants, and use your will to avoid depressing thoughts.

Challenging regenerative spiritual endeavors combined with studies and social interaction could prove to be beneficial then. Do not let the nasty Dragon's Tail pull in your house of wishes and friends get the best of your body and mind. The positive Dragon's Head in Pisces will induce a variety of circumstances to meet interesting, either younger or older people, and promote the affairs of the 5th house of love and romance. Within the next few months, karma will be burnt and you may be forced to face the world with a new and much better partner.

Those new partners will offer great opportunities where foreigners will play an important part of your life. Foreign business association contracts, partnerships, traveling and luck in general will be offered by the new Dragon's Head in Pisces for you. Providing you keep busy and avoid nurturing pessimistic thoughts about previous partners, a very progressive time is ahead of you. As a rule, those born in November strive for power, education, traveling and health. Pluto may be slow in his rewards but when he does it is usually big. Keep in mind to respect the Universal Law of the moon and your personal dragon windows as this awareness will become a major contribution for your success or failure in life. The opportunity to make serious progress with business and love is available to you this year. This celestial process will bring you much luck if you take on the challenge of investing in computerized education, metaphysical pursuits, traveling, and if you associate with new partners provided by the Dragon. Those shining stars above your head are on your side.

In the year 2006, the great Jupiter (luck) will cruise through the sign of Scorpio in your 1st house and will bring new depths, new study to your life and may force you out of religious groups that are not giving you true light or real wisdom forcing you to travel and deal with foreigners. Much progress is to be expected in this area especially where study and spiritual growth is concerned. Jupiter may also bring a lot of study and with it stress, take the time to relax. Shortly after Jupiter's entrance into Scorpio you can expect serious changes or advancement with travel, partnerships and your financial endeavors in general. Be ready for new associations and great business deals with foreigners. If you never experienced Dr. Turi's gifts you must do it now as this new Dragon will impose incredible challenges and knowing about it in great details can only bring more power to you and avoid depressions. You may order your taped 90mn Full Life Reading or your Progressive reading to find out more about the upcoming changes in your life. Visit www.drturi.com and use our system or call our office for more information. Good luck to all of those born in November.

Jupiter Governs the Philosophical and Educated Constellation of Sagittarius

I have traveled the worldwide
With naught but the law on my side
Yearning for the higher knowledge
All of God's creation as my college
I am SAGITTARIUS, child of Jupiter.

Characteristics For Those Born In December

The planet Jupiter and the sign of Sagittarius govern the month of December. You are a philosopher, a natural teacher and classified in Divine Astrology as a "Truth Seeker." You would do well in learning or teaching computers, aeronautics, law, religion, communications, radio, and language. You are also attracted to holistic healing, animals, Indians, and the world of sports. Your desire to travel to foreign lands is quite strong. Doing so will take you far away, giving you the option to return with incredible knowledge to teach to the rest of us. You were born with the gift of teaching and you will always promote a form of purity and organization in life. You can do quite well in office work and you can be extremely organized. You inherited a quick mind from the stars and you can keep up with anyone willing to discuss knowledge and philosophy. You need to realize the importance of education and you must focus on your chosen goals. Jupiter, "The Lord of Luck," will throw you many blessings in your life. With discipline and determination you have the potential to produce interesting books, even novels. The young Sagittarius soul is too concerned with finances and must learn to give so that he may receive help from the accumulated good karma. You must adapt to the saying, "to be a millionaire, you must act and think like one." Your sign rules the wilderness, the desert, and the Indians. This also represents some of your past lives with the Incas, the Sumerians and Atlantis where you had a position of spiritual power. A word of caution: Souls born with an overbearing Jupiterian energy must guard against the codification of thoughts (books) and biblical materials; your lesson is to realize that God cannot be confined to any man-made buildings, deities or archaic doctrines. The advanced ones (truth seekers) will lead the rest of us towards the reality of God's manifestation through the stars. Remember to respect the Universal Law (see Moon Power), as your awareness of Moon planning will become a major contribution to your happiness and success. The location of your natal Dragon's Head or Tail will seriously alter the strength or weakness of Jupiter in your chart. (See Nostradamus Dragon Forecast for more information). You can learn much more about yourself or anyone else by ordering my books entitled "I Know All About You", "The Power Of The Dragon" or "And God Created The Stars".

2006 — Forecast For Those Born In December

Personal: The Dragon's Head entered the sign of Aries on Sunday December 26, 2004 and will stay in the Aries/Libra axis until Thursday June 22nd, 2006. Then the Dragon will enter Pisces Virgo axis until December 18, 2007. The Dragon's Head in Pisces can be a blessing if you use your personal Yearly Dragon windows and the Moon fluctuations to further all your wishes, this is a new service and it is strongly recommended for you to do so.

A new way of thinking about the way you perceive your security and your old days will be induced by the Dragon's Head. Many souls born in December operating in the real estate or food industry will also be promoted to a higher place and gain a position of responsibility. The passage of the Dragon in both the sign of Pisces and Virgo will open exciting new doors in both houses and all affairs related to those houses within the spiritual and physical worlds. This promises many new business endeavors and rewarding financial contacts. The Dragon's Tail location in your house of career will induce a general restructure of your occupation where much work will be accomplished from the home and travels to far away places. This could induce quite a lot of activity and social interaction during the waxing moon periods. Some lucky Sagittarius will expand the family circle with new arrivals. As a rule Sagittarius are dedicated and career oriented parents.

During the new and Full Moons of March and September 2006 (see Moon Power publication for dates), serious positive or difficult happenings based upon your personal karma will take place. Again, you are strongly advised to use your will and avoid depressing thoughts. Regenerative spiritual endeavors combined with studies, exercise and social interaction could prove to be beneficial at those moments. Do not let the nasty pull of the Dragon's Tail affecting your career get the best of your body and mind. The positive Dragon's Head in Pisces has much to offer and will induce a variety of opportunities to improve your health and working life right from your base of operation. Building and promoting a group or some kind of club from home can only prove beneficial in the long run. Within the next few months or so, the fruits of many years of hard work will begin to pay off as you may be forced to service the world on a much higher level.

The Dragon will also offer great opportunities where security and family matters will play an important part of your working life. Foreign business associations, contracts, partnerships and traveling are also ahead. The new Dragon's Head in Pisces the sign of drugs could also induce depressions and abuse with anti depressants, be cautious especially after the Full Moon. Providing you keep busy and avoid nurturing pessimistic thoughts about your new career, a very progressive time is ahead of you. As a rule, those born in December strive for success, education and a place of respect that often brings lots of responsibilities and challenges. Jupiter is particularly great to bring any project to fruition and when he does they last forever. Remember to respect the Universal Law (see Moon Power) and use your personal dragon windows dates as this wisdom becomes a major contribution to your success or failure in life. The opportunity to make serious progress this year is available to you. This celestial process will bring you much luck if you take on the new challenge and invest in education, metaphysical pursuits, traveling, and if you associate with new partners. Those shining stars above your head are on your side and you can make the most of them. Many people born in December will also be promoted to a higher position.

Many December writers will be able to publish their light work to the world. This will open exciting doors to promising new business endeavors and rewarding financial contacts. The Dragon's Tail's location in Virgo your 10th house (career), will still force you into a general restructure of all affairs ruled by this house. Wrong partners or impractical associates will produce physical and mental stress during the waning moon periods of the current year. During the New and Full Moons of December and June 2006, serious happenings based upon your career and relationships will take place. You are strongly advised to steer clear of drugs, alcohol and relaxants, and use your will to avoid depressing thoughts.

Challenging regenerative spiritual endeavors combined with studies and social interaction may prove to be beneficial during those times of depression. Do not let the nasty Dragon's Tail get the best of your body and mind. Within the next few months, karma will be burnt and you may be forced to face the world with a new and much better partner and a much better career position if you ask for the changes.

Those new partners will offer great opportunities where foreigners will play an important part of your life. Foreign business association contracts, partnerships, traveling and luck in general will be offered by the new Dragon. The opportunity to make serious progress in your career and even with love is available to you this year. This celestial process will bring you much luck if you take on the challenge of investing in computerized education, metaphysical pursuits, traveling, and if you associate with new partners provided by the Dragon. A new way of thinking about the way you want to project yourself in a new career and/or your love to others and to the world will be induced by the new Dragon. Those shining stars above your head are on your side.

In the year 2006, the great Jupiter (luck) will cruise through the sign of Scorpio your 12th house of secret affairs and subconscious matters. Much progress is to be expected in all affairs involving the divine this year. You can expect serious changes or advancement with study and in your working life in general. Be ready for a new romance or great business deals with those born in June, August or April. You may order your taped 90mn Full Life Reading or your Progressive reading to find out more about the upcoming changes in your life. Call 602-265-7667 or visit my site and fill out the order form or call our office for more information. Good luck to all of those born in December.

> He is wise who understands that the stars are luminaries, created as signs. He who conquers the stars will hold the golden keys to God's mysterious universe
>
> — Nostradamus

****

Astro ~Weather ~ Service

First SUPERNOVA window:

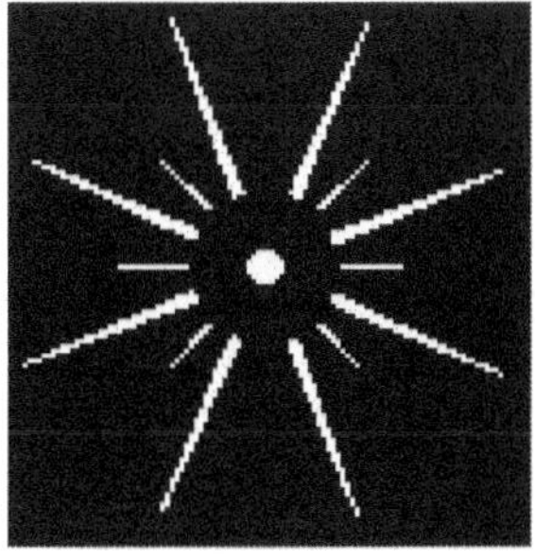

From Sunday, December 14th 2003 through Sunday January 11th 2004.

EXPLANATION OF A SUPERNOVA WINDOW

Concentration of negative celestial energy approaching

Concentration of negative celestial energy approaching Be extremely prudent in driving, and expect chain-reaction accidents. Be prepared for delays, strikes, and nature producing awful weather, including hurricanes and tornadoes. The same energy that produced the Titanic disaster, the Northridge, Los Angeles, and Kobe, Japan, earthquakes is approaching again. Double-check all your appointments, and if you can, postpone traveling and flying during this Supernova "window".

Communication and electricity will be cut off, and a general loss of power is to be expected. Appliances, computers, telephones, planes, trains, cars, all of these "tools" will be affected by this energy. They will be stopped in one way or another. The people of the past will make the news and will reenter your life. Expect trouble with the post office, education, students, strikes, prisoner's escape, newspapers, broadcasting industries and computer viruses may bother us again.

Many a failed mission and expensive electronic equipment (Mars probe etc.) and our tax dollars have been wasted because of the scientist's lack of knowledge of the stars. As usual NASA, which is not aware of the science of astrology, will waste our tax money with failed missions due to bad weather and electronic malfunctions. In the name of ignorance a few years ago, in the Challenger explosion seven astronauts lost their lives when NASA launched the shuttle under a "Supernova Window".

Note: Regardless of Dr. Turi's expectations posted on his website for the second time and his desperate attempts over the years to make NASA officials aware of dangerous Super Nova Windows, the Columbia was also launched during this window and re-entered the last night of it producing the death of all courageous astronauts.

Marine life sharks, whales etc may also beach themselves due to Mercury retrograde affecting their natural inborn navigational systems. All these malevolent predictions and waste of lives and equipment do not have to occur. Those predictions do not have to affect you directly as they unfold. Instead, they are printed to prepare you for setbacks and frustrations, thus advising you to be patient and prudent during this trend. There is no room for ignorance, and those who are not aware of the celestial order, including the NASA space-program management team, will continue to pay a heavy price. In all mankind's affairs, ignorance is true evil. Why any scientists who are against my research do not honor the word science, which is based upon solid investigation, is solid proof of mental snobbery. By omitting any physical or spiritual laws can only bring penalty; for science's purpose is to explore all possibilities, even those laws written in light via the stars.

Your 2006 Moon Power "Starguide"

Welcome to

Your Day - to - Day Guidance

For January 2006

February 2006 — Mars in Taurus: Wherever your Mars is located in your chart indicates the best man for a woman or how a man "goes hunting" for a woman. Mars regulates your desire principle and a strong Mars produces sportsmen. Mars will always promote the soul towards dangerous and competitive career endeavors. Famous author John Gray (a Libra) uses a catching title for his book "Men are from Mars, women from Venus". A few years ago we met in San Francisco, I gave him a reading and he bought all my books and my introductory course in Astropsychology (Divine Astrology). Be cautious with Mars cruising a specific house and sign in your chart. Danger and aggression is its signature. It may be a good idea for you to know where "The Lord of War" in Greek Mythology is located in your chart at birth, or where it is now, so that you can use his energy constructively. Souls born now will be extremely artistic with a strong desire to establish security. Taurus rules Switzerland (banking capital of the world) and many financial corporations subconsciously use the symbol of the bull to represent security and solidity.

SUN., MON., TUE. — JANUARY 1, 2, 3:

RULERS —Saturn (career matters) and Uranus (explosions/surprises):

Work, Career and Business: With Jupiter's touch in Scorpio, you should be confident in all your transactions. Expect this transformation to become a new beginning for your career life. Great Jupiter may induce foreigners to play an important part of this trend. Listen to your intuition and keep a positive attitude at all time.

Partnerships: New partners are on the horizon for some, while others must learn from previous errors. Money and general security will also be on your mind, serious decisions will have to be made soon. Be patient and wait for the upcoming New Moon, nothing comes easily in this life and one must strive and plan if one is to succeed. Letting go and rebuilding is a must. Expect excentric behaviors from some of your partners.

Family and Friends: Jupiter's optimistic spirit will replenish you with hopes and a new approach to life. Spend some time with family members or dear friends, and be ready to listen to a wise soul. Enjoy the family and the good food offered to you, fight depression, and invite a friend over. Because of the waning Moon, a night out will not bring you much pleasure; better stay home, relax watch a movie or read. An old friend may stimulate your life; this will make you happy and further an important wish later on. Some souls born with the moon crossing the dragon's Tail will suffer needlessly. The "Lucky Dragon Dates" service (see home page banners) would do miracles for planning.

Love Affairs: Someone much older or much younger may enter your life soon and will teach you great wisdom. You may look for love these days; there is plenty to gain if you socialize and the stars are supporting you. You will feel spiritual and some of the questions of life will trigger your imagination. If you were born in October an Aries, a Gemini or an Aquarius will need you. A friend born in June may be interested in you. Old people will be in need for love.

Travel and Communication: Expect your telephone to be busy and be ready for good surprises. If you have to drive be cautious and take extra time to get there. Some will travel to deal with the future or to gather New Age information. Be aware on the road anything can happen and flying is fine. The "Lucky Dragon Window" could make a huge difference in your existence, be advised, be safe, such a little investment that could save your life).

Environment: Mother Nature may become capricious and surprise us with weird weather soon; tornadoes and earthquakes are on the list. Environmental groups will become active and will find support from the media, in saving the earth from uncaring corporations. Interesting news may come from foreign grounds (Japan France or the Middle East). Expect this type of news - 07/23/05 - Strong quake jolts Tokyo, injuries reported- 07/23/05 - 7.2 quake shakes Indian islands. 07/23/05 - CNN - 07/23/05: 85 dead - Bombs kill scores in Egyptian resort town. CNN - 07/23/05: Explosion hits Beirut

Famous Personalities: A well-known foreign personality involved in communication or writing will gain international attention where sorrow, tears and memory will make many followers cry.

Events: Some militant groups from a faraway continent will try to disturb the peace and could become dangerous. Surprising explosions and eartquakes/volcanoes news are on the way. Also expect sad news such as; November 4, 1997 when a dual typhoon lashed the Pacific islands and destroyed all on his passage. Also in CAMDEN, New Jersey — 6/25/2005 Three young boys missing for two days were found dead in the trunk of a car by one child's father, who jumped away screaming and sobbing after his grim discovery.

Shopping: A good time for the gamblers; however, if you happen to be in Las Vegas, keep the spending in control. The Moon is still waxing (positive);make the best of the remaining new moon while you can.

January 4, 2006 — Mercury enters Capricorn: Souls born with this celestial position will be gifted in engineering and will aim for a position of mental achievements. Their powerful intellectual natures combined with strong desires for respect and honor could lead those souls towards the Army and the Navy. Some interests are also with architectures, history and could also include large corporations. Souls born with this Mercury location possess a scientific logic mental process where intuition or objectivity could be lacking. Expect some serious beginning or endings taking place where career and home are concerned.

WED., THU., FRI., SAT. — JANUARY 4, 5, 6, 7:

RULERS — Neptune (Middle East/ drugs) and Mars (war/Germany).

Work, Career and Business: Make good use of the information printed in Starguide; this work translates the energies ahead of us. With the waxing moon with us for a few more make the mmost of your days. Sign important contracts, and expect important meeting to be fruitful. All seem to work your way at the start of the New Year. Expect some new beginning and new faces around.

Partnerships: Do not let anything bad happen to your psyche; avoid Neptune's deceiving nature. With Mars around, you'd better use a diplomatic attitude in all your endeavors and avoid any confrontation with co-workers or your supervisor. Time to rescue some depressed spirits without letting yourself be affected by their personal problems. A good movie or a great video will rebuild your spirit.

Family and Friends: Friends and family may suffer Neptune's pull and may call you. They might be experiencing anxiety in their relationships; provide them with your support. Talk about Neptune's impact upon their lives and psyches and mention my book. Expect a thorny time where you should be prudent and patient with others. The depressing power of Neptune also affects your friends; sadly enough some of them will abuse alcohol and may pay a heavy price. DO NOT DRINK and drive and if you do drink, designate a safe driver or have a cab take you back home. Even in a waxing moon period Neptune could seriously blind your vision and with Mars' impatience you could visit the emergency room (or the cemetery!). Don't take a chance on your life; stay clear of chemicals and use tons of patience on your family members.

Love Affairs: A secret love affair may be a temptation to some but it will bring deception to the unaware initiator. Time to give strong support to your mate, especially if they are water signs, as Neptune will make them sleepy or moody. If you are a Pisces, Cancer or Scorpio expect much with love, romance or with your children. Just be patient, control your imagination and do not nurture guilt from past endeavors. A long walk to the mall or the sea will keep your mind away from Neptune's depressing cries.

Travel and Communication: The majority of people is not yet aware of the power of Mars and Neptune upon their psyches and will become aggressive emotional robots. Drive slowly, be alert and most of all stay calm in any situation. Be very forthright and patient in your speech, as miscommunications with authority now could have disastrous results. Further love and understanding and all will be fine.

Environment: This celestial duo has in the past produced oil spills, chemical plant explosions. A trip by the sea will make many happy. Interesting news about chemicals, exotic places and flooding is to be expected soon.

Famous Personalities: An interesting new but deceiving movie will be promoted. Elizabeth Taylor and many other water sign celebrities including the Pope will make the news soon. Some famous people's bad habits will be made public while religious figures will insist on their personal religious views and wars. A strong message with the new Pope and changes in the church is reflecting the ending of the deceiving age of Pisces (deception/illusion/religions/poisoning of the body mind and spirit). A new light is upon the world produced by Uranus/Aquarius (genius/the future/UFO/technology/astrology) is upon the world and the future of mankind. The dark religious age of Pisces did die with the old Pontife.

Events: Neptune rules news about the Navy, deception, jails, hospitals, the Middle East, oil, and all religions combined together. Under his illusive power on May 3 1997, the Pope made an important announcement. VATICAN CITY — When Pope John Paul II makes a choice for sainthood; it's often to make a point. On Sunday, he draws attention to a long neglected and often despised group in Europe, beatifying a Gypsy for the first time in the history of the Roman Catholic Church. Beatification is the last step before possible canonization or sainthood. With Mars in action the weather could turn real nasty again and water and slides could be a serious threat to some regions of the US.

Shopping: News about gas is on the way and good deals could be found in a garage sale or your local flea market. But anything related to water and fix the pool or the water system in your house. Keep an eye on the children near water and stay clear of anti depressants and prescriptions.

SUN., MON., TUE., WED. — JANUARY 8, 9, 10, 11:

RULERS — Mars (Army/Navy) Mercury (traveling) and Venus (dedication):

Work, Career and Business: Control Mars' fighting spirit or he may slow down some of your projects. With the new moon around, you may also use his power constructively to improve your business endeavors. This fortuitous timing will strengthen your chances for success in the near future. Trust your ability to communicate with Mercury and follow your intuition. The next few days will be vital to launch yourself and Venus' lucky touch will bring additional developments. With the waxing Moon at work, the next two weeks should be used to the maximum to promote your business life.

Partnerships: Remember, Mars is also around and you should use his strength and concentrate your efforts to get things done. The future promises to bring about good results from interviews, employment applications, promotions and other job opportunities. A pivotal turning point is to be expected this week in a key relationship. As always consider the long-term implications and respectability of the offer before making up your mind.

Family and Friends: We are still under the power of the New Moon and Mercury the "Lord of communication" you can expect your telephone to be busy. Everybody will have something to share with you. Use Venus' loving touch in your verbal exchanges and avoid Mars' invective remarks about an unlucky friend. Don't be shy; pass on your message, be confident and direct in your approach, your impact on others will surprise you. Do all this with "savoir faire." Take the family out and enjoy the wilderness with the children. As always keep an eye on them as Mars will make them restless and accident-prone.

Love Affairs: Use the kind-hearted touch of Venus to your advantage; you may decide to treat someone you truly love with your best intentions. You're apt to make significant progress with love this weekend (especially close to the water) and you should really make the most out of this trend. Social life and romance is up; a trip is on the way for some. If you were born in June, a Sagittarius, a Libra or an Aquarius may fall for you. Go out don't waste this celestial energy and ask for love you may be surprised.

Travel and Communication: You may be asked to take a trip or one of your trip could be a lucky strike. This week promises to be worthwhile for the more creative souls and your writing skills will improve dramatically. Under Mercury and Venus' auspices, especially in time of a new moon, a new book could be started or finished. A trip to your past will pay off for some. Don't let Mars make you impatient or accident-prone on the road; be patient and be courteous with other drivers. Take care of your car before taking the road or it could let you down anywhere.

Environment: Mars' destructive temper may produce tornadoes, explosions, high winds or flooding. Be aware, don't take any chances the red planet of danger will be felt somewhere in the world and hurt lots of people.

Famous Personalities: Listen for news to come to light about great projects from many famous people. Some important legal problems for Michael Jackson but money and fame does help criminals.

Events: Remember, Mars is around; don't take any chances with confrontations or the police. A positive attitude and diplomacy will keep you out of trouble. Impending breakthroughs with religion, the Government , the Pope, medicine or science are to be expected soon.

Shopping: It's a great time to buy interesting books and telephone appliances for your business. As Mercury rules transportation, it would be a good idea for you to take care of your wheels or invest in a new car.

THU., FRI. — JANUARY 12, 13:

RULERS — Mercury (rational power) and the Moon (endings):

Work, Career and Business: The Moon is nearly full (difficult) and the universe won't further new opportunities for much longer. This may force you into a change with your business endeavors. Use Mercury's mental power to promote yourself or clarify a difficult situation with others. For those involved in sales, this lunation will not bring worthwhile arrangements and some of us will have to deal with important legal documents. During the upcoming waning moon, you may be forced to sign important paper work if you decide to get rid of a situation (or a person!).

Partnerships: Nothing is made to last forever, not even relationships and you may be able to see what's ahead of you. This process will impose many changes, prodding you towards new experiences and valuable knowledge. Do not hold tightly to your past; you only make yourself miserable until you can't take it any more. Only when the changes are accepted will the stars shine upon you and your new destiny. Keep a positive attitude no matter what.

Family and Friends: Many will enjoy good food and the family circle these days. If you decide to dine out it would be wise to make reservations, as the local restaurants will be busy. It is a good time to enjoy wide-open spaces with children and pets. Expect news from mom brothers or sisters.

Love Affairs: Do some listening; avoid talking too much about you or your past. Nurture positive thoughts about life in general. A trip close to nature or the water would be great for both of you. Candlelight, good wine, great food, and soft music are there for you to enjoy with your partner. Take some pictures and have fun. If single, go out with friends you know and do not be too trusting of a stranger's words. Participate with life wisely. Those born in January will be attracted to older or younger people born in September, July or May.

Travel and Communication: Do not expect much good news to arrive via mail or telephone close to a Full Moon. A person you know who is going in a direction that you disapprove of, could benefit from your advice. This individual might need more emotional support to deal with past experiences; don't let this affect your own psyche and learn to say no. Soon depressed friends may need more support from you; don't expect much reward from them. Avoid being critical with old friends as your remarks could be misinterpreted and could haunt you for a while. Be aware if you're invited to a party this weekend, don't believe in all that you hear. Be nice and happy; impress everyone with your attitude. With a bit of luck one of your wishes can be granted before the Full Moon, if you mean business with your subconscious. A trip to your past could bring you joy. Keep in mind to service the car before leaving your city, and drive safely.

Environment: Thousands of people will be forced to relocate during this type of celestial configuration soon. Nature may decide to throw a nasty message to man; quakes, volcanoes, tornadoes, explosions, floods are very high on the list. Let's hope for the sake of many that this lunation won't be too difficult.

Famous Personalities: Many prominent people will come in or out of a situation, business or a bad marriage. The beginning or ending of important phases of life is active for all of us. Famous or not, they are under the same stars and will suffer the reality of life.

Events: Be ready for the government (foreign or the U.S.) to make important decisions. Some elected officials might be forced to depart from office. The United States, France and Japan could be touched directly.

Shopping: Avoid spending too much money on anything. If you need a new answering machine or a new telephone, wait for the next new Moon. Purchase books now that could teach you something spiritual.

January 14, 2006 – Full Moon in Cancer: — The Full Moon will mature in the loving, family-oriented sign of Cancer. Expect some serious career or personal developments to take place. Some will be starting new jobs, and others will drop them; this may also include a business relationship. Promotion or deception, whichever happens to you (or others) will mark an important part of your life. Just be ready to accept the upcoming changes with faith in your new future. Be ready to provide a supportive shoulder to the victims. Nature may also decide to do some nasty tricks in some states, promoting bad weather or earthquakes. The government will have to take serious steps to keep peace in some parts of the world. The Moon rules this sign. Expect the beginning or ending of important phases of your life. This lunation could represent a very important part your destiny. You may be forced to let go of your past, accept your new future with confidence. Many will be affected and forced to move on around you. The US will be touched directly and the dramatic impact will affect many families in the long run. Keep a positive attitude and have faith in the government decisions for the future. Do something for someone you care and offer my book to them, remember Moon Power is a limited edition and many people get really frustrated when they can not get their copy of Moon Power. Think of it as a present and realize how much help you are offering the people you care most with my guidance.

Lunation impact on all signs

Aries - Relocation ahead and changes in your home life and career soon. Accept those changes.

Taurus - An important letter or disturbing news from your siblings. Use your stamina and have faith.

Gemini - You will be forced to spend money for home or your family. You'll be glad you did it.

Cancer - Serious business or emotional stress is ahead of you. Changes are needed in your life.

Leo - Let go of your past, move on. Time to look for that position you deserve, be ready.

Virgo - You need to go out with your friends. New ones will bring you love and wishes soon.

Libra - Great career changes are ahead of you. You might have to go or look somewhere else.

Scorpio - A trip or someone far away will need you. Big business must be done.

Sagittarius - A legacy or a present is in store for you. Give if you want to receive some money.

Capricorn - You will have to work on yourself and your partner soon. Promotions and endings are ahead.

Aquarius - A great new opportunity to serve the world will be offered to you. Move on.

Pisces - A chance to find new love is offered to you. A friend will need your help.

SAT., SUN., MON., TUE., WED., THU. — JANUARY 14, 15, 16, 17, 18, 19:

RULERS — The Moon (endings) Sun (love) and Mercury (words):

Work, Career and Business: With the Full and waning Moon upon you, do not expect much luck these days. A new job or a better position may be what you need and could be attained in the near future. Renew your confidence and support to your worldly ambitions and don't let the waning moon affect you negatively. Keep a low profile for now.

Partnerships: Come clean with what you mean with a partner; mis-communication does happen and usually leads to trouble. Go easy in expressing your feelings; don't let the sad Moon blur your vision or your words. Re-schedule an important meeting.

Family and Friends: Don't expect much with family members or friends either. Expect disturbing news from them and help them to get on with their lives. Avoid stressing about them, and let them know when they overuse your telephone. Children will also be a bit unmanageable and nervous. Use lots of patience with them and remember their sensitivity if they are teenagers. They could be hurt with your attitude and this could damage your close relationship later in life. Discipline them carefully, assist their young wills, and help build their self-esteem.

Love Affairs: With the waning moon above your head, a reliable love relationship won't be available for a while. An unexpected invitation to a gathering could bring an interesting person into your life. Use your head, not your heart, and you'll be fine. The Sun's revitalizing power should be used to rekindle your feelings for some of the friends or lovers you really trust. A good romantic movie will help you release some feelings you may have for someone you care about. If you are single, and born in February, spend valuable time with those born under the sign of Leo, Gemini or Libra.

Travel and Communication: As always with Mercury in charge, take good care of your car and drive cautiously. You may be unexpectedly asked to drive somewhere soon; wherever you want to be drive slow and be aware of the waning moon and don't take any chances with the cops. Avoid gossiping about someone close to you. Words travel fast; be aware as you may lose that person's friendship.

Environment: With the waning Moon in progress, Mother Nature might respond to our closest satellite's disturbing magnetic field. Some lives may be swept away with flooding. Some surprising developments will make the news on CNN. Explosions and volcanic eruptions are on the way. Some naturalist groups will be concerned and active in making the rest of us aware of nature's wonderful blessings.

Famous Personalities: A famous person will see the surprising end of his/her life and many will miss the great soul. Under the same type of energy on February 19 1997, Beijing China formally declared six days of mourning for Deng Xiaoping as the nation began to come to terms with the death of its leader of two decades.

Events: This is the type of occurrence with these energies at play: 1/23/2005 - NEW YORK (CNN) — Howling winds and blinding snow blasted the Northeast on Sunday, closing Boston's airport and forcing airlines to evaluate whether to cancel flights in other cities slammed for a second day by blizzard conditions.

Shopping: If you are an investor, hold on to your gold assets or you may be stuck in a bad transaction and lose. Presents will be offered to those deserving loving souls. Do not invest right now in a specific interest or creative study. A garage sale is where great bargains are available now.

January 23, 2006 — Mercury enters Aquarius: If you inherited this Mercury position you are a free thinker. You also regenerate in investigations, health, metaphysics, and anything related to the new age. Work on your inventiveness and don't be afraid to use computers. You will gain fame because of your originality and your ability to communicate. Invest or design some software and investigate astrology. The near future promises to divulge surprising news pertaining to Japan, France, electronics, aeronautics, NASA, inventions and UFOs. This Mercurial position creates geniuses. Note that Mercury in Aquarius is dignified and supports futuristic and original thinking and endeavors – I, Dr. Turi was born with this Mercurial position!

Note: Attention Pluto is back with us — With Mars now in the sign of Taurus just after the Full Moon, expect dramatic happenings all over; control is a must. The Lord of Hades doesn't forget and doesn't forgive; don't be a victim. Be aware of Pluto's destructive power.

FRI., SAT., SUN., MON., TUE. — JANUARY 20, 21, 22, 23, 24:

RULERS — Venus (hot love) Pluto (drama/secrets):

Work, Career and Business: Don't let Pluto tempt you to take any form of unlawful shortcut, consider the dramatic impact and the potential for disaster, even death. These days will bring about wake-up calls for many unaware people. Do not expect anything to go your way, as people will show the worse traits of their personality. Be easy with your words, avoid meetings with strangers, and don't take any phone calls or threats lightly. Don't let Pluto and Mars sting everyone and everything to death. Use your intuition in all you do and be ready for concealed financial or sexual business to surface. Early plans have to be suddenly abandoned and this means business and career momentum could be lost.

Partnerships: Spend time reorganizing the home and the office, throw old things away and look busy at all times. The boss or co-workers are also affected by those negative stars and could make your life misery. Someone may try to show you the error of your ways on your dietary habits, perhaps a co-worker or a critical friend. The stars want you to consider, re-think and be cautious. You may have to slow down now and put on your thinking and rational judgment caps concerning key partnerships. Be diplomatic, as your weakness or errors won't go unnoticed. You may want to listen carefully to what is said for or against you; those comments deserve your attention. Pluto will damage your partnership if you do not consider, re-think or be cautious. You may have to use your rational judgment concerning key partnerships. Some changes are imminent.

Family and Friends: Some of your friends will experience dramatic endings to some portions of their lives and your supportive shoulder will be requested. At home or at work expect arguments, making these days miserable. Aggravations that could continue into the evening hours could have serious repercussions and may bring police into the neighborhood. Keep your head cool; stay calm and patient.

Love Affairs: Be ready for secrets to surface; however, bits and pieces of information may be wrong or missing. Do not make important decisions about a situation or a person just now. Concealed love trysts will be taking place all over, and will keep a bunch of insidious investigators active. Don't trust strangers; Pluto always induces drugs, alcohol and rapes. Protect yourself at all cost if you're sexually active now; the signature of Pluto is death and AIDS! If you were born under the sign of Pisces, those born in September, November or July will be strongly attracted to you. Use your head, not your heart!

Travel and Communication: Avoid long trips by air, plane or ship, the stars are not positive and do not care about anyone — they just do the work they were intended to do by God's higher order.

Environment: Be ready for nasty surprises, especially the ones with nature's forces at work. Expect events such as — A powerful 7.3 earthquake shook southwest Pakistan early Friday, killing at least 40 people in an impoverished area dotted with flimsy homes made of sun-baked mud. During this Plutonic time another quake killed 100, injures 250 in northern Iran. See the power of Pluto by investigating my site and how this disruptive planet affects the world .

Famous Personalities: Pluto rules secrets, sex and likes to take away famous personalities when in charge. Expect a well-know figure to pass away soon.

Events: Awful news involving tragic accidents, the police, mass murderers, suicide and drama will plague the media. Everything you say or do now will have serious repercussions later on. ST. PAUL, Minnesota (AP) — Police said they are investigating an incident in which an officer pepper-sprayed an 85-year-old man during a traffic stop. 6/19/05 -SELLERSVILLE, Pennsylvania (AP) — A man who had recently left a mental health facility killed his wife after an argument and was shot to death by the couple's 15-year-old son, police said.

Shopping: Invest in anything that will help you to destroy any form of life, this should be efficiently used. Insecticides and other things to get rid of insects and household nuisances should be high on your list now. If you need to purchase a firearm, you are strongly advised to wait until after the New Moon, if not it could be used against you or kill a family member. And for the sexually active: Preservatives will stop any chance of sexually transmitted diseases.

Mimi Fahnestock says she had an affair with JFK

June Carter dies

Robert Stack dies

WED., THU., FRI., SAT. — JANUARY 25, 26, 27, 28:

RULERS — Jupiter (Foreigners/Religions) and Saturn (Uncle Sam/Adjustments):

Work, Career and Business: We are still on a waning Moon period; caution is advised in all you do. With the guardianship of Jupiter, the finances, resources and expertise of others could spell a profitable opportunity, especially after the upcoming New Moon. Real estate deals, trades, and credit approval will be among workable developments then. However, with the waning Moon still with us, better keep a low profile and avoid asking too many favors. Be ready for the beginning or ending of an important portion of your business life. Surprising even destructive news is ahead of you; be ready to welcome any changes. Life is a constant process of change and your existence on this dense physical world has specific purposes. Be patient and promote your business life only after the next New Moon.

Partnerships: Saturn may make you feel depressed, especially during the very last days of the waning moon. Do not put any strain on your relationships, and don't put stress on your significant other. Be ready to provide spiritual support to those close to you, and learn to say "NO" if needed. Work toward your heart's desire and don't let Saturn drag you down. Don't make too many demands on your partner and don't be too concerned with little details. No one will do things right just now. Errors are parts of your business life; don't hate yourself if you make some. Get involved with computers or learn a different program to make your business life easier.

Family and Friends: As usual in a waning Moon period, assign your spiritual help but do not involve your personal feelings about a difficult situation with a family member or a trusted friend. Give practical directions and don't be too pessimistic about the end. With freedom-oriented Jupiter above these days, an out-of-doors trip for the family will be rewarding. A trip to your local church on Sunday could also give you a sense of faith in the creator and in your future. Hope and believe and a wish will come true.

Love Affairs: That Waning Moon will induce stress in your psyche; caution in your speech is advised. Expect surprising news soon, related to a legal situation, a marriage or a divorce. If you happen to be the victim, be patient and sooner or later you will find peace of mind and true love with the right partner. If you were born in April, a Leo, A Sagittarius or a Libra will be strongly attracted to you. An Aquarius or Leo friend could make one of your wishes a reality soon.

Travel and Communication: Be careful on the road as the waning-moon brings bad tempers to some "lunatic" drivers. No one attracts bees with vinegar; use honey instead! Avoid arguments at all costs and use diplomacy to save situations which could turn dangerous on the road. Be careful driving; don't trust anyone and keep your eyes on your speed. The Cops will be watching you with their electronic eye.

Environment: Gloomy news may come from Mexico, Japan and some faraway continents. Nature may decide to stretch herself and do harm to people in different places. She will produce a bad quake or a volcanic eruption within the next few days.

Famous Personalities: Some well-known entertainment figures may make dramatic news.

Events: A prominent political person either from the US, France or Japan will make an important announcement. Important meetings will take place to bring calm to certain parts of the world. The government may come up with important news or decisions that could affect many families in the future.

Shopping: Use this trend to find great Indian or foreign bargains in a garage sale or enjoy shopping your local antique shop with a Capricorn, Taurus or Cancer friend. Do not invest in anything new or any plants now; the ones that you will pick won't stay alive for long.

New Moon — January 29, 2006 in Aquarius: The New Moon will mature in the futuristic sign of Aquarius. Expect surprising developments everywhere. The waxing "positive" moon means it is a progressive time to launch any new project. The next two weeks are going to be full of surprises, and a good chance to move forward will be offered to those asking for progress. Try anything now, aim as high as you are capable; coincidence be will magical. Don't waste this great lunation; be original, ask and you will receive! Expect incredible news involving explosions, nature's forces at work, electronics, UFOs, celestial bodies, etc. soon! A perfect time to apply your will and decide to start a spiritual Astropsychology, Kabalistic Healing or Astro-Tarot course (Get a super deal - see www.drturi.com or call the office at 602-265-7667 and help us set a seven days crash course in your area).

Lunation impact on all signs:

Aries - A good friend will bring a great opportunity to grow and travel. You're lucky.

Taurus - A new career opportunity is ahead of you, master computers, TV soon.

Gemini - More opportunities to travel and study will be offered to you.

Cancer - A wealthy partner will offer financial support and will promote your business.

Leo - Big changes in your business and emotional life are ahead of you.

Virgo - You are due for some significant changes at work, be ready.

Libra - Your love life will turn surprisingly positive, opportunities are ahead for you.

Scorpio - You may be forced to move and your home life will undergo positive changes.

Sagittarius -Be ready to travel physically and spiritually. Learn and use computers.

Capricorn - Positive financial changes are ahead, electronic knowledge is a must.

Aquarius - A new door is about to open to you, be ready, you can't loose.

Pisces - Your perception of the future will be right, be positive. Swim upstream.

SUN., MON., TUE. — JANUARY 29, 30, 31:

RULERS — Uranus (Surprises/explosions) Neptune (Religion/water):

Work, Career and Business: With the New Moon upon us you will encounter interesting people and incredible situations. Neptune may induce a trip for business close to the water. Many of us will be forced into new circumstances involving career moves or jobs. Get out now! Many Saturnian people will be standing next to you and could further your wishes; don't be afraid to start a conversation with an older person. Don't take anything personally if some of their comments seem harsh; they might know better than you. Use this progressive trend and invest some thought into new business opportunities. A change in schedules or rules could affect you, take chances now. Keep busy and be courteous to the Boss and pleasant to everyone, you're being noticed for your gentle nature. Be easy on yourself, don't be too critical of anyone in the office; nobody is perfect.

Partnerships: Be ready for a wave of surprising news coming your way. Karmic Neptunian souls will not benefit from that unexpected news, and some will be forced to accept the realities of life. Listen to an older person, he may play an important part in helping your emotional life and will give you good advice. Uranus, "the Lord of surprises" and Neptune "Poseidon" could also bring about boating misadventures; be aware if you happen to get close to the river or the ocean this weekend. Avoid drinking heavily and watch your possessions.

Family and Friends: Trust the waxing Moon and the upcoming changes; be confident in the new situation, as it will affect your security and your finances positively. Keep an eye on the children; Uranus will make them behave irrationally, they will be overactive and you do not want anything bad to happen. An adolescent or a younger friend may need your support and may ask for direction. Do not turn down invitations, and you may also invite a long-standing friend to spend valuable time in your company. Some of those friends will bring your wishes home; be active on the social front. Wishes can only take place if you participate with life fully.

Love Affairs: Neptune may grasp the spirit of a person close to you and induce emotional stress and confusion. Be considerate or you may lose that person in the future if you do nothing. Expect some people to fall for Uranus' erratic personality and to surprise you in public places. Love is in the air for many while for others, Neptune may lead them into a secret love affair. Be aware of weird souls hanging around, but you can still enjoy their original company. Again, don't fall for Neptune's deceiving powers, avoid drinking during the late hours, as your emotions will run unusually high and could alter your driving or behavior. If you were born in July, Capricorn, and Scorpio will be strongly attracted to you. A Pisces friend will provide a wish.

Travel and Communication: With Uranus' eccentricity, be aware of crazy drivers while driving to trips or work during this trend. Take plenty of time to reach your destinations and be ready for some driver's unexpected behavior on the road. Neptune may make you feel sleepy, rest or walk a bit along the way.

Famous Personalities: Expect startling developments with some well-known people trying to get more publicity. This energy doesn't stop with famous people; regular souls may act oddly too. News of love, marriage, and children will make many famous people happy and ready to throw expensive social gathering.

Events: New moon or not, Uranus will surprise many of us with nature's destructive forces. Be ready for earthquakes, tornadoes, volcanic eruptions or incredible weather developments soon. Here is a quatrain I wrote and posted on my forum using Nostradamus' methodology.

Earth belly fury will surprise many

Mother Nature rules unleashed power

While wind fire and water will join

In a dance where all evils rejoice

Results: Devastating floods in Peru blamed on El Niño - 70 dead, 22,000 homeless; worst flooding in 50 years. Uranus might also disturb sophisticated electronic equipment and produce aeronautic disasters. Under his power many U.S. military cargo planes and helicopters crashed under fire or trying to land. Many soldiers were killed under Uranus command. Expect news of explosions and earthquakes.

Shopping: This is a good time to visit your favorite spiritual for his divine guidance. Spend on anything electronic now; this will prove to be beneficial for your business life in the long run.

Memo - On January 29th, 1998 Neptune entered the sign of Aquarius: This dreamy and deceiving planet will cruise through the genius-like sign of Aquarius until April 5, 2011. In the incredible sign of Aquarius (UFOs/microchips), Neptune's creative energy will be used to the maximum. A wave of new electronic devices will be used within the cinematography industry (Titanic/Matrix and many other movies were produced since then!). The communion of Uranus (electronics) and Neptune (imagination) can only create incredible effects and super movies. Some will or did involve UFOs and/or Apocalyptic messages. Neptune (movie industry/make believe) in Aquarius (ingenuity) will promote a serious increase in creativity and a solid progressive restructure within the cinematography industry. The Neptunian world of creativity and imagination fused with the futuristic sign of Aquarius has a lot to offer to cinemagoers. On a higher level, the spiritual essence of mankind's religious belief systems is undergoing a rebirth, where the dogmatic religious views of the past will be replaced by more practical awareness of god divine celestial order and will bring forth more cosmic consciousness to society at large. From that day on the true Universal face of God and his celestial manifestation will be revealed to mankind.

Welcome to
Your Day - to - Day Guidance

For February 2006

February 1, 2006 — Venus enters Capricorn: The great planet of love and wealth is in the practical sign of Capricorn. On a positive side this position produces high-class musicians and great artists who will work hard to bring their talents to the world. On the negative side, Venus will make them promiscuous and will use people with money and power to get positions of power or recognition. However Saturn is watching and karma is always repaid.

WED., THU., FRI., SAT. SUN. — FEBRUARY: 1, 2, 3, 4, 5:

RULERS — Mars (Hostility/War) and Venus (Love/ Friends):

Work, Career and Business: The New Moon will exert a revitalizing pull that will be felt in your business affairs. You may use this lunation to perhaps resolve conflicts in a difficult situation with a person of authority or a co-worker. Control Mars' opposing tendencies; don't let him affect your words, your attitude or your emotions. Practice patience during this Martian trend and use diplomacy; if you do so you'll make serious progress. You may also use the tough energy of Mars to do some needed tasks around the office such as removing furniture; in any case, don't get hurt.

Partnerships: Even with the Waxing Moon, learn to keep Mars' impatience under control and use Venus' diplomatic gifts to save difficult situations. Everyone is so intent on having their own way and there could be little cooperation around you. It's time to practice tact with the same dedication as a diplomat. Impatience could be detrimental to you and others, so use the knowledge found in this publication accordingly.

Family and Friends: With Venus' blessings upon us, you should try your creativity at home. Your fruitful Venusian imagination will lead you to creations of perfect interior designs. Realize your limits with troubled friends, and don't allow them to rely too heavily on you. As always, give spiritual support but avoid getting emotionally involved with their personal problems. You and your mate or family member can gain through financial endeavors, but discuss all possibilities before making any commitments. You might have an idea yourself that could be used; talk about it. Use what's left of the waxing Moon, so plan and enjoy a gathering this weekend.

Love Affairs: Don't let your relationship becoming shaky because you sense that the person in question may be deceiving in some way. Do not fall for your own insecurity, false information or a wild imagination. Avoid guilt in any of your decisions, and if you feel a change is unavoidable, trust your future. Expect much from a night out on Friday or Saturday if you take a chance on someone. Enjoy social life but don't drink and drive. Mars (action) and Neptune (deception) are not great cohabiters. When alcohol and speed are mixed, it can produce serious accidents. If you are a Gemini, then Aquarius, Sagittarius and Libra will be strongly attracted to you. A friend born in April has a surprise for you.

Travel and Communication: Be vigilant if you must drive, and don't take chances on the road, as Mars' energy could make you careless. Don't let his aggressive nature make you complain about a person, and use your words cautiously. Venus has much more to offer, and it's your choice; so use your will and your knowledge. Someone from your past may call.

Environment: Some people will learn about fire the hard way. However, many thoughtful people will use Mars' power to further environmental knowledge on preventing fires in nature. As usual, Mars, the red and violent planet, doesn't seem to care much for the waxing moon. He may decide to pull a nasty trick with nature's devastating forces, where all the elements could be invited for a destructive dance. Explosions and fires are common during his reign, be aware.

Famous Personalities: The oblivious rich and famous may be Mar's victims or make sad news involving accidents, drugs or alcohol. On a positive note, Venus will shine and induce love to those often-lonely famous souls.

Events: The Martian energy is tough and has in the past produced explosions and accidents of all sorts; be prudent. Venus will put up a serious fight against her destructive brother and may save many souls. Violent and dangerous sports will attract many people challenging their respective sides. Some unsuspecting souls may fall victim to Mars, and suffer head injuries.

Shopping: Invest in anything involving love, creativity or the arts. Show for whom you someone you care, the depth of your love. Under Mar's power, dangerous tools and machinery bought now will bring financial opportunities.

MON., TUE., WED., THU., FRI. — FEBRUARY 6, 7, 8, 9, 10:

RULERS — Mercury (News/Siblings) and the Moon (Mother/Changes):

Work, Career and Business: The blessings of a waxing moon are on the way in a few more days; you should fight lethargy and depressions. Be confident, as much needed change is ahead for you and those you care. You may also consider using Mercury's mental agility to pass on new ideas to improve your business or communicate with the family. You could use these waning days to re-write or plan new advertisements or publicity. The telephone will be particularly busy but the news could be depressive. Don't leave the office upset you do not need to bring stress at home. Stay active and be mentally alert.

Partnerships: Dealing with others has and will always be a challenge for us all. Some of you have learnt hard lessons and the scars takes time to heal; don't re-open them again. Move on to better ground, the future has always better to offer. Keep a positive attitude in your conversations and promote only the great times of your past. Some karmic souls will have to experience a rebirth of their relationships. Whatever unfolds, accept the changes with confidence; the truth is that, life is a constant process of change and it always seems to be for the better.

Family and Friends: Mercury is fast and rules communication, so expect family members to get in touch with you via mail or telephone. Some will be invited to enjoy great cooking at their friend's homes. "The messenger of the Gods" loves to talk and throw jokes all over. Control Mercury's desire to exaggerate and do not fall for the negative things you may hear now. Keep in mind that your friends have the potential to fulfill all your wishes; get active in the social arena after the new Moon. As always, you might have a karmic debt with a long-standing friend; if so, you may have to experience annoyance. Try to clear it all up and you'll win the person back.

Love Affairs: Be ready for the beginning or ending of important love phases of your love life. Keep your eyes and ears open on the people you know as the Moon affects everybody. If you were born in July, someone much older or younger than you born in March, November or January will be attracted to you. A friend may bring you sad news soon.

Travel and Communication: Use Mercury's mental powers accordingly. Time to write those letters, as Mercury improves your mental faculties. He will reward you favorably if you decide to invest in your education or start a book after the upcoming new moon. Control his strong desire to be a "chatterbox," and save money on your telephone bill. Mercury rules transportation and general motion; he also makes people restless on the road. Under his command you should be a defensive driver. It's time to plan for your future travels, or visit parts of the world via great books. Wait for the next New Moon to launch the trip. You'll be glad to know and respect God's Universal Laws.

Environment: We are coming into a Full Moon period and some will soon experience severe weather systems in some states. If you are into videotaping lightning, storms, volcanic eruptions, earthquakes, etc., be ready for those soon.

Some will see the beginning or ending of dramatic times. This may force thousands of people to relocate. Be ready for disturbing news soon where thousands of people will be forced to flee nature's destructive forces.

Famous Personalities: Too close to the Full Moon for comfort, thus some famous artist or important political figure will experience shame with love, and their children will be directly affected.

Events: Prominent political personalities either from the Russia, US, France or Japan will make an important announcement. The government may come up with drastic news or decisions that could affect many families in the future. Let's hope for the best.

Shopping: Invest faithfully in anything to clean the house or the office. Equipment purchased now will bring trouble to its owner. This is a perfect time to take care of your car. Mercury also rules literature and great deals on old books will be available under its influence.

Full Moon - February 13, 2006 in Leo: Be gentle with affairs of love and watch over the children. Keep Mrs. Pride and Mr. Ego in control if you intend to sustain your loving partner's relationship! Disturbing and surprising news with children are ahead be ready for agonizing happenings but learn not to dwell on them. Life is a constant process of change; the future has better to offer. Expect earthquakes above 6.0, and avoid flying. Be patient, take chances and as a rule promote your life only after the next New Moon.

Lunation impact on all signs:

Aries - A rebirth of your love life or stress with children is ahead. Accept the changes.

Taurus - An important decision about home or family matters is ahead. Use your stamina and have faith.

Gemini - Your mind is on love, children, and your family. Don't get too stressed.

Cancer - Serious financial or emotional stress is ahead. Changes are needed in your life.

Leo - Let go of your past, move on. It's time to look for that position or a new love, be ready.

Virgo - A secret love affair can only bring you more trouble. Clean it all and start fresh soon.

Libra - Some friends will put stress in your life. You might have to go or look somewhere else.

Scorpio - A decision about your career and love must be made. Use your intuition.

Sagittarius - A study or a trip or sad news could bring depression to you. Be patient life goes on.

Capricorn - News of legacy or death is ahead. Hopefully it is just a contract for business.

Aquarius - An opportunity to look for a new business or emotional partners. Move on.

Pisces - A chance to improve your health or your work is offered to you by the stars.

February 9, 2006 — Mercury enters Pisces: Souls born with this celestial position will be gifted in the arts, spiritual endeavors, and medical pursuits and will use their incredible imagination in exotic places. Their sensitive natures combined with strong religious intonations could lead many young March souls towards the ministry pulpit. The advanced ones will swim upstream and turn into great light workers, while others less advanced type will develop into (religious terrorists or ministers). On a negative note this Mercurial position produces mental ailments such as phobias, fears, drug and alcohol addictions, confinement, depressions and religious fanaticism. This planetary position will lead the soul towards creative imagination; true spiritual values, the performing arts and great success can be achieved if the intellectual energy of Mercury in Pisces is applied positively.

SAT., SUN., MON., TUE.— FEBRUARY 11, 12, 13, 14:

RULERS —The Sun (love/Children) and Mercury (Health/Nature):

Work, Career and Business: Some surprising developments are on the way, but with the Full Moon upon us don't expect them to make you happy. Progress will still be made in the few weeks ahead of you, but be ready for a bumpy ride. Take on new technical studies, or improve your knowledge of computers, as this endeavor will give you better opportunities later.

Partnerships: Don't take any chances these days, keep a low profile; use Mercury's creative power to clean up a business situation. Important legal papers might come your way; sign them only if it is to get rid of an unhealthy situation. Whomever you come in contact with, don't misbehave in public.

Family and Friends: Keep busy with close friends and family; watch the children, as they will be accident-prone. In the past, many of them got in trouble or had accidents during this type of lunation. It's a great time to enjoy the people you know well, but because of the waning Moon, avoid overcrowded public places.

Don't expect new people met under this lunar cycle to bring many of your wishes. Some friends have surprising even disturbing news for you and could affect you emotionally. Again, watch the children. They are accident-prone, especially on the road with fire, weapons and explosives.

Love Affairs: Expect aggravating surprises coming your way and learn to let go of deceitful people. Do not invite interlopers into your home, and socialize only with the friends you know well. Make good use of the waning moon; learn to relax, enjoy nature and the sea, and look for inner peace. If you're single, a chance to find the "right one" will be given to you at a later date. What you may perceive as love, may enter your life but without much to expect. Use your head on Friday night, not your heart. If you were born under the sign of Leo, an Aries, an Aquarius or a foreigner born in December could be a source of trouble in your life. Wait for better auspices.

Travel and Communication: Not a time to take chances at flying; many karmic souls will pay the ultimate price. Expect all sorts of little problems arising, which could turn lethal for some unlearned souls. Anticipate disturbing telephone calls from friends in trouble; as usual, provide spiritual help but know your limits and stay clear of depression. Under the same energy in BROOKSVILLE, Florida (AP) — 15 hurt in school bus accidents. Two school buses flipped over Wednesday morning in Florida and West Virginia, injuring 13 children and both drivers. FORWARD THIS TO THE SCHOOL MASTERS ALL OVER THE US PLEASE, HELP ME TO PASS ON MY MESSAGE. Also under the same lunation on April 8, 1998 the news reported that in CHAPPELL HILL, Texas — A loaded school bus was hit from behind by a tractor-trailer truck on a Texas highway injuring at least 22 children, some of them seriously.

Environment: Earth activists will feel this puritanical lunation and will do all to protect nature and its wild life; some may fall victim to ill-advised conflicts with unscrupulous large organizations. Expect unusual oceanic or earth activity soon that could prove disastrous for the environment. Not good times to play with fire, as explosions are very high on my list of trouble for this specific trend. The news may bring about startling explosive developments.

Famous Personalities: Certain famous people will find themselves in difficult situations. Some will try anything to get the attention they need. Eccentricity is in the air and could lead to the use of force or involvement with the law. Under this lunation Pop star George Michael was arrested for lewd conduct on April 8 1998, in Beverly Hills California: On that day, the news reported that pop star George Michael, the British-born heartthrob whose hit songs include the too-hot-for-radio "I Want Your Sex," was arrested on suspicion of committing a lewd act in a park restroom.

Events: Expect massive power outages without readily known causes. On the positive side, some high-tech scientific news as well as great medical breakthroughs is on the way. Expect news from space too such as PHNOM PENH, Cambodia (Reuters) — A 4.5 kg (10 lb) meteorite that landed in a former Khmer Rouge zone of northwest Cambodia started fires across rice fields and prayers from villagers who saw it as a divine omen of peace.

Shopping: Do not invest on anything electronic; you will not get a good deal. Do not invest in toys for your children now; they could prove to be fatal at a later date. Some will plan to travel to Europe.

February 18, 2006 — Mars enters Gemini: The Lord of war in the sign of communication will instigate a sharp tongue. Be concerned with other feelings and be diplomatic at all times. If not, someone might give you a kick in the mouth, and you would have to learn the hard way to control Mars' aggressive verbal power. On a more productive note, use this powerful planet to start a book, take a long trip, or use your mental power for any spiritual task. Winds are forecasted producing devastative tornadoes soon. Drive slowly and beware of crazy blind souls that will fall victims to Mars' speedy nature. Souls born with this celestial gift will be geared into sales, mental exploration, writing, broadcasting, general communication and speed. This Mars position breed dares devils, racing drivers, boxers who break bones.

Note: Pluto will become very destructive in this waning Moon period; — You can expect dramatic happenings with nature all over; control is a must. He has produced much sensational news including the California Rancho Santa Fe mass-suicide. Mass murderers are again on the lookout for innocent victims as Pluto always stimulates the criminal element, the insane and the police force fighting all ill purposes. Don't be victims; be aware of Pluto's destructive power. Secrets from the past will return to your life.

WED., THU., FRI., SAT., SUN., MON. FEBRUARY 15, 16, 17, 18, 19, 20:

RULERS —Mercury (Words/Traveling) Venus (Love) Pluto (Secrets/Passion):

Note: Pluto will become very destructive in this waning Moon period; he is still with us — You can expect dramatic happenings with nature all over; control is a must. He has produced much sensational news including the California Rancho Santa Fe mass-suicide. Mass murderers are again on the lookout for innocent victims as Pluto always stimulates the criminal element, the insane and the police force fighting all ill purposes. Don't be victims; be aware of Pluto's destructive power. Secrets from the past will return to your life.

Work, Career and Business: Chances are that your boss may not be aware of the power of Pluto and could make your life miserable. Odds are also that many country's leaders are totally ignorant of the power of Pluto and may decide to make hasty decisions that will bring death to many of their faithful followers. Do not take anything too personally and forgive anyone's sharp sarcasm and destructive tempers. A wake-up call for some karmic souls where reality must be accepted is around the corner.

Partnerships: On a waning moon period, never take a Pluto trend lightly as his impact is usually dramatic and could produce serious stress in your partnership and its future. Use all the diplomacy you know as anything you say or do will have serious repercussions. Not a time to play with anyone's emotions; stay cool in all you do. Changes must take place, as life is a constant process of change itself.

Family and Friends: Secrets will pop out from a person close to you; be sure to keep silent if you intend to keep this relationship. If you decide to speak up and force the truth on this person, keep cool and do the clean up gently. Don't expect anyone to be sensitive or respond to your needs. Instead, be ready for bitterness and harsh comments. Don't let Pluto's sarcastic nature destroy the serenity of your home life. Many ignorant souls will pay the heavy price of ignorance and lose much in the process.

Love Affairs: A surely stressful time is ahead for some, with Pluto's desire to demolish it all. Beautiful Venus will make you quite magnetic these days. You could become a prime target for some Plutonic soul's thirst for sex. If you become active on the dating scene, don't take chances on strangers; protect yourself and avoid heavy drinking. Pluto knows how vulnerable you are to his power when under the influence, and he will teach you one of the hardest lessons in your life. Relationships started now could be of a destructive nature, filled with jealousy and drama, and could lead you to harm or even death. This dramatic relationship could also be of a karmic nature but hopefully short lived. Be very aware out there and avoid negative group situations. Your intuition will be very accurate and should be followed with full trust. For those born under the sign of Pisces, a Scorpio or a Taurus will be strongly attracted to you. A Cancer friend has disturbing news for you.

Travel and Communication: We are under a Supernova period so be smart and patient on the road. Avoid the sarcastic remarks of others, and be aware of Pluto's desire for drama. Some people may call you for advice or share their secrets. Better keep it a secret for now, as Pluto does not like to talk. Pluto may decide to take many human lives in dramatic accidents.

Famous Personalities: You will most likely hear more about the infamous than the famous under Pluto's command. Venus will try everything she can to subdue her violent brother and smooth things out. The great loss of an old and eminent political, religious or entertainment figure will vex the media.

Events: Expect dramatic headlines like the following: Botched L.A. bank heist turns into bloody shoot-out — February 1997 — Manhunt on for suspects. "It was like the OK Corral." Or, New York — The crash of China Airlines Flight 676 on Taiwan, killing 205 people. The same energy was active when flight 800 was blown out of the sky, killing all people on board. Pluto rules death and secrets involving death. On May 15th, 2003 Moon Power read Note: Attention: Pluto is back with us - Expect secrets to surface and news from the police force.

Hundreds of grieving relatives gathered today at a mass grave discovered about 55 miles from Baghdad, Iraq. A forensic team working at the site says up to 11,000 bodies may be buried there. The dead are thought to be mostly Iraqis — killed during an uprising against Saddam Hussein in the wake of the 1991 Gulf War.

Shopping: Buy now anything related to sex, spying, metaphysics, and especially healing products. Do not purchase guns, knives or anything that could kill humans under Pluto's power. They may be used against you or your loved ones. Invest in dangerous pesticides to use in and around the house, they will work perfectly.

Iraq grave may hold 11,000

TUE., WED., THU., FRI. — FEBRUARY 21, 22, 23, 24:

RULERS — Jupiter (Middle East) Saturn (Politics) and Uranus (Chocking News):

Work, Career and Business: Pluto's legacy is dramatic experiences, and the acceptance of the transformation will open new doors to you. With Jupiter's touch, you should be confident in all your transactions. Expect this transformation to become a new beginning for your career life. Great Jupiter may induce foreigners to play an important part of this trend. Listen to your intuition and keep a positive attitude until the worst is gone.

Partnerships: New partners are on the horizon for some, while others must learn from previous errors. Money and general security will also be on your mind, serious decisions will have to be made soon. Be patient and wait for the upcoming New Moon, nothing comes easily in this life and one must strive and plan if one is to succeed. Letting go and rebuilding is a must.

Family and Friends: Jupiter's optimistic spirit will replenish you with hopes and a new approach to life. Spend some time with family members or dear friends, and be ready to listen to a wise soul. Enjoy the family and the good food offered to you, fight depression, and invite a friend over. Because of the waning Moon, a night out will not bring you much pleasure; better stay home, relax and read. An old friend may stimulate your life; this will make you happy and further an important wish later on.

Love Affairs: Someone much older or much younger may enter your life soon. Don't look for love these days; there is plenty to gain in yourself, and the stars want you to be in isolation for a while. You will feel spiritual and some of the questions of life will trigger your imagination. Indians affairs will strive. If you were born in October an Aries, a Gemini or an Aquarius will need you. A friend born in June may be interested in you.

Travel and Communication: Expect your telephone to be busy but do not hope for super-positive mail to reach you just yet. If you have to drive, be cautious and take extra time to get there; don't rush as the police could spoil your day. Don't be depressed about anything that may come your way; the stars have better for you on a later date.

Environment: During the last breath of the waning moon, Mother Nature may become capricious and surprise us with bad weather soon. Environmental groups will become active and will find support from the media, in saving the earth from uncaring corporations. Sad news may come from foreign grounds or the Middle East soon.

Famous Personalities: A well-known foreign personality involved in communication, television or writing will gain international attention where sorrow, tears and memory will make many followers cry.

Events: Some militant groups from a faraway continent will disturb the peace and become dangerous. Surprising destructive explosions are on the way. Also expect sad news such as; November 4, 1997 when a dual typhoon lashed the Pacific islands and destroyed all on his passage. Moon Power memo; Prediction - WED., THU. - MAY 21st, 22nd 2003: RULERS - Uranus (shocking news). Environment: Stay clear of thunder and lightning; Uranus takes many lives without warning. Expect him to throw a quake, a tornado or blow up a volcano soon.

Shopping: Not a good time for the gamblers; however, if you happen to be in Las Vegas, keep the spending in control. The Moon is still waning (negative); be patient and make major moves only after the fast approaching new moon.

New Moon — February 28, 2006 in Pisces: With the Head of the Dragon in Pisces and Uranus in Pisces expect surprising terrorist's activities on the US and its allies. Disturbing news about religious fanatics, abortion or oil is ahead while the weather will be nasty over land and the ocean. Many diplomats will be active on the political front, trying to avoid proliferation of religious wars in different parts of the world. With Mars in Gemini fueling acts of destruction in transportation trouble and death is the aim of every terrorists. Prominent politicians of the Middle East run the risk of assassination and some unlucky souls will not survive this dangerous trend. Expect progressive news involving science, chemical research. Meanwhile, it is a sure sign that drastic change is in store for parts of the Middle East and Asia. Nature and the weather could also turn out particularly difficult and may sink ships, produce devastating oil spills and flooding. However, with the waxing moon (positive) we can only hope for less damage than anticipated. Push now, be confident and like the fish swim with the upward tide.

Algeria Quake kills over 1100

Quake over 7.0 spares lives

Lunation impact on all signs:

Aries - A secret about your past will be divulged to you, your intuition is accurate.

Taurus - A new friend will enter your life and further one of your important wishes.

Gemini - Be alert, an opportunity to further your career is ahead of you.

Cancer - A trip close to the water will be bring you joy and a foreigner will please you.

Leo - A great opportunity to make more money or a legacy is ahead of you.

Virgo - A new business or emotional partner will be close by, don't miss this option.

Libra - A new job opportunity or a promotion is around the corner, simply ask for it.

Scorpio - A new business offer, a new love or a child will make you happy.

Sagittarius -Thinking about buying a house or moving, the family needs you.

Capricorn - A new study and a trip is on the agenda. Make the most of it.

Aquarius - A deal will bring you money, but be practical in your spending.

Pisces - A new start in many areas of your life will further your position. Move on.

February 26th, 2006: Today is your astrologer's birthday and because it unfolds within a new moon period I am going to enjoy a great birthday. Again thank you for all your good wishes and wonderful birthday cards. Each year I am getting more and more birthday cards and incredible amount of emails from all of you. It is an honor to receive so many blessings from all around the world. Please forgive me if I do not personally answer you, but it is from the depth of my heart that I sincerely thank you. God bless all of you. Dr. Turi

There will be three major negative SUPERNOVA windows in the year 2006. Each destructive "window" is operational for three to four weeks, thus caution is strongly advised during this period. Heavy loss of lives due to nature's devastating forces, aeronautical disasters and structural damage is to be expected. Once more realize that I do not use traditional dates found in popular ephemera.. Years of practical observation lead me to extend the Mercury retrograde motion and period of time.

July / August: Second SUPERNOVA window - From Saturday July 1st through Wednesday August 2nd 2006.

October / November: Third SUPERNOVA window - From Saturday October 21st through Tuesday October 21st 2006.

EXPLANATION OF A SUPERNOVA WINDOW

There is a celestial concentration of negative celestial energy bombarding the earth for a few weeks. Be extremely prudent in driving, and expect chain-reaction accidents. Be prepared for delays, strikes, and nature producing awful weather, including hurricanes and tornadoes. The same energy that produced the Titanic disaster, the Northridge, Los Angeles, and Kobe, Japan, earthquakes is approaching again. Double-check all your appointments, and if you can, postpone traveling and flying during this Supernova "window".

Communication and electricity will be cut off, and a general loss of power is to be expected. Appliances, computers, telephones, planes, trains, cars, all of these "tools" will be affected by this energy. They will be stopped in one way or another. The people of the past will make the news and will reenter your life. Expect trouble with the post office, education, students, strikes, prisoners' escape, newspapers, broadcasting industries and computer viruses may bother us again.

Many a failed mission and expensive electronic equipment (Mars probe etc.) and our tax dollars have been wasted because of the scientist's lack of knowledge of the stars. As usual NASA, which is not aware of the science of astrology, will waste our tax money with failed missions due to bad weather and electronic malfunctions. In the name of ignorance a few years ago, in the Challenger explosion seven astronauts lost their lives when NASA launched the shuttle under a "Supernova Window".

Note: Regardless of Dr. Turi's expectations posted on his website for the second time and his desperate attempts over the years to make NASA officials aware of dangerous Super Nova Windows, the Columbia was also launched during this window and re-entered the last night of it producing the death of all courageous astronauts.

Again in July 2005 NASA repeated the same error regardless of many failed attempts to launch the space vehicle. As expect foam from the fuel tanker damager the shuttle forcing astronauts to take an historic unplanned space walk costing millions of dollars for the tax payers once more and risking another disaster. When will NASA learn?

Marine life sharks, whales etc may also beach themselves due to Mercury retrograde affecting their natural inborn navigational systems. All these malevolent predictions and waste of lives and equipment do not have to occur. Those predictions do not have to affect you directly as they unfold. Instead, they are printed to prepare you for setbacks and frustrations, thus advising you to be patient and prudent during this trend. There is no room for ignorance, and those who are not aware of the celestial order, including the NASA space-program management team, will continue to pay a heavy price. In all mankind's affairs, ignorance is true evil. Why any scientists who are against my research do not honor the word science, which is based upon solid investigation, is solid proof of mental snobbery. By omitting any physical or spiritual laws can only bring penalty; for science's purpose is to explore all possibilities, even those laws written in light via the stars.

MEMO FROM WWWDRTURI.COM 2005 JULY SUPERNOVA WINDOW

WHEN WILL THE PEOPLE LEARN NOT TO FLY DURING A SUPERNOVA WINDOW?

CNN 8/14/05 - ATHENS, Greece (CNN) — A Cypriot plane with "no sign of life" in its cockpit while approaching Athens crashed into a mountain on Sunday, killing all 121 people on board, Greek officials said.

CNN 8/3/05: Canada Air France crash flight recorders recovered -Toronto on lightning alert when plane crashed!

CNN 7/31/05: 31 injured in truck-bus collision.

CNN 7/30/05: Death toll from India flooding climbs to 853.

CNN 7/30/05: AVON, Connecticut (AP) — A fiery crash involving 20 vehicles, including a commuter bus, killed at least four people Friday and injured at least 14, officials said.
MEMO - WED., THU., FRI., SAT. - JULY 20, 21, 22, 23: RULERS -Saturn (creditability) and Uranus (extraordinary news/explosions): Luckily for all of us ignorant NASA scientists suffered a bad dose of a "Supernova window" confining the shuttle to its launching pad saving the lives of the astronauts. Expect news from space too.

Expect news from space too .CNN 7/30/05 - Astronomers claim discovery of solar system's 10th planet.
7/27/05 - WHEN WILL NASA SCIENTISTS LEARN TO NEVER, EVER SEND A SHUTTLE UNDER A SUPERNOVA WINDOW? Debris came out of the fuel tank during the launch. Let's pray for the courageous astronauts, as NASA responsible never heeded my warnings over the years...

WHY WASN'T I SURPRISED???

Large foam shedding "surprised" mission specialist Andrew Thomas and Commander Eileen Collins. When will those educated imbeciles learn once and for all what a Supernova window is all about and stop killing astronauts?

READ THE SUPERNOVA WINDOWS - SAVE YOUR LIFE, BE AWARE!

SAT., SUN., MON., TUE. — FEBRUARY 25, 26, 27, 28:

RULERS — Uranus (Explosions/Chocking News) Neptune (Deception/Religion):

Work, Career and Business: The new moon in Pisces is upon you and she will bring a high level of emotion into your business affairs. Set up a difficult situation now to avoid a conflict later. Don't let Neptune's deceiving powers affect your attitude with life in general; be positive and listen to your intuition. Beware of get-rich-quick schemes, clean up your act and invest in new equipment that may let you down soon. Use the ingenuousness of Uranus to do some investigation around the office and let him provide you with great ideas with computers to promote your career. Progress is to be made now.

Partnerships: Keep Neptune's complaining attitude in check and control your thought processes. Think positive and your wishes will come true. Expect much from co-workers but Neptune may induce daydreams. Supervise yourself closely; you might forget something important, errands or returning vital telephone calls. Everyone will feel the "dreamy" side of Neptune, so be patient in your dealings with others. It's time to build others' confidence and practice tact with the same dedication as a diplomat. Be aware of Neptune sensitivity and be tolerant.

Family and Friends: As always, with Neptune in charge, you may dwell on your intuition but you must control your imagination. With Uranus driving next to him, your psychic abilities are enhanced; just tune in and you will receive the wisdom of the stars. A friend may become difficult; do not let this person rely on you too much and avoid getting too emotionally involved. Both Uranus and Neptune strive in new-age endeavors; you may decide to share your own psychic knowledge with a friend. You could gain through new-age financial endeavors if you educate yourself in metaphysics. Do not allow Neptune's deceiving tendency to make your life misery. Clean your thoughts; you have a choice, be happy.

Love Affairs: A romantic relationship may fall short of your expectations, mainly because your intuition tells you differently. Did you meet that person on the waxing Moon? If your Neptune is badly aspected by Venus (love) you will sense that perhaps the person may be deceiving in certain ways. Someone may try to lead you into a secret love affair, do not fall for it. Don't be deceived, especially if the person in question happens to be married. Avoid any form of guilt in your decision and stay miles away from alcohol during the night hours. With this new moon, expect much from weekend dating and social plans. If you were born in May, Pisces and Virgo will be strongly attracted to you. A Cancer friend has a good advice for you.

Travel and Communication: Neptune and Uranus may decide to strand you somewhere with the police. Wherever you go, keep an eye on your possessions; the crooks will be active. Enjoy life in many ways this weekend; go after your wishes but don't drink and drive. Uranus and Neptune are not great co-habitants and when alcohol and speed are mixed, it produces serious accidents. Be cautious if you must drive a long way; take plenty of rest as Neptune's energy could make you sleepy. Chew gum, it will keep you more alert. Don't let Neptune grasp your spirit and complain; use positive words and keep busy to avoid depression or guilty feelings from your past.

Environment: Uranus (explosions) will be strong and with the Head in Pisces (water) expect bad surprises with nature's devastating forces. Crazy people and all the elements will be invited for a mad dance. This energy will be quite strong and will disturb electronics and could produce aeronautic disasters.

Moon power memo: Prediction: 2006/7 will be the worst year for death and suicide attacks, dam terrorist acts and natural disasters (volcanoes/eruptions/earthquakes and water damages since 1948).

CNN - Forecasters predict severe hurricane season in 2006

Famous Personalities: Some rich and famous people may make sad news and be involved with drugs or alcohol. Moon Power memo:

Events: Uranus, the Lord of Surprises could also bring about explosions and misadventures, especially if you happen to get close to the river or the ocean this weekend. Under the same celestial energy on October 1996 — BLUE ISLAND, Illinois — An explosion rocked an oil refinery south of Chicago, jolting neighborhood homes for miles around and sending clouds of black smoke into the air.

Shopping: Invest in anything related to the arts, fishing, metaphysics and electronics. Put a big smile on your face and use your will and your knowledge; the New Moon will sharpen your spiritual values. Visit an old friend and spend time by the water.

Welcome to Your
Day - to - Day Guidance

For March 2006

WED., THU., FRI. — MARCH 1, 2, 3:

RULERS — Mars (Action) Venus (Love):

Work, Career and Business: control Mars' fighting spirit or he may slow down some of your projects. With the new moon around, you may also use his power constructively to improve your business endeavors. This fortuitous timing will strengthen your chances for success in the near future. Trust your ability to communicate with Mercury and follow your intuition. The next few days will be vital to launch yourself and Venus' lucky touch will bring additional developments. With the waxing Moon at work, the next two weeks should be used to the maximum to promote your business life.

Partnerships: Be ready for some people of your past to re-enter your life, with all the activities around they can only further your wishes. Remember, Mars is also around and you should use his strength and concentrate your efforts to get things done. The future promises to bring about good results from interviews, employment applications, promotions and other job opportunities. A pivotal turning point is to be expected this week in a key relationship. As always consider the long-term implications and respectability of the offer before making up your mind.

Family and Friends: With the new Moon and Mars (the warrior) in charge these days control your emotions. Everybody will want something from you. Use Venus' loving touch in your verbal exchanges and avoid Mars' invective remarks about an unlucky friend. Don't be shy; pass on your message, be confident and direct in your approach, your impact on others will surprise you. Do all this with "savoir faire." Take the family out and enjoy the wilderness with the children. As always keep an eye on them, as Mars will make them restless and accident-prone.

Love Affairs: Use the kind-hearted touch of Venus to your advantage; you may decide to treat someone you truly love with your best intentions. You're apt to make significant progress with love this weekend (especially close to the water) and you should really make the most out of this trend. Social life and romance is up; a trip is on the way for some. If you were born in June, a Sagittarius, a Libra or an Aquarius may fall for you.

Travel and Communication: This week promises to be worthwhile for the more creative souls and your writing skills will improve dramatically. Under Mercury and Venus' auspices, especially in time of a new moon, a new book could be started or finished. A trip to your past will pay off for some. Don't let Mars make you impatient or accident-prone on the road; be patient and don't trust other drivers.

Environment: Mars' destructive temper may produce tornadoes, explosions, high winds or flooding. Be aware and don't take any chances on the road. Moon Power memo:

Prediction Environment: The police will be needed in some situation where nature will get out of hand. Let's hope Venus will slow down Mercury's windy nature and stop him from producing hard weather or tornadoes.

Famous Personalities: Listen for news to come to light about great projects from the old or forgotten famous.

Events: Remember, Mars is around; don't take any chances with confrontations or the police. A positive attitude and diplomacy will keep you out of trouble. Impending breakthroughs with religion, the Pope, medicine or science are to be expected soon.

Shopping: It's a great time to buy interesting books and telephone appliances for your business. As Mercury rules transportation, it would be a good idea for you to take care of your wheels or invest in a new car.

05/31/03 - Two dozen twisters damage Illinois

SAT., SUN., MON., TUE. — MARCH 4, 5, 6, 7:

RULERS — Venus (Affection) Mercury (Conversation) Moon (Changing Cycles):

Work, Career and Business: Be ready for a variety of new starts concerning some areas of your career and your life. Some dutiful souls will land on a great opportunity for a new career. This energy will affect the "executives," so meeting one of them can seriously promote your career. Make the most of those days and have faith in all you do. Venus may send you an opportunity for a party or some flowers.

Partnerships: Venus' gentle touch will improve your magnetism and make you desirable to many. Expect the beginning or ending of important phases of your emotional life. Keep your eyes and ears open and listen to your friends, this new moon (changes) combined with Mercury (communication) and Venus (love) will affect them too. Many will be forced into new partnerships or marriage where a commitment will be asked. This is a great lunation for many lucky people. Spend those days in the outdoors close to the water or in the high mountains. The wilderness will do great healing on your spirit and recharge your soul for future challenges. Be aware of Mercury's tendencies to talk too much and listen to your partner a little more.

Family and Friends: You will be in demand from your active friends, calling you to join them in a social gathering. Don't turn down any invitation from friends; many of your wishes may come true through them. Some close friends or children, not without tears, will have to move away and carry on with their independent lives. Expect the family circle to be emotional, busy, with Mom and the kids to be the center of attraction. Enjoy the warm family circle, the food and all the children around you. They would love you forever if you decided to take them to the zoo soon. Happiness will rule these days and you should make more plans for the near future.

Love Affairs: Many mercurial spirits will be out there enjoying what life has to offer. Do not be afraid to take chances on anything or anybody now; these stars are extremely lucky and your competitiveness will pay off. Do not stay home this weekend; you may have to wait a long time to get this type of positive energy around again. Go out, ask and you may even find true love. If you were born in December, foreigners will play an important part of your life. An Aries or a Leo will want to know you and a Gemini will be strongly attracted to you.

Travel and Communication: Mercury will make you curious and will help you to communicate adequately with others. Your telephone will be busy, as this rare beautiful trio energy will boost everybody around you. Enjoy your life and if you have to be at work, be ready for an interesting meeting with some beautiful people after work.

Environment: Expect the weather to be decent or windy, as Venus will soon show off her finest garments. Control speedy Mercury to avoid freak accidents.

Famous Personalities: Good news pertaining to children and love is to be expected from famous people.

Events: Let's hope this trio and the new moon will stop any dramatic happenings but it could also mean that thousands of people may be fleeing nature, forced to relocate to start a new and better life.

Shopping: Invest in anything and everything for your children. Tools used for the home or the arts will also bring luck to future projects. Purchase your plane ticket now if you need to fly far away this summer.

March 5, 2006 — Venus enters Aquarius: With the planet of love in the independent sign of Aquarius, an opportunity to fall for an original even powerful person will be given to you. This trend will allow many freedom-oriented souls to find intellectual, new age partners, and to enjoy their magnetism and the respect they worked so hard to establish. Some lucky souls will be given the opportunities to enjoy electrifying love experiences; they may end up with memorable moments to cherish for the rest of their lives. If your natal Venus is in a hard aspect to Uranus, your desire for freedom and experience will take over the real feeling and need for true love. If she is well aspected, then an incredible and solid marriage will take place and surprise many people. Souls born now will be given the opportunity to experience love on an intellectual level and will have to learn to show more emotion and compassion. Again, If Venus is badly aspected; the soul will suffer many disturbing and short relationships with abusive partners, who will behave badly especially on a sexual level. Intellectual exchanges, honesty and freedom are needed with this position. Blessed with such a universal love, Venus in Aquarius will offer the soul an opportunity to attract an incredible, loyal, creative, intellectual even original partner. This position makes for one of the most original and magnetic partners. Usually artistic talent in writing, talking, photography, acting, and mental medicine is present with this position. This is a top position for those involved in the artistic, medical or scientific and research fields. Souls born now will travel the world in their lifetimes. They will be attracted to beautiful, intellectually stimulating partners and will be inclined to marry foreigners.

WED, THU., FRI., SAT., SUN. — MARCH 8, 9, 10, 11 12:

RULERS — The Moon (Graduation Ceremony) and the Sun (Love and Children):

Work, Career and Business: Some people will see the end and the beginning of a business situation. New people will move in to replace others. The Moon is still waxing (positive); make the most out of these days ahead and have faith in your ability to deal with any changes. Hope and faith will take you places.

Partnerships: This lunation means a great new start, relocation, and a promotion, even the start of a brand new life. Those changing stars do not care about your sadness, guilt or anything else; don't turn back, move on to your future. Your situation or feelings do not match your wishes; changes must take place. You'll be glad you did it. Remember life is a constant process of change, so go for it.

Family and Friends: Mom may get in touch with you, and your past is calling you back. The moon will make the children quite emotional; they will need your attention and will be demanding. With the Sun's vitality invest some time with them and do something special; they will cherish these days in their heart forever. A surprising new involvement with a child or love is ahead of you. A friend surprises you with an invitation; restaurants will be busy, so you'd better make a reservation if you do not want to stand in line for a table.

Love Affairs: Control your feelings about the past and let them lead you towards your future. Some relationship might end with sorrow, but the stars are on your side. Promote your next section of life without delay. Expect some surprises too and go full speed after your desires; anything incredible can happen especially during the weekend and you shouldn't stay home. These surprises should be positive and unexpected and there is much to gain if you interact with others. Visit friends, socialize or throw a party to celebrate this great solar and lunar energy. It's time to do your cabalistic candles ritual, white for the purification of the spirit, green for the purification of the physical, and blue to pray and ask favors of your guardian Angel. Don't forget to burn some sage and the use of the circle of salt. This lunation has the potential to bring about one of your greatest wishes. Again, don't waste it, go out there now, push and have faith. If you were born in July, a younger or older person born in January, November or March won't be able to resist your magnetism.

Travel and Communication: Expect news from brothers and sisters; be part of the action and communicate with those you love. Use plenty words of love and care for others; somehow you'll be rewarded. Bring your camera; great things and great surprises are imminent.

Memo; Bangladesh floods kill 45

Environment: Many people are forced to relocate during this celestial energy, sometimes due to nature's destructive forces. Typhoons and other water disasters are to be expected. Let's hope the new moon will alleviate drama and make the transition safe for many souls.

Famous Personalities: Famous and powerful personalities will be ending or starting a very important part of their love lives. Some will have finished their work on this physical plane, and will work as guides for whom they cared on earth.

Memo; Katharine Hepburn died

Events: Foreign governments will have to make important decisions soon. This type of energy was present on October 20, 1997- Typhoon Winnie killed 140 people in east China and forced relocation for many. Under the same star pattern, in June 1995, worried about its capital's growing population, the North Korean government reportedly began moving hundreds of thousands of people out of the city of Pyongyang. DHAKA, Bangladesh (AP) – June 2003 - Monsoon floods battering parts of Bangladesh have claimed 45 lives in the past four days, washed away many houses and displaced thousands of villagers. Thus, as predicted in Moon Power for these dates, thousands have and will have to be forced into a new part of their lives due to forced relocation.

Shopping: Only real estate endeavors from your past are protected; a new house bought now could bring much trouble to the new owners. If you do so, make sure to do a candle ritual. Burn white, green and blue candles, and mix them with incense to clean up some psychic residues left behind by disturbed souls. Some of your local stores may also be affected and may rebuild or close down completely.

Full Moon — March 14, 2006 in Virgo: Be ready for the ending of a portion of your working life. Disturbing news is ahead of you, be ready to accept these changes, as you might have to service this world in a different manner. Life is never stagnant so learning to embrace change is part of the whole lesson. Don't be too critical with your or other people performances. Naturally health oriented Virgo, Taurus, and Capricorn: this Full Moon will affect your mental processes and could make you prone to worry about your health. If you were born with a Moon in an earth sign, this applies to you too. Instead of anxiety or hurting your self-esteem, use this lunation to join a club and rebuild your physical figure. On a negative note you can expect oil spills and aeronautic accidents, so avoid flying if you can. Not a time to take chances, forestall signing important contracts. To travel or start new projects, wait until the next New Moon.

Lunation impact on all signs:

Aries - Don't worry too much about your health; expect some changes at work soon.

Taurus - Don't be too critical about a lover and don't worry about the children too much.

Gemini - Planning on a move? Don't let your family put too much stress on you.

Cancer - Keep your imagination in control, no one is perfect. Paper work must be done.

Leo - Be ready to positively spend money on your health or your image. Look good.

Virgo - Love or business may bring stress, don't be sarcastic and you'll be fine.

Libra - Some affairs of your past my surface, don't nurture guilt, move on.

Scorpio - A friend may deceive you; wait for a while for one of your wishes to come true.

Sagittarius -Career and traveling plans must be changed; the next New Moon will bring joy.

Capricorn - Difficult news from foreign lands, don't stress in any of your studies.

Aquarius - Money spent against your will, difficult news if your stars are afflicted.

Pisces - A business or emotional partner makes your life misery, clean up time.

MON., TUE., WED., THU., FRI. — MARCH 13, 14, 15, 16, 17:

RULERS —Mercury (Knowledge) and Venus (Sweetheart):

Work, Career and Business: The Moon is now waning (negative), and opportunities to further your position in life will depend on your interaction with others. Social contacts will pay off at a later date if you use Venus' gentle touch in all you do. Remember the power of your own thoughts; don't be crippled by your own fears and anxieties, or you may attract setbacks to your life. Go after what you really want and don't be afraid to communicate your feelings. Expect some deceiving developments soon. Contracts will be signed and will bring great financial rewards if you decide clean up and start again.

Partnerships: Do not assume the worst without first finding all the facts, nor break your spirit by suppressing all faith in your abilities. Mercury could make you talkative; listen to your partner a little more. Keep an open mind and be receptive when direction is being offered, especially if the person in question is older than you. Being patient and working harder to attain your goals is the key. If you are inquisitive enough, secrets of a financial nature may be revealed to you. Important legal paper work to clean up your past may be on the way for you to sign; be confident in doing so as the future has better to offer.

Family and Friends: Use your exceptional insight into the secret motives of a friend close to you and avoid all unnecessary gossip. Be patient and practice diplomacy with loved ones. During a waning moon, Mercury may promote intellectual challenges, even confrontations. Use plenty of words of love to those for whom you care, and keep your eyes on the children. Friends may ask for financial favors; provide help, but watch your own security.

Love Affairs: Those stars above your head are tough, but your knowledge is well placed; use your will in all occasions. The kind-hearted touch of Venus can only alter those nasty stars if you have faith in the right people and yourself. Avoid being too critical about someone you value; no one is perfect, not even you. Learn to love yourself and concentrate on the qualities you and others possess. If you were born in August, an Aries will help you but a Scorpio could be giving you trouble.

Travel and Communication: Venus' diplomatic powers will be felt in your words and will further many of your requests. Just remember, no one attracts bees with vinegar. Invest in your own thought power and do not expect too much from others. Many souls will be forced to deal with their past, and some will have take a long and difficult journey. You will learn about people getting in trouble with the law or getting a divorce soon.

Environment: As usual with the waning Moon expect dramatic news soon with Mother Nature. Let's hope that with the gentle touch of Venus, nature will be quiet. Many environmentalist groups will be active; some may get out of hand while trying to get their message out.

Famous Personalities: A prominent person will promote a new diet or a specific product. It will use only natural goods and be very Eastern in conception. Some will announce a new baby's arrival.

Events: Some disturbing, even shocking news will arrive soon pertaining to unhappy people willing to start trouble. College students or the post office may make the news.

Shopping: Now is the perfect time to invest in a diet or a health program to lose those unwanted pounds. You may also find great deals with children's second hand products.

SAT., SUN., MON., TUE., WED. — MARCH 18, 19, 20, 21, 22:

RULERS — Pluto (Death) Venus (Love Drama) Jupiter (Law):

Note: Attention Pluto is back with us and we can only expect dramatic happenings; control is a must. Do not be one of his victims; be aware of Pluto's destructive power. Anything you say or do under his power will follow you for the rest of your life. Time to use extreme caution in all you do.

BE CAUTIOUS SCORPIO MOON & SUPERNOVA WINDOW

January 25th 2006, through Thursday March 30th, 2006.

He who reigns himself and rules his passion, desire and fears is more than a king.
—Goethe

Work, Career and Business: Don't take chances, be cool, be smart, pull in a safe place and be quiet for a while; that is the best advice I can give you now. You are at the time of the month when you must wait for the green light; keep a low profile and all will be fine. Watch the dramatic news during this trend and realize the importance of having your Moon Power close by. As always, if Starguide works for you, it also works for others, so don't be afraid to tell others to "cool" down. We are all under the incredible will of the cosmos, and Pluto will punish some unlucky souls for their ignorance of God's universal rules.

Partnerships: Be courteous with everyone as your true motives, feelings and desires are sure to be heard and felt. This is the time to use your will and apply your knowledge of the stars. Avoid outbursts of emotion, even if your partner gets completely out of hand with jealousy or bad temper. With Jupiter and Venus' protective presence these days, some of the upcoming dramatic news and predictions might pass by without harming your relationships.

Family and Friends: After a full Moon, Pluto will enjoy himself and will become destructive; use Starguide's wisdom or you may be very sorry you didn't. Many of us will undergo some form of metamorphosis as Pluto gives serious wake-up calls. If friends and family members need help or guidance, share your knowledge for the common good. Not a time to plan a visit or get away from home; wait for better stars. Many disturbances are reported during this trend, especially the ones with domestic violence, and the police will have their hands full. Keep a low profile with all, you have the right to be scared, Pluto means business and will hurt you if he has to.

Love Affairs: These days could bring an element of drama, and you are advised to stay clear of other people's problems. Be ready for some secrets to surface. Some people for whom you care may become very uncooperative or decide to fight with you, and could lead you to depression. Better enjoy your own home and cooking on the weekend nights. Social life can only bring unwanted situations as Pluto may send one of his awful children to teach you a lesson. Don't take chances with sex and stay clear of strangers. In the game of love, protect yourself. If you were born in September, a Taurus or a Capricorn could be difficult to deal with. If you are having trouble with a person who is a water sign having problems with alcohol, move on and look for a better soul.

Travel and Communication: Do not travel unless you absolutely have to. Your car may decide to let you down, so take care of the wheels before taking a risky journey. Double-check all plans and arrangements to avoid further hazards. Now is the time to speak clearly and concisely, as you're prone to miscommunication. Do not broach subjects that are controversial these days, with emotions running high and logic out the window. For those who find themselves in a difficult spot communicating, it may be better to save the subject for later and excuse yourself before it's too late. You will usually find that the argument occurred as a result of what might happen rather than what will. Lots of secrets will come to light and money will be a disturbing topic for some.

Environment: Remember Pluto. Under this planet's immense destructive power, chemical plants explode, airliners crash, nature goes crazy, products are tampered with, and potentially dangerous technology is sold to hostile powers. It's now time to get close to God in your local church and pray for the unaware victims of deadly Pluto. On April 16th, 1997 I posted a "window" for April 23rd on the Internet saying "Be ready with nature's devastating forces and quakes well above 6.0." Results — 4/23/97 - Santa Cruz Islands. (8.0Mb), 4/23/97 - Tonga islands. (6.5 Mb), 4/23/97 - Trinidad (6.5)Ms, 4/23/97 - Vanuatu Islands (6.1) Ms, 4/23/97 - Mariana Islands (6.3) Mb.

Famous Personalities: The world will lose a famous personality under Pluto's command. He may also decide to do it dramatically (assassination). Pluto will not stop with famous people, so watch yourself and choose your environment carefully.

Events: This disreputable planet has always promoted dramatic news involving the police, sex, drama and death. Be ready for a bumpy ride. Pluto is also a factor that stimulates and dramatizes ethics issues and makes them even more complex. 1/6/2005-JOHANNESBURG, South Africa (Reuters) — South Africa's Nelson Mandela, one of Africa's most committed campaigners in the battle against AIDS, announced that his only surviving son had succumbed to the disease. 1/5/2005 - Sheriff posts snipers after firings - Georgia judge orders workers reinstated. JONESBORO, Georgia (AP) — On his first day on the job, the new sheriff called 27 employees into his office, stripped them of their badges, fired them, and had rooftop snipers stand guard as they were escorted out the door. 1/6/2005 - Ute fans angry with police for electrical shocking -SALT LAKE CITY (AP) — Some Utah fans are upset that police responsible for security at the Fiesta Bowl used 50,000-volt electric devices to zap fans trying to storm the field after the win. All these dramatic news happened under the destructive power of Pluto, the Lord of death and drama, so be aware and don't be his victim.

Shopping: Buy now anything related to the unknown, magic, candles, and incense. Some old souls will be busy writing their wills. Visit your favorite psychic or astrologer and deal with the unknown. Invest in anything that will bring death to pests but stay clear of weaponry, it could be used against you or a family member.

THU., FRI.,SAT., SUN. — MARCH 23, 24, 25, 26:

RULERS — Saturn (Politicians) Uranus (Explosions) Neptune (Drugs/Religions):

Work, Career and Business: We are on the waning time (negative) and faith could be quite low for many. Hold on a little longer for the upcoming New Moon and life will improve for us all. Use patience with everyone around, and wait before launching important business or signing documents. Don't trust any business propositions now and don't take any chances with your finances. The worse is now over, just be patient.

Partnerships: Don't let Saturn's gloomy nature affect your psyche and try smiling if you can. Moon Power mentioned a concentration of negative influences with this last Pluto impact and some of us had to experience a rebirth in partnerships. Again do not to fall prey to depression or self-destruction. Use all your abilities to deal with your new life and help the ones you care about. Enjoy a good movie and a good bottle of wine at home in the evening hours.

Family and Friends: You may not like it but a friend or a family member's surprising visit has you scrambling to make your home presentable in advance of the arrival. This person may bring a lot of excitement but also some unhealthy news. If you decide to socialize, keep an eye on your possessions and lock your car. During a waning Moon and under Uranus' grip expect bad surprises, as crooks become active. Get rid of unwanted things: have a garage sale or give it away to the Salvation Army to the unfortunate. Now is a good time to clean, take care of your gardens or even your houseplants. Don't fall for guilt; avoid depressing thoughts of your past. Look for happy people and try to enjoy what life has to offer for now. Keep an eye on the kids especially if there is water around, as Neptune may play tricks on them. An introduction to harmful drugs is always a possibility with them now.

Love Affairs: Stay clear of strangers, especially if alcohol is offered. Not a good time get involved sexually; take precautions. Bad aspects to Neptune in your horoscope will promote even induce sexually transmitted diseases and narcotic abuse. Secret love affairs may start now, but if you are in one, make sure you are not taken for a ride, as all those promises may be too good to be true! Be practical and review any promises with common sense. If you were born in October, an Aries or an Aquarius will find you quite attractive and may bring more trouble than love into your life.

Travel and Communication: Traveling now may be too risky for comfort; be sure you're prepared for any road emergency or difficult weather. If you must take a long journey, be very careful on the road and if possible avoid flying. With the waning Moon your energy level won't be that high and if you must drive, take plenty of rest before hitting the road. Keep to the speed limit; the police will be out there ready to penalize you. Avoid drinking at all costs during the evening hours and keep a positive attitude in all you say. Your imagination will be high and must be kept in control.

Environment: Uranus (surprising disruptions) Neptune and Saturn (karma) are not a good combination under a waning Moon and will upset the poor unaware human on earth below. Many eruptions have taken place under this energy and the weather won't cooperate. April 29, 1997 Mexico City — The Popocatepetl volcano erupts near Mexico City and — April 30, 1997 — Explosion at Albanian weapons depot kills 20 — TIRANA, Albania — At least 20 people were killed Wednesday when a weapons depot exploded in a central Albanian town. Be aware don't take chances.

Famous Personalities: Sad news will be coming from famous people and their involvements with deceiving activities. Some will live this world and others could be incarcerated or receive emergency care.

Events: On a large scale disturbing news is to be expected and may disturb the population. The government may be forced to make very important decisions that could affect us. Expect news from Japan, France and about nuclear endeavors and devices soon. 07/23/05 - Strong quake jolts Tokyo, injuries reported - 07/23/05 - ROME, Italy (Reuters) Italy and France announced on Friday - they were boosting security to try to stave off terrorist attacks. - CNN - 07/23/05: 85 dead - Bombs kill scores in Egyptian resort town. CNN - 07/23/05: Explosion hits Beirut

Shopping: Difficult energy coming from the Universe will manifest itself, thus not a time to deal with metaphysics or trust psychics. Neptune may blur their vision of the future. Avoid investing in Uranus' tools (computers/electronics).

New Moon — March 29, 2006 in Aries: The New Moon will mature in the sign of Aries. Explosive and destructive news about fires, wars, and explosions is to be expected soon. Mother earth is alive and may stretch her self vigorously, producing powerful volcanic or earthquake activity. Souls born with this celestial identity will be competitive, aggressive and will use their inner leadership abilities to gain positions of power during their lifetimes. Discipline and patience must be induced at an early age to avoid serious head injury. Many endeavors will be launched successfully within the next two waxing weeks and you should be confident of the outcome.

Lunation impact on all signs:

Aries - This lunation is on you, a new start of a section of your life is imminent.

Taurus - A secret will come to light soon and relieve some guilt of your past.

Gemini - A new friend will bring you an important wish, you're lucky this month.

Cancer - Your career will see some great developments use this new moon accordingly.

Leo - A trip or a study will help you to deal with foreign affairs.

Virgo - A partner will help you to make money, a legal action or a contract is ahead.

Libra - A new business deal or a new emotional partner is on the horizon.

Scorpio - Changes at work, don't stress and your health will improve for sure.

Sagittarius - A new hobby or a child will make you happy and love is in the air!

Capricorn - You will have to re-structure your home or move, be aware of fire.

Aquarius - Great news by mail or telephone is ahead of you, a sibling needs you.

Pisces - A new way to make money or invest in your education is on the way.

MON., TUE., WED., THU., FRI. — MARCH 27, 28, 29, 30, 31:

RULERS — Neptune (Magical Hopes) and Mars (War Action):

Work, Career and Business: The new moon will make you lucky but Mars could upset your plans. Be nice with others at work; use your knowledge and don't expect your boss to be aware of Mars' impatience and irritability. The waxing Moon will provide you many opportunities soon. Neptune may make it difficult for you to concentrate these days. Try to be more practical in your endeavors, important matters related to finances will be on your mind, and all will be fine soon.

Partnerships: As always communicate my work to others and make good use of Starguide. You may also suggest it to your partner, as two souls aware of the stars are better than one. Using Neptune's intuitive power may save a situation, but avoid complaining and do something about it. Control Mars' impatience and understand the needs of your partner too.

Family and Friends: In time of a New or Full Moon, people have some problems sleeping. Use tons of diplomacy with the children; Mars will want to keep them up late. A great time is to be expected soon as the New Moon is now shining on us all. Enjoy the love and good food provided by those who really care for you. Spend some time with the children; teach them love and harmony as Mars may make them play rough. Remember, dangerous Mars is with us and with Neptune nearby, be aware around water.

Love Affairs: Avoid any intense Martian situation with your partner; support, love and respect will take you miles. Use Neptune's soft values to apologize to someone you deeply care for and control your imagination. Offer a present or some flowers; this always works. If you were born in November, a Pisces or a Cancer will want to know you. A trip close to the water or a movie will make you feel good.

Travel and Communication: Mars' speedy nature may affect your driving and response to others. Be courteous, psychotics and lunatics share the same road with you and one of those dangerous drivers may get you in trouble. As always, under Neptune's power, stay clear of alcohol if you take a long trip, and rest if you feel tired. Anticipate this New Moon to be great and put a big smile on your face.

Environment: Combined with Mars' accident prone nature and Neptune's absent-mindedness, expect sad news from water, oil or the Middle East. Once more, Mars' destructive instinct is unpredictable, so avoid dangerous situations, especially if you spend time close to the water this weekend.

Famous Personalities: Life is a constant process of change, and like all of us, famous figures must also accept the sad reality of demise. Light will be brought up to some famous people's hidden problems with alcohol or unlawful endeavors. Soon, the end of a notable person's life will reach the media.

Events: With Mars, even on a waxing positive Moon, fires, destruction, violence, war and nature's devastating forces at work are on the agenda. Difficult weather including explosions, tornadoes or flooding may affect some of the states and surprise a number of people. Much of the difficult news may be coming from Japan, Germany, the Middle East and the US.

Shopping: Now is the perfect time to purchase sharp tools, a camera or get a good deal on any form of chemicals or paint. A new car can also be bought now, but with its Martian nature, controlling speed will be difficult. With Neptune on those wheels, you may be asking for trouble later, if you drink and drive fast.

Welcome to Your
Day - to - Day Guidance

For April 2006

April 6, 2006 — Venus enters Pisces: This is the ideal celestial position to invest in an artistic or spiritual study. Empower yourself with spirituality and display your creativity to the world. Souls born now will inherit natural gifts in music and the arts. This is a great astrological position and the option is given to the soul to become a leader in the artistic fields. A weak or badly asserted Venus in this sign will induce deception in love, abuse of alcohol and drugs leading to secret love affairs and deception in the long run. If you're born with Venus in Pisces, you are strongly advised to learn to love with your head, not your heart, to avoid the awful guilt. When well assisted by other celestial bodies, this is a perfect position for total commitment and endless love. Many souls will choose to serve "Poseidon, Lord or the sea" and will work and serve marine life.

SAT., SUN., MON., TUE., WED. — APRIL 1, 2, 3, 4, 5:

RULERS — Venus (Affection) Mercury (Siblings) Moon (Big Changes):

Work, Career and Business: This long trend lunation will be progressive and may force you into many changes; no matter how painful they may seem to be, those changes are for the best in the long run. Thus be ready for a variety of new starts concerning some areas of your career life. Some dutiful souls will land on great opportunities for new careers. This energy will affect the "executives," so meeting one of them can seriously promote your career. Make the most of those days and have faith in all you do. Venus may send you an opportunity for a party or some flowers.

Partnerships: Venus' gentle touch will improve your magnetism and make you desirable to many. Expect the beginning or ending of important phases of your emotional life. Keep your eyes and ears open and listen to your friends, this new moon (changes) combined with Mercury (communication) and Venus (love) will affect them too. Many will be forced into new partnerships where commitment will be asked. Enjoy the outdoors close to the water or in the high mountains. The wilderness will be a great healer to your spirit and recharge your essence for future challenges. Be aware of Mercury's tendencies to drive too fast or talk too much. Listen to your partner a little more.

Family and Friends: You will be in demand from your active friends, calling you to join them in social gatherings. Don't turn down any invitation from friends; many of your wishes may come true through them. Some close friends or children, not without tears, will have to move away and carry on with their independent lives. Expect the family circle to be emotional and busy with Mom and the kids to be the center of attraction. Enjoy the warm family circle, the food and all the children around you. They would love you forever if you decided to take them to the zoo soon. Happiness will rule these days and you should make more plans for the near future.

Love Affairs: Many mercurial spirits will be out there enjoying what life has to offer. Do not be afraid to take chances on anything or anybody now; these stars are extremely lucky and your competitiveness will pay off. Do not stay home this weekend; you may have to wait a long time for this type of positive energy to come around again. Go out, ask and you may even find true love. If you were born in December, foreigners will play an important part of your life. An Aries or a Leo will want to know you and a Gemini will be strongly attracted to you.

Travel and Communication: Mercury will make you curious and will help you to communicate adequately with others. Your telephone will be busy, as this rare beautiful trio of energy will boost everybody around you. Enjoy your life and if you have to be at work, be ready for an interesting meeting with some beautiful people afterwards.

Environment: Expect the weather to especially beautiful as Venus will soon show off her finest garments. Control speedy Mercury to avoid freak accidents.

Famous Personalities: Good news pertaining to children and love is to be expected from famous people.

Events: Let's hope this trio and the new moon will stop any dramatic happenings, but it could also mean that thousands of people may be fleeing nature, forced to relocate to start a new and better life.

Shopping: Purchase your plane ticket now if you need to fly far away this summer. Tools used for the home or the arts will also bring luck to future projects. It's the right time to buy anything and everything for your children. Those stars also support anything, which involves the mastering of any form of spiritual light. Dr. Turi needs your help to pass on his very important star message to the world. See www.drturi.com or call 602-265-7667 to help us to set a crash course in your area on Astropsychology, Kabalistic Healing or the Astro-Tarot.

> MEMO – On June 22nd, 2006 the Dragon's Head will move into Pisces and will stay in this sign until December 16, 2007: Expect a complete re-structure of the affairs ruled by the house where Pisces or Neptune are located. You are strongly recommended to order a

90mn taped Full Life or Progressive Reading to find out about this incredible and dramatic impact in your or someone else's life. Visit www.drturi.com click on "readings" or call the office at 602-265-7667 for more information. Remember: "Knowledge is power; there is no room for ignorance in your life. Power means your option to establish emotional, financial and spiritual stability!"

—-Dr. Turi

THU., FRI., SAT., SUN. — APRIL 6, 7, 8, 9:

RULERS — The Moon (Real Estate/Changes) and the Sun (Love/Surprise).

Work, Career and Business: The week starts on a note of faith with many new financial breaks ahead of you. You can expect serious beginnings or endings of important phases of your and others' lives. Be ready for those upcoming progressive variations and prepare to accept them. Life is a constant process of change and the stars are, even if you don't agree or realize it, working for your benefit in the long run.

Partnerships: Let go of the wrong people and depressing situations; take a chance on your new future with faith. Many will experience the sad endings of their relationships and their lucky souls may see the new beginnings. However, under a positive moon there are no excuses; just get on with it. Many of your wishes may see the light soon, be confident.

Family and Friends: The Sun rules love, romance and children and with the waxing moon surprising news is ahead of you. If something wrong happens to a child under a good moon, maybe you should check out when you had bought the toy that was used. The Sun gives life to anything that he touches but for some mystical reasons, fatalistic experiences involving children can still happen. As usual, watch over them, especially close to the water. On a more positive note he will put his undiscriminating light on the incredible UFO manifestation. You may hear about someone's heart problem or surgery.

Love Affairs: Be ready for new starts in love matters and provide spiritual help for the victims suffering painful broken hearts. The right partner might not be the one you want to be with. You should use your newfound freedom to look for someone who deserves your love. With the waxing moon, keep looking for that special person and by miracle it will happen. Some teenagers may find their first love or suffer the heartbreak of it. If you are born in January, a much older or younger person born in September or July may want to let you know how much you mean to them.

Travel and Communication: If you decide to take the children with you, be aware on the road; you are responsible for their young lives. Order them to put their seat belts on and be ready for anything. Enjoy all that nature has to offer and be prepared for surprises; enjoy — a great time is ahead of you.

Environment: What was once built by man (cities/homes) or nature (forests), somehow with time will have to be destroyed. What was once born must eventually die; this is the great cycle of life. Be ready for surprising explosions as experienced on February 24th, 1998 in a Rome apartment-Three people were injured Tuesday when an explosion, possibly caused by a gas stove, ripped through an apartment in a historic district of Rome, according to the Italian news agency ANSA. There is nothing else to do than to accept the ultimate changes imposed by God, and usually the future offers better. The Sun regulates fires, so be aware and be prudent if you happen to go into the wilderness.

Famous Personalities: Expect interesting, even weird surprises with children and the rich and famous. Be ready for the unexpected with their words and actions. You may take some calculated chances with the Sun in charge but understand your limits.

Events: Terrible tragedies such as the Kobe, Japan earthquake and many volcanic eruptions are around the corner, as the 2nd Supernova energy will soon reign upon the earth. If early, this Supernova window will force thousands of people out of their homes because of nature's destructive forces. Let's hope the powerful life-giving Sun will slow or stop tragedy.

Shopping: Buy anything for children as long as it is new. Invest in gold or expensive items; you may also invest in computers or anything involving creativity and the arts.

MON., TUE., WED., THU. — APRIL 10, 11, 12, 13:

RULERS — Mercury (News/Traveling) and Venus (Love Affairs).

Work, Career and Business: Just a few days away from the full moon, make the most of Venus' new fresh breath of life and be aware. With Mercury's vital intellectual genius, push your business now. Advertisements, important calls, traveling, and meetings will pay off before the upcoming Full Moon. Respect the Universal Law, use Moon Power and your knowledge and have faith in your abilities.

Partnerships: Mercury rules the mail, telephone and communication in general; expect drama and secrets coming your way soon. Venus may decide to offer you a get-together after work but Mercury will have everyone "gossiping." Promote only faith and love, and pass on your message to the world around you.

Family and Friends: Use what's left of the New Moon to provide a generous shoulder to those who suffered karmic experiences the last few months. However, let no one exhaust your spirit, and avoid being frustrated with loved ones.

Some of those friends really need spiritual regeneration or a helping hand. Do so, but realize your limits, especially where money is concerned.

Love Affairs: Your sense of perfection will expand with Venus in charge until the Full Moon. Don't be too picky or demanding with your loved ones; no one is perfect. You may feel like starting a diet; but don't get too concerned with your appearance or your health. Work first on yourself, and the results will stimulate those close to you. Venus hates cigarette smoke, so with her help, apply your will and try to give up smoking. By doing so, the opportunity to find real and healthy love will be given to you. If you were born in February, someone born in August or June may fall in love with you.

Travel and Communication: Get your wheels in action; traveling and shopping are under protection until the Full Moon. Use Venus' touch of love to show your affection to those you care for, and offer them flowers. Mercury will get your telephone ringing, and much of your important mail should be sent now. Further happiness and love, and you will benefit from your own positive attitude.

Environment: You need to recharge your batteries; a trip in the wilderness is strongly recommended if you have been under stress lately. Venus' energy will make you appreciate the beauty of Mother Nature and the people around you. Many animal rights activists and environmentalists will make serious progress and gain the attention they deserve when passing on their important message.

Famous Personalities: A new diet is on your mind; a famous person will promote a new health product.

Events: With the New Moon still upon us, Mother Nature may decide to relax a bit and keep the approaching Pluto's destructive power under control. Some large financial corporations may decide to merge to secure themselves against competition.

Shopping: Great bargains will be offered if you want to invest in products to improve your life and body. Some may decide to join the local gym or enroll in a weight loss program.

Full Moon — April 13, 2006 in Libra: The next two weeks are going to be a trying time for many of us. Keep a cool head, as changes in business and partnerships are a part of this lunation. Be ready for the beginning or ending of a portion of your business or emotional life. Disturbing, and surprising news is ahead of you from the government. Be ready to accept those dramatic upcoming changes. The world is getting ready for serious drama where many young lives will be wasted and death for some innocent souls is inescapable. Keep in mind that, life is a constant process of change, and the future usually has better to offer. Take chances, sign contracts, travel and promote your life only after the next New Moon. Be ready for a bumpy couple of weeks ahead of you. Be strong, you'll need to be, for when all is said and done you and the world will be in better positions. Some foreign governments will work hard to avoid wars.

Lunation impact on all signs:

Aries - A full restructure of your business and emotional life is ahead. Be patient.

Taurus - Don't be concerned or too worried, your work and your health are connected.

Gemini - Stress and changes with love, business and children are a part of life.

Cancer - Problems at home, and your security should not keep you depressed for long.

Leo - Control your speech, important contracts are ahead so use diplomacy.

Virgo - Money and commitment is a thought, important paper work and your signature is ahead.

Libra - Your emotions and imagination runs high, a new relationship for you?

Scorpio - Let go of wrong associations, a secret love affair could bring trouble; move on.

Sagittarius - A wish can not come true with the person you are with now, change ahead.

Capricorn - Career commitments, contracts and changes are best for you.

Aquarius - A trip must be canceled, a partner gives you trouble, you'll see through it.

Pisces - Someone has or will let you down soon, you deserve better association for your money.

April 14, 2006 — Mars enters Cancer: Wait for the upcoming New Moon to launch any financial or real estate endeavors. Home improvement, buying or selling a beautiful house is on the agenda for some. Souls born now will be geared by Mars to be involved with matters related to construction, the Government, and general country and family securities. They will invest time and money in hotels and restaurants and real estate endeavors. Many of them will strive to find total security and a husband or wife with protective qualities. Some will have to learn to let go of wrong relationships without drama and tantrums. This Mars position makes the soul very sensitive to home and family. Usually a gift in building and cooking is to be found in this position. Those souls are born to feed the world with food and love. Under stress, this Mars position produces overwhelming stomach acidity and ulcers.

April 17, 2006 — Mercury enter Aries: With the planet of communication cruising through the aggressive sign of Aries, be aware of your speech and your speed. On a more positive side, your intellectual potential will regenerate with new studies. This is a perfect time to launch a magazine or any form of study involving the mind or new topics. Souls born with this celestial signature will be extremely competitive, intelligent, curious and great communicators. They will need to discipline their minds and learn to listen to others. An opportunity to make an impact in the world of speed and communication is offered to the soul. Dr. Turi needs your help to pass on his very important star message to the world. See www.drturi.com to help us to set a crash course in your area on Astropsychology, Kabalistic Healing or the Astro-Tarot.

Note: Attention: Pluto is back with us — As always with the Lord of hell in charge of this trend, better think twice before saying or acting on impulse. With the second Supernova window in action, expect many affairs of the past and secrets to be divulged. Affairs and foreign leaders will soon make the news again while man and nature's destroying forces will be felt all over the world. The police and blackguards will make the news. More than ever, use diplomacy, as whatever you do now will have very serious repercussions in your future.

FRI., SAT., SUN., MON., TUE. — APRIL 14, 15, 16, 17, 18:

RULERS — Pluto (Death/Drama) and Jupiter (Law/Foreigners):

Work, Career and Business: You are now walking on fire! You'd better use all the "savoir faire" you know if you are to go through this lunation without trouble. A serious wake-up call will come to many abusers, as the heavy hand of karma will fall on the victims. The possibility to lose and rebuild it all will be a serious matter for some karmic souls. Not a time to deal with money matters: keep a low profile until the next New Moon.

Partnerships: The offensive secret life of a person may surface; you may learn something valuable about a partner. Whatever it is you find out, do not divulge the secret. Stinky moneymaking schemes will play an important part of this trend; listen to your intuition in all you do. Stay clear of dark alleys; your life hangs upon your awareness. Many people will learn the hard way these days.

Family and Friends: Do not expect anyone you care about to be diplomatic with you during this trend. Do not fall for Pluto's destructive or sarcastic remarks; words of love and support will pay off in the long run. Be ready for some dramatic news from someone close to you. Whatever happens, be strong; life must go on as Pluto has important work to do and he is part of the celestial design devised by God. Time to further my work and offer knowledge to those for whom you care by letting them read Moon Power.

Love Affairs: Secret affairs of sex and passionate love may be divulged to the public, forcing people to take a stand in destroying and rebuilding relationships. This might happen to you too. In any case use tons of diplomacy to save unwanted trouble in your love life. If you are a water sign or have any planet in Scorpio, be ready for a wake-up call of some form. Stay clear of any new relationship, stick with the old one or refrain from social interaction.

Travel and Communication: Expect news pertaining to secrets, sex, the police force, and medical discovery. Be careful of what you do or say during this trend. Drive carefully; stay clear of strangers and strange places. Be ready for dramatic news to plague the media.

Environment: Pluto will have fun destroying it all, but remember he belongs to the divine family and has a specific work to do. His dramatic impact on this earth (and people) is needed. As Pluto demolishes he also gives opportunities to rebuild stronger and better bridges and buildings. Be ready for dramatic news with the police and nature's forces soon. CNN 5/22/05 — Police have arrested the pastor of a defunct church in Ponchatoula, Louisiana, his wife and six former congregants in a sexual abuse case involving as many as 24 children, authorities. CNN 5/22/05 - A children's sleepover ended tragically early Saturday when fire swept through a two-story home, killing nine people, including seven children.

Famous Personalities: Some famous people will be called back to God. Sometimes famous spoiled children get involved with the wrong crowd, and some are found shot to death alongside a road. Pluto couldn't care less about famous people. CNN 5/22/05 - ATLANTA (AP) — Former Los Angeles Rams running back David Lang, who also played on the Dallas Cowboys' Super Bowl XXX championship team, was killed in a shooting, police said Saturday. Lang, 37, was shot and killed following an apparent argument with an acquaintance Thursday near his Stone Mountain home, about 20 miles northeast of Atlanta, said police Lt. L.J. Florea. .

Events: Hopefully knowledgeable Jupiter will slow down Pluto's rampage and thirst for blood. Under his power a plane plowed into crowd at air show. Under Pluto jurisdiction plane crash, avoid flying and be ready for a repetition of the past soon. A Bell 212 helicopter belonging to the Mexican Attorney General's Office crashed upon landing in rural Mexico killing the navigator and injuring five people. 6/18/05 -LOS ANGELES, California (AP) — Leonardo DiCaprio was hit with a bottle while attending a Hollywood party given by Paris Hilton's ex-lover and needed about a dozen stitches to close a wound near his ear, People Magazine reported Friday on its Web site. 6-18-05- (06.18.2005) . An unauthorized user may have accessed the names, banks and account numbers of up to 40 million credit card holders, MasterCard International Inc. said. CNN) — A gunman opened fire inside a Chicago, Illinois, nightclub early Saturday, killing three people and injuring at least five others, according to a police spokesman.

Shopping: All water and earth signs will see an important part of their business or financial life taking a specific direction within this lunation. With Jupiter here too, the worst might be avoided by some miraculous development. A visit to your local church to pray for Pluto's victims will be of benefit to you. Do not invest in weapons, if you do so you might have to use them against crooks later. Anything bought now that can be used for metaphysics will bring unusual power to you.

WED., THU., FRI., SAT. — APRIL 19, 20, 21, 22:

RULERS — Saturn (Uncle Sam/Career) and Uranus (Shocking News/Explosions):

Work, Career and Business: Expect a forced ending passed to your service to the world or your career. Something must be done, something must change; be ready. The undertaking that you are doing leaves you unsatisfied and is a source of stress; you might be forced to modify your direction. Resolve to find a new way of handling your career soon and for the lucky ones expect a well-deserved promotion. The unlucky ones will be forced to realize their limits.

Partnerships: Don't let anyone pressure you into using their ideas instead of your own. You came across this plan to stimulate you and your entrepreneur spirit to become more independent. Meditate to understand where this partnership is going in your life. Did you make the right choices and can you live with them? If not, there won't be a better time to deal with those questions; these days will help you to change it all. Some surprising news is ahead of you.

Family and Friends: Your friends will be requesting your presence and may invite you to a gathering. Enjoy this opportunity, but you will be amazed with what you are about to hear. Uranus also makes the children very active and accident-prone; watch them closely. They will lean heavy on you; be patient with their young demanding spirits. Let them enjoy Uranus' world of miracles, maybe by going to a place you went before like Disneyland or the Zoo. Keep your eyes on everything they do and everywhere they go and you will have a smashing time.

Love Affairs: Expect spicy consternation during these days, as many people will surprise you. With Uranus' disturbing touch these days, avoid going places or doing things you never did before. Stay with what you do or know best. Karmic love is around the corner for some, especially if you were born under an air sign. Someone from your past will be attracted to you. If you are an Aquarius, a Leo or a Gemini may bring someone much younger or older in your life.

Travel and Communication: Here are some ideas for a small trip not far from town. Uranus rules electronics, the future, astrology, psychic phenomena, and UFOs. If you want to see something unusual, talk about it and do it now. However be aware of the negative Moon as you may attract wrong experiences. If you're lucky Uranus may decide to grant one of your wishes. Stay clear of storms; sudden blackouts and danger coming from lightning is very real.

Environment: Under Uranus' surprising explosive power, large earthquakes and incredible news tends to take place. Many eruptions have taken place under this energy. 3/8/05 - CNN Mount St. Helens coughs up ash. 3/8/05 - Severe cyclone hits Australia.

Famous Personalities: Be ready as expected, for unusual types of news coming from extroverted celebrities. Much will be done for children during this trend but the negative tendency could touch some of them. Let's hope I am wrong, I hate to say anything drastic about the children. Sadly enough, Uranus or Pluto couldn't care a bit about my personal feelings and will do whatever pleases them. A famous person will provide and help to make important decisions pertaining to the younger generation, computers and education.

Events: On a sad note, keep in mind that Uranus rules explosions, earthquakes and volcanoes. He may also decide to throw a tornado or produce violent explosions or induce crazy actions on some weak mind. CNN - 05/30/05 - On the same day he was to attend his high school graduation ceremony, Scott Moody, 18, shot five friends and relatives to death and wounded another before killing himself, Ohio police said. The weather will turn really nasty and will induce serious chain reaction accident.

Shopping: You may feel like spending time and money on your appearance; it's a great time to shop for second hand wardrobe items, or consult a beautician if you experience any skin problems. Not a good time to pay a visit to your local psychic; stay practical and use your own intuition.

SUN., MON., TUE., WED. — APRIL 23, 24, 25, 26:

RULERS — Neptune (Middle East) and Mars (Danger/ War).

Work, Career and Business: Make good use of the information printed in Starguide; this work translates the energies ahead of us. With the waning moon upon us it is time to slow down and do some clean up around the office. Avoid signing important contracts, and postpone every important meeting until the approaching new moon. Slow down, be patient; there won't be much that you can do, apart from finishing up or preparing your next move. Anything else could be a waste of your time and money.

Partnerships: Do not let anything bad happen to your psyche; avoid Neptune's deceiving nature. With Mars around, you'd better use a diplomatic attitude in all your endeavors and avoid any confrontation with co-workers or your supervisor. Time to rescue some depressed spirits without letting yourself be affected by their personal problems. A good movie or a great video will do for tonight.

Family and Friends: Friends and family in trouble will call you. They might be experiencing anxiety in their relationships; provide them with your support. Talk about the moon's impact upon their lives and psyches and mention my book. Expect a difficult time where you should be prudent and patient with others. The depressing power of Neptune also affects your friends; sadly enough some of them will abuse alcohol and may pay a heavy price. DO NOT DRINK and drive and if you do drink, designate a safe driver or have a cab take you back home. Neptune could seriously blind your vision and with Mars' impatience you could visit the emergency room (or the cemetery!). Don't take a chance on your life; stay clear of chemicals and use tons of patience on your family members.

Love Affairs: A secret love affair may be a temptation to some but it will bring deception to the unaware initiator. Time to give strong support to your mate especially if they are water signs, as the waning moon will make them "moody." If you are a Pisces, Cancer or Scorpio do not expect much with love, romance or with your children. Just be patient, control your imagination and do not nurture guilt from past endeavors. A long walk to the mall or the sea will keep your mind away from Neptune's depressing cries.

Travel and Communication: The majority of people is not yet aware of the power of Mars and Neptune upon their psyches and will become depressed or behave like aggressive robots. Drive slowly, be alert and most of all stay calm in any situation. Be very forthright and patient in your speech, as mis-communications now could have disastrous results. Further love and understanding and all will be fine.

Environment: This celestial duo has in the past produced oil spills, chemical plant explosions and will produce extremely high tides. Avoid the sea if you can to be safe, as many vessels will go down to Poseidon's world. Stressing news about chemicals and flooding is to be expected soon.

Famous Personalities: An interesting but deceiving movie will be promoted. Elizabeth Taylor, Mohammed Ali and Michael Jackson could make sad news. The Pope and the church could give us sad news as abortion and religious groups will insist on their personal wars. Neptune rules news about the Navy, deception, jails, hospitals, the Middle East, oil, and all religions combined together. Under his illusive power on May 3 1997, the Pope made an important announcement. VATICAN CITY — When Pope John Paul II makes a choice for sainthood; it's often to make a point. On Sunday, he draws attention to a long neglected and often despised group in Europe, beatifying a Gypsy for the first time in the history of the Roman Catholic Church. Beatification is the last step before possible canonization or sainthood. With Uranus (shocking) in pious Pisces (religion/Middle East) expect anything weird again soon to take place. The church authorities will find another way to probe into society to grasp more sinners (Gays/Gypsies) to pay for their enormous legal battle and failing abusive financial infrastructure. The age of ignorance, manipulation and religion is giving place to the more advanced universal and brilliant sign of Aquarius.

Events: Mars (the warrior) rules Germany and parts of Europe; disturbing news may come from there. The weather could turn real nasty again and water and slides could be a serious threat to some regions of the US.

Shopping: Sad news about gas is on the way but good deals could be found in a garage sale or your local flea market. But anything related to chemicals to rid the house of pests or the garden of unwanted weeds. Avoid buying any hard medicines and stay clear of heavy prescriptions.

New Moon — April 27, 2006 in Taurus: Taurus is ruled by the peaceful planet Venus. The emphasis will be on general security. This lunation will affect the banking industry. Hopefully, gracious Venus will stop her turbulent brother Mars from disturbing the earth's equilibrium. Use this lunation to further your finances, and utilize Venus' diplomatic power to deal with others. If you play your cards right she might also reward you with love. Money and security will play an important part of this lunation.

Lunation impact on all signs:

Aries - An opportunity to reshape yourself and your finances is ahead, don't miss it.

Taurus - This lunation is right on top of you and your wallet, a new start for you.

Gemini - A money secret will come to light and a person needs help from you.

Cancer - An important security wish will be granted by a friend, be active.

Leo - Positive changes in your career will make you happy, stay on top of a deal.

Virgo - A new opportunity and a far away trip is in store for you, be confident.

Libra - A legacy or a money deal will turn in your favor and foreign people are with you.

Scorpio - A new relationship or a new business venture will be offered to you.

Sagittarius - Your health and your work will improve and you are lucky these days.

Capricorn - Good news from love, business ventures or children, invest now.

Aquarius - Traveling or doing something important for home, visit the family.

Pisces - Interesting surprises by mail or telephone, a new deal and a trip is ahead.

THU., FRI., SAT., SUN. — APRIL 27, 28, 29, 30:

RULERS — Mars (Hazard) Venus (Cherished) and Mercury (Traveling).

Work, Career and Business: Mars is still active, so emotional reactions in the office should be avoided. Use patience and diplomacy with who ever is around, and good progress will be made. Make plans for the future and act upon them while the moon is new. Money and communication will play an important part of this trend.

Partnerships: Some interesting news may come your way. You have free will so don't allow Mars to let anyone force his opinion on you. With Mercury's sense of exaggeration, do not fall for all you hear, and don't be afraid to challenge people's information. You need to use your intuition, and sensitive Venus can help you in doing so. Use words of love and be patient with everyone; the new moon will induce a new energy in them. Time to proceed forward, you are protected.

Family and Friends: In the anticipation of the upcoming weekend, Venus will bring an element of love and joy. Mercury will make us very communicative, and Mars will further a desire for action. This trend will be an interesting one where friends and family members will try to get in touch with you all at the same time. Make the most of those beautiful stars and enjoy life. Listen to a young person's needs.

Love Affairs: If you use Venus' "savoir faire" in any situation, you will win over Mars' argumentative temperament. A great time to show love and affection to those you care for. Avoid depressing conversations of your past, stay in the future, and look to the bright side of life. If you were born under the fiery sign of Leo, keep a cool head with someone born in April or November. An Aquarius may fall in love with you. Get going and reach your wishes now.

Travel and Communication: Don't let this trio drive you crazy, as you will have a million things to do at the same time. The strength of Mars combined with the speed of Mercury may bring trouble in your driving, so slow down. Use precautions and take your time if you have to travel far; don't let accident-prone Mars create obstacles. Be alert and slow down and nothing wrong will happen. Make your future plans to travel now.

Environment: Keep in mind that impatient Mars is also with us and he doesn't care for any of your plans; he may decide to create an earthquake or produce disturbing weather. If Mars wins over Venus and Mercury, his destructive power will be felt with explosions. "Mars, the Lord of War will show is power, while none suspect, the surprise of lightning will strike"— Note: Algeria train bombing kills 18- A bomb exploded under a passing train, killing 18 people and injuring 25, state radio reported. It was the latest in a new wave of attacks the government blamed on Muslim militants.

Famous Personalities: This powerful threesome may take the life of an important political person. Someone famous person may also meet a sad fate in the water or on the road. Be aware and be prudent.

Events: Pluto (ultimate power/ life and death) is still in the sign of Sagittarius (religion). He will keep enforcing a slow but sure decay of dogmatic religious doctrines. Religions as they are known at present will be completely transformed. The rebirth will result in one Universal religion based on man's direct cosmic consciousness with God. This celestial configuration will bring real spiritual leaders to the fore passing on their inborn gift of teaching the fundamental laws governing all life in the universe. Disturbing news from the Pope or the Middle East is ahead.

Shopping: Invest in tools or anything brand new, as great deals await you. Be confident in spending large amounts of money on clothes or jewelry now, they will bring you luck or the magnetism you're looking for.

Welcome to Your
Day - to - Day Guidance

For May 2006

May 3, 2006 — Venus enters Aries: Time to use your head not your heart in dealing with love. Aries is much too impulsive and impatient to look thoughtfully into others people values or motives and some young people will get hurt in the process. On a more positive note, souls born with this celestial signature will be quite artistic and extremely magnetic. The aggressive attitude of Mars (ruler of Aries) will be toned down by his diplomatic sister Venus the planet of love. All fire signs (Leo/Sagittarius/ Aries) will see an improvement or changes in the love area. For all other signs, wherever Venus is cruising through by sign or house, expect to find love or happiness. Souls born with this Venus position won't wait for you to make a move to find love. Aries and Mars needs to be first in any area in your chart.

May 5, 2006 — Mercury enters Taurus: It's a perfect time to review a new financial endeavor or investigate the possibility of future investments. Empower yourself to structure your financial security and sign the legal forms after the new moon only. Souls born now will inherit a natural gift to handle corporate money and will slowly and surely secure themselves financially. These souls are born financial planners, and much of their patience will pay in the long run. A top position offered to the soul to lead corporation involving the communication the arts and beauty. They must learn to let go of the wrong people without resentments. Taurus rules the throat and Venus will endow those lucky souls with musical talent, some great singer will be born today.

MON., TUE., WED., THU., FRI., SAT — MAY 1, 2, 3, 4, 5, 6:

RULERS — The Moon (Result of Correcting) and the Sun (Spirit of Love).

Work, Career and Business: Do not try to hold on to your past; accept the upcoming changes with faith. The stars' pattern and changes are imposed by God to continually promote experiences and a better life. This will be an interesting Universal trend full of changes and surprises for us all. With the waxing Moon, try anything new and take chances on new opportunities. Someone's advice regarding an investment may be worthwhile. Examine all business propositions carefully and sign the paperwork now. With the Sun around, expect some surprising progress in the near future.

Partnerships: Be ready for the beginning or ending of an important part of your life. It is a strong possibility to find a new business partner. You may feel comfortable with the person involved and sense that you can succeed with his inborn talent. Make a full commitment to succeed and work harder to get there. If the people you are with do not fit your wishes, the new Moon will induce new ones, so go out now.

Family and Friends: The Sun will give tons of radiant energy to the children. If you don't take them out to the park, your hands will be full for a couple of days! Let them get rid of their surplus solar energy, and be sure to keep your eyes on them. Many kids get hurt under this energy. You may be requested to enjoy Mom's great food at home in the security and safety of your own family. The family circle will be active these days and mother would be happy to hear about your progress. Expect an element of surprise coming your way by a friends' surprising arrival. You may want to plan a special gathering for a person to whom you are close. Great food, love and joy are on the agenda. Make the most of these rare and beautiful stars.

Love Affairs: Use this new Moon fully. Romance is on your mind more than ever, and a meeting with some friends could lead to an exciting love affair with an interesting stranger. Visit or call your friends; they need to share interesting news pertaining to love, romance and children. During the night hours, enjoy the artistic intonations of the Sun with a great show. If you are a Capricorn, Virgo, or a Taurus, a much younger or older person needs to know you.

Travel and Communication: Again, this is the time where anything you really want could happen if you ask hard enough. The Moon is waxing and your trips are protected if you take precautions on the road. Flying is also under good auspices and planning for trips now will add more protection.

Environment: Some dramatic happenings related to nature will force the government to make decisions about a situation. Many will be forced to relocate and start a new life due to natural catastrophes. Let's hope the new Moon will slow down any structural damages. Food and clothing could also be needed and sent to some parts of the world.

Famous Personalities: Many famous people will take part in charity events and many will donate money to alleviate the suffering of the world. Great news pertaining to new arrivals will make the family happy. Children could also be affected, so watch over them. Jan. 24 2005 - A Brazilian woman has given birth to a baby weighing nearly 17 pounds.

Events: The Sun's expansive power may affect a number of organizations. Expect some conservative groups to make the news about the earth, abortion or religion. NEW YORK (AP) – Nicole Dufresne - An aspiring actress and playwright whose work explored life's darker sides was shot and killed as she confronted an armed robber during an early-morning street holdup.

Shopping: Invest in gold; the stock market will take some by surprise. Anything charming and beautiful bought now will further fame or love. Use the light of the Sun to further your creativity and invest in any form of healing art now. Dr. Turi needs your help to pass on his very important star message to the world.

SUN., MON., TUE., WED., THU. — MAY 7, 8, 9, 10, 11:

RULERS — The Sun (Children) Mercury (traveling) and Venus (love):

Work, Career and Business: This trio will make these days quire interesting in terms of action and news. You will be occupied trying to cope with all the demands made upon you. Local errands will keep you busy and bring you in contact with interesting people. Don't rush if you feel you won't make progress or if things don't go your way; all will change soon. Use the waxing moon to your advantage and be patient.

Partnerships: Expect new partners to show you their talents, and be patient with them if they cannot follow your pace. The deserving hard-working souls will benefit soon with well-deserved promotions or new opportunities for growth. Your wishes could be granted if you mean business and become active on the social scenery.

Family and Friends: A family member or a friend in need may request your advice. Be willing to consider the issues from their point of view, but try to avoid emotional outbursts and do not force your opinion on them. You may receive an invitation to be part of a gathering; use this opportunity to get some of your wishes. You miss some people you know well who have moved away. You may decide to relocate soon yourself.

Love Affairs: Don't be insecure or shy; go after the person you are attracted to. Propose to dine out or offer flowers. With the great Sun in charge your romanticism will be accepted. Use positive words and further your life now. With Mercury in the air, get on the phone; you will use a convincing approach to stimulate someone you care about. Your words can make a difference with a person who has lost some of the feelings they had for you. If you were born in July, a curious foreigner born in March or November may be looking for your love. Keep busy on the social scenery.

Travel and Communication: Some lucky people will decide to take a trip to Las Vegas and enjoy the nightlife. The waxing Moon (positive) may bring you luck.

If you plan to travel, always make all your plans within the New Moon to protect yourself and further your wishes. Enjoy the wilderness and enjoy the best of what life has to offer. Use the growing new moon's energy to your advantage.

Environment: Wind could be a problem and speedy Mercury could produce sudden tornadoes in some parts of the US. Expect activity from environmentalists fighting for the survival of wildlife and the earth.

Famous Personalities: Much talk and gossip will be available from celebrity magazines. A brother, a sister or a pair of twins may make the news.

Events: Hopefully Venus will stop any damage from explosions. News from France or Japan or the Middle East could be troublesome. Interesting new developments in biology, science and research are to be expected soon.

Shopping: Gifts offered to those for whom you care will bring much luck to their happy owners. You can find a good deal on a big-ticket item by comparison shopping. Offer Starguide as a birthday gift, and bring the light of true predictions and guidance into someone's life.

Full Moon — May 13, 2004 in Scorpio: Use extreme caution. The next two weeks are going to be trying and dramatic for some. Be ready for a rough journey. Disturbing news from foreign lands is to be expected. Pluto (suicide/drama/death) will bring a dance of destruction to this world where fanatic religious young souls will impose their deadly, righteous, dogmatic views on others. Powerful transformations in the world of faith and the church are ahead. The previous wake-up call provided by Pluto's impact on the WTC on 9/11 will induce a form of awareness, but also a death and rebirth for some people. Pluto will bring to light the shameful manipulation, sexual and financial secrets of organized religions and some of their religious leaders. As always with the Lord of hell in charge of this trend, better think twice before saying or acting on impulse. Expect nature's devastating forces to be active, and secrets, affairs of sex, and finances to be divulged. The police and blackguards will make the news. More than ever use diplomacy, as whatever you do now will have serious repercussions in your future. Time to keep a cool head and be aware in all you do or say. Pray for the souls of the poor victims and let's hope my message gets out to the world at large this time.

Lunation impact on all signs:

Aries - News of life and death and trouble with corporate money is ahead. Be patient.

Taurus - Partnerships in business or marriage will become serious problems you need to clean up.

Gemini - Stress and change with your health or your work, use your will and win.

Cancer - Problems with love, romance and children; don't respond to the negative moon.

Leo -Important change at home or with the family is ahead, use diplomacy, you'll win.

Virgo - Be aware of your words and your speech, or a sexual encounter could bring trouble.

Libra - Finances will cause worry, don't hurt your self-esteem, be positive.

Scorpio - Time to use all your will to avoid drama in all areas of your life, be the Eagle.

Sagittarius - Let go of your past, a secret will come to light and good change is ahead.

Capricorn - Sad news and secrets from friends will bother you, be strong.

Aquarius – A setback to your career but so much more for you later on. See through it.

Pisces - A study or a trip will become stressful and wake up calls from a foreigner.

Note: Attention: Pluto is back with us — Be ready for dramatic happenings all over; control is a must. Don't be Pluto's victims; be aware of its destructive power. Anything you say or do under his power will follow you for the rest of your life. Time to use extreme caution in all you do. Killers, rapists, psychotics, and the worst of society will be active. While Pluto reigns, you'd better stay home and let the ignorant get killed. Make good use of my work and pass on this site to those you care for solid guidance. Expect secrets to surface and news from the police force soon.

FRI., SAT., SUN., MON. — MAY 12, 13, 14, 15:

RULERS — Pluto (drama/death) Venus (forgiveness) and Jupiter (foreigners).

Work, Career and Business: In time of a Full Moon, don't let Pluto make you too direct or radical until you really know what you're talking about. Be cautious in all you say and do. Pluto stimulates the animal nature in man and will make us behave accordingly. Be aware that whatever you say or do now will have serious repercussions in your life. Stay on the side of the law and make a good use of Venus' diplomacy or you could end up sorry. Money will play an important part of this trend; use your intuition and turn down a hazardous business proposition.

Partnerships: Pluto is very choleric, and nothing will stop him from inducing trouble in your life. Death, secrets, power, manipulation, sex and extra-marital affairs are his favorites. Venus is no match for her powerful brother Pluto and this duo will change you into a walking sexual magnet to others. Be aware and stay close to the one you trust.

Family and Friends: Be aware of everything and everybody around you. Keep an eye on the children; Pluto takes their young lives swiftly. Be patient with family and friends, avoid gossiping, and help by cooling things down. This is the perfect time to mention my work before this celestial trend; the skeptics will receive a full wake-up call pertaining to the stars' impact in their lives.

Love Affairs: With Jupiter around, a foreigner you know will play an important part in the next dilemma of your life. Pluto will also make you highly sensual and magnetic; you should take all the precautions needed to avoid sexually transmitted disease. A love affair started now will have a profound, even dramatic impact on your life. All water and earth signs, especially Scorpio and Taurus, will be affected by this plutonic impact; be aware, be prudent. Better stay home and watch TV.

Travel and Communication: Not a time at all to plan a long-distance trip or even to travel to faraway places. Use diplomacy in all your conversation and listen carefully; you will hear about secrets. Understand the limits to your investigations, and let neither sarcasm nor the Scorpio's stinger affect your self-esteem. Stay clear of psychotic leaders and crowded places loaded with maniacs suggesting castration, suicide or drugs.

Environment: Nothing will stop Pluto from his tragic assaults to the earth. Be ready for some serious messes from the worst of our society who will shock the media. NEW YORK (AP) — Two teenagers — one a 14-year-old girl — were charged Tuesday in the shooting death of Nicole DuFresne an aspiring actress who challenged a group of muggers on a Manhattan street.

Famous Personalities: Many financial or sexual secrets about a famous person will reach the media. Some unlucky souls will get wake-up calls from the dramatic planet. A public figure will make dramatic news or may be called to God. WASHINGTON (AP) — Rosemary Kennedy, the oldest sister of President John F. Kennedy and the inspiration for the Special Olympics died, she was 86.

Events: As usual, be aware of the power of Pluto, as dramatic news will plague the media. Expect news pertaining to the police force, sex, scandals, earthquakes, secrets, abortion and AIDS. The police will be busy trying to catch the villains. Hopefully none of the brave public servants will die doing so. The police force will make the news as they always do when their Plutonic ruler is in charge. In the past, I have sent certified letters to many prominent governmental figures and police chiefs, before and after dramatic happening unfolded. Copies were sent of both pages 87 and 36 of Starguide 1996/1997 where I predicted (over a year before) the "Rancho Santa Fe mass suicide" of March 26th 1997 and "Bill Cosby's loss." No reply ever came. None of those "educated" high board of directors had the decency or the courage to answer my mail. Even with the plain facts in their face, none of those public executives ever acknowledged my work in predictive astrology. Fear of ridicule kills your children and our police officers. I hope and pray that someday they will train our valiant and courageous policemen on the incredible dangers they face when Pluto is in charge. My research is unarguable and too many police officers have died in the name of their superiors' ignorance and fear of ridicule. In ignorance of Pluto's laws, too many lives have been wasted in vain by the "Death Wish Generation" where children kill teachers and classmates (see my book, "The Power of the Dragon" and learn more about it).

Shopping: Avoid investing in dangerous tools, weapons or ammunition. Pluto's awful signature of death should not be stored in your home. Doing so could kill your own children or family members. Beware of what cannot be seen or understood yet in terms of metaphysics could greatly cost you or your loved ones. You may invest in anything that can be used to kill nuisances. If you buy dangerous substances, keep them well away from children. Share my valuable forecast from www.drturi.com or accurate guidance for someone's birthday or offer a comparison chart for a newly wed couple.

May 20, 2006 — Mercury enters Gemini: Speedy Mercury enters his own sign of Gemini. You will feel like talking about traveling or furthering your business and emotional relationships. Be prudent on the road as Mercury rules cars and speed. Many people driving with you are not aware of this celestial activity and could pay the price of their cosmic ignorance. Make good use of "Moon Power" and keep reminding yourself of this fact and your real knowledge. Your telephone will be red hot and action will be everywhere. Mercury rules all the motion parts, your arms, fingers, shoulders, etc. Don't let him crack some of your bones because of impatience. Be prudent and be patient in all you do and you will be protected. Investing in a car after the New Moon may protect you from violent death or serious accident.

TUE., WED., THU., FRI., SAT. — MAY 16, 17, 18, 19, 20:

RULERS — Saturn (Uncle Sam Decisions) and Uranus (Explosive News).

Work, Career and Business: With a waning Moon (negative) many of your wishes won't be granted just yet. Don't invest in your future; you may regret it. Do not turn down an invitation offered by friends that you know well; they may require your presence at a gathering. Chatter from those you meet now should not be taken seriously. Those of a certain age will offer valuable intellectual guidance. Be patient until the next New Moon.

Partnerships: Expect the beginning or ending of important parts of your life and be ready for surprising developments. Your life at work may be unstable now but those changes will give you the opportunity to focus on plans for a better future. Support your partner with words of courage. Don't let Saturn's depressing thoughts get to you.

Family and Friends: The weekend could be spent with family members, good friends and Mom's good food. Some will prefer to dine out with lovers or business partners, but the experience could be troublesome. This is the time to practice patience with everyone around, and avoid doing anything original. Help a younger spirit in need.

Love Affairs: Absolutely anything great can happen if you are lucky enough to be involved with the right partner who really loves you. Don't gamble on anything or try to reach for your dreams just yet. Throw a party, but avoid new faces; old friends have the best to offer. Participate with life to avoid depression. If you are a Capricorn, then a Cancer or a Virgo may fall for you. If the person is new in your life then don't dream, use your head.

Travel and Communication: Make the best of Saturn and "Moon Power" in your life by planning future trips and by being prudent on the road. Curiosity is the pathway to fulfillment and happiness and Saturn will reward you for your celestial planning. Take care of the children and let them participate in all the great activities. Be aware of eccentric Uranus affecting them; have a good time and enjoy it all. Some may have to relocate to different residences; make sure you do your Astro-Carto-Graphy before then, as these "new" stars may affect you positively or negatively. Read the section on Astro-Carto-Graphy at the end of the book, and if you need more information don't be afraid to call the office at 602-999-3010. Being at the right place at the right time has a lot to do with your progress in terms of opportunities. The knowledge found in Astro-Carto-Graphy would be a major contribution to your success (or your failure) in one of these new locations. Keep this opportunity in mind and give it a try — it works!

Environment: Stay clear of thunder and lightning; Uranus takes many lives without warning. Expect him to throw a quake, a tornado or blow up a volcano soon. Let's just hope you won't be in his way! Explosions in Japan, France or the US are to be expected soon. Under Uranus power - TOKYO — A bomb damaged the home of an official at Tokyo's international airport, police suspected leftists, who have long opposed the airport.

Famous Personalities: Crazy behavior by some famous people in public is high on the list. Some will become engaged, or married in very large gatherings, and others will expose their strong desires for freedom.

Events: Under Uranus' power in CONROE, Texas — A fire ignited a small oil tank causing several explosions outside an Exxon oil refinery and forcing the evacuation of 40 refinery workers and nearby residents. Disco death Philippines

— 150 people died in a discotheque fire. Alaska fire burns 'out of control'. HOUSTON, Alaska — Fueled by gusty winds, a wildfire has swept "out of control" in south-central Alaska, where it has engulfed 7,000 acres and destroyed as many as 100 homes. Expect earthquake and volcanic activity soon. CNN - 05/30/05 - Bombers hit Hilla police - A pair of suicide bombers, wearing vests packed with explosives, detonated themselves Monday in Hilla, killing 27 people — many of them police — and wounding 118, police said.

CNN - 05/30/05 - YUKON, Oklahoma (AP) — A small plane crashed Sunday while performing aerobatics, seriously injuring the pilot, the Federal Aviation Administration said.
Shopping: Invest in Uranus now: visit your astrologer or favorite psychic only if you know him/her well. Don't bring a new spiritualist into your life at this time, especially if you have never dealt with him before. Unless you feel strongly or know otherwise about him, don't do it. Any of those light workers are karmically attracted to you and the reading could be one of your best or your worst psychic experience. Stay with the professionals, some of those psychics needs more help than you do! Uranus rules astrology and if you are attracted to the stars there won't be a better time for you to realize what the old science has to offer you.

SUN., MON., TUE., WED. — MAY 21, 22, 23, 24:

RULERS — Neptune (Oil/Ocean) and Mars (Assault/War).

Work, Career and Business: As usual with Mars' aggressive personality, expect all sorts of trouble with business partnerships. You are strongly advised to use diplomacy to avoid serious complications, especially during a waning Moon. If you are experiencing some trouble in your career, a serious change may be ahead of you. Neptune will make you absent-minded; try to concentrate. A little walk by the water would do your spirit good. Be patient, we are getting closer to the next New Moon.

Partnerships: The Lord of dreams may make your spiritual life busy and some of your dreams may come true in the near future. Learn to translate your subconscious impressions and write down your dreams first thing in the morning. You or your partner may be responding to Neptune's power, so you may want to reach your inner self asking for God's help in your prayers. Some may feel tuned into the universe and miraculously guided out of a bad situation. Provide spiritual support to those in need.

Family and Friends: As usual with Neptune's sad touch and combined with the waning moon, sensitive friends may get depressed. Be there to help, but don't let their problems get to you. The lonely old ones will feel the impact of Neptune and its accompanying deception upon their lives. Give a thought and pay them a visit or send them a little card. This gesture will make them feel less lonely and will make their own world more exciting. Be ready to offer a strong shoulder and realize the impact of Neptune upon your world. If you are a Pisces or a Gemini a positive friend could help you.

Love Affairs: Keep your eyes on your possessions as things may "disappear" now. Don't let yourself into a deceiving business deal or worthless situation; learn to love with your head first and give your heart later. Your intuition will be sharp; use it to your advantage. A secret love affair may start for some earth signs and might last a while.

Travel and Communication: Remember, Neptune is also part of this trend and if you have to drive, you MUST stay clear of any alcohol. Neptune leads many unaware people to jail, left with DUIs to deal with. If you were born under a water sign stay clear of trouble if you feel depressed, don't drink tonight.

Environment: Venus will try to stop her violent brother from stirring the earth's innards, as Mars loves earthquakes, explosions, volcanoes and mass disasters. Sad news may come from the ocean, the Middle East and oil spills. Mother earth is alive, resourceful, and must heal.

Famous Personalities: Some prominent people may be caught in secret sexual or love affairs. Their dependency on chemicals, drugs or alcohol will be made public. The lucky ones will promote new movies. Under Neptune's power — WEST HOLLYWOOD, California — Sheriff's deputies pulled over Eddie Murphy early Friday and arrested a transsexual prostitute who was riding in his car, authorities said. A spokesman for the actor maintained Murphy was just being a "good Samaritan" by offering the transsexual a ride.

Events: Under Neptune and Mars' powers, CAIRO, Egypt — A powerful sandstorm tore through southern Egypt Saturday, killing at least four people. The storm comes a day after the worst sandstorm in 30 years blasted across the country. With Mars' aggressive nature, expect this type of news again. Villains will be active during this trend; do not trust strangers and do not put yourself in any situation that could make you a potential victim. Avoid dark streets and keep your personal alarm (intuition) on all the time.

Shopping: Try to participate in volunteer work to provide love and help to the needy. Shop in places promoting good causes; they need your financial support. Not a good time to invest in prescription drugs or decide to visit your spiritual advisor, unless you know him/her very well.

New Moon — June 27, 2006 in Gemini: Now is the perfect time to start any intellectual pursuit, begin or finish a book, learn photography, a foreign language, find a publisher and communicate your feelings to all. With the new Moon upon us soon, you may plan to invest in a new car or anything related to communication. Traveling and foreigners will play important parts of this lunation. Plans made to travel under this New Moon will bring excitement and many wishes. On a larger scale, combined with the New Moon, witty Mercury will help in promoting better relations with other countries around the world.

Lunation impact on all signs:

Aries - A letter or a telephone call will make you happy soon. Your sibling needs you.

Taurus - Great news involving money or a business endeavor is on the way.

Gemini - The Moon shines on you, make the most of it, you're lucky for a while.

Cancer - A secret will come your way but don't talk too much about it later.

Leo - One of your wishes will come true because of a friend, good news ahead.

Virgo - Your career gets you very busy, lots of opportunity in communication. Write.

Libra - Good news from far away and a gambling trip will bring luck.

Scorpio - Corporate money, a contract, legacy, and a deep spiritual study is coming.

Sagittarius - A new business or emotional relationship is about to start.

Capricorn - Your health and your work will improve and good opportunities are ahead.

Aquarius - Love and creativity are on the way, good news from the children.

Pisces - A change of residency or a new set of wheels will make you happy.

THU., FRI., SAT., SUN. — MAY 25, 26, 27, 28:

RULERS — Venus (Dying love) and Mercury (Upsetting News).

Work, Career and Business: The Moon is still waning for a few days; forget about making any progress until then. This is a time where you should clean up the past and make new plans. Maybe you should try to relax while you can; you will feel better for the new challenges and you would enjoy the break. Keep your head out of the swarm of stress, let go for now and put a big smile on your face. People tend to react positively to a smiling face and a happy heart. Better times are on the way; the new Moon is not too far, just be patient.

Partnerships: Someone close to you is upset. Perhaps you should apologize with a romantic dinner; don't expect it to be perfect, but it would help your situation. Mercury will pass on all sorts of news including some financial or sexual secrets. Improve your cosmic consciousness and do some inside soul-searching. See what makes you so different and what can be done to make your lives better. Don't believe all you hear.

Family and Friends: Save a difficult relationship with a friend or a family member; now is the time to use diplomacy and understanding. Expect disturbing news with brothers or sisters and take the time to reply to the mail. Mercury rules communication and will help you pass on your thoughts deeply and correctly. Don't let the waning moon sap your faith; stand strong, tomorrow is always better. Life is changing around you and you know it.

Love Affairs: Just before the New Moon the energy is quite low. This trend may induce stress and may require both of you to control destructive emotions such as jealousy and suspicion. Love Affairs started now could be stressful and unproductive in the long run; use your head, use Starguide's knowledge. This energy will also force many unsuited couples to get out of their unhealthy relationships. The worst of both of these planets is to be expected mainly due to the fast dying Moon. Now is the time to use all the diplomacy you were born with to save your relationship before it's too late. If you are a Libra, don't be too critical about an older or younger person born in February or June who may be attracted to you.

Travel and Communication: Many police officers will meet with trouble in speedy chases and dangerous confrontations, while trying hard to stop lunatics. Venus will help those who are willing to use her gentle touch of love in all they do. If you were born with a passionate Venus in a water sign, you will be challenged by this celestial trend. A very high level of depressing energy will be imposed upon many souls these days. Stay clear of chemicals, drugs and alcohol if you decide to take a trip.

Environment: The police will be needed in some situation where nature will get out of hand. Let's hope Venus will slow down Mercury's windy nature and stop him from producing hard weather or tornadoes.

Famous Personalities: Nothing good will come before the New Moon pertaining to the rich and famous. Scandals, sex, drugs and all the tools used by the "devil" will be made public. A very famous but unlucky person may also be assassinated or found dead.

Events: Be aware, use Moon Power Starguide wisely and if you know someone involved in Law Enforcement, let them read this book. With Pluto (death) still cruising through the sign of Sagittarius, different religious agendas and destructive passions will run high. A nasty confrontation with foreigners could be the outcome. The diplomats will work hard to form a common agreement to stop the madness.

Shopping: You may purchase anything dealing with cleaning the environment. With Venus' desire for peace and love, buy flowers and give fresh love. Take serious precautions if you happen to be in the dating game with a stranger met in a public place. Invest and wear the protective item. Think of Starguide as a solid gift to help someone you care.

July 17th, 2005 - Saturn entered Leo: Many deserving souls benefitted from Saturn's passage into the sign of Cancer and invested in real estate. Many important contracts have be signed and secured, and many progressive investments will be added to the general security principle. Saturn is a karmic planet, so those who have used and abused others of society will be forced to lose their homes and start from the scratch to repay their karmic debts. Others famous political figures or CEO's have been brought down from their high positions of fame to disgrace, and thrown back to the bottom. Children born with this placing will gain positions of power in all affairs involving the arts, teaching children and political fame. In times of stress they will experience problems with their heart and should avoid eating rich food or drink heavily when upset. With Saturn in Leo a general insecurity about raising children will plague the world. Parents should not overload their children with work and /or they own expectations for greatness and fame. With karmic Saturn in Leo the entire spectrum of Leo (*children/art/education) will be restructured. Thus expect tremendous changes wherever Leo or the sun resides in your chart. A 90-mn Full Life or progressive reading will be a must for many experiencing a strong urge to change career and deal with stress with love, romance and children. You are also strongly advised to order a 90 MN Children Character logy/Astropsychology tape to find the true potential of your child before forcing him or her into a career or study that may not fit the purpose and fate of that child.

May 30, 2006 — Venus enters Taurus: Souls born with this celestial gift will need emotional security at all times. Unless the partner is solid and strong insecurity will bring about a swift break. Great ability is often found in money-making schemes, the arts, poetry, writing, photography and drawing. A natural zest for diplomacy and diplomacy is often found with this position. The soul could also marry wealthy and operate in an artistic environment during the course of this reincarnation. Expect presents, love and general uplifting news where your Venus transits your housing system. This is a perfect time to concentrate on improving your wardrobe and shape the body, invest in your desire for beauty and perfection. Souls born now will be possessive in matters related to love, and lucky with money. As the Bull is stubborn, many of them will have to detect wrong relationships and learn to let go and trust again. This is the ideal celestial position to invest in an artistic study. Empower yourself with spirituality and display your creativity to the world. Souls born now will inherit natural gifts in music and the arts. This is a top position to become a leader in the artistic fields for some. When well assisted by other celestial bodies, this is a perfect position for total commitment and endless love. This position makes for one of the most beautiful woman of the Zodiac. A sincere gift in loving, creating and a distinguished magnetism will lead her to a successful career. These souls were born to reach emotional, financial and spiritual security, teach genuine love and be loved back. A top position involving financial security, communication, writing, and success in any artistic fields is offered to these lucky souls.

MON., TUE., WED., THU., FRI. — MAY – 29, 30, 31 — JUNE – 1, 2:

RULERS — The Moon (Changing Life) and the Sun (Light of Love).

Work, Career and Business: Let go of your past and take chances, you have two great weeks ahead of you. Examine all business propositions carefully and if they fit your rational mind, then go for it. The Moon is now waxing and progress is to be expected soon. Some may be forced to relocate, start or finish a business. Many of the stars are on your side and you should be confident in the outcome. Invest in your business now.

Partnerships: Either the beginning or ending of an important part of your life, or a business partnership is a strong possibility within the next few days. As you know, nothing is made to last forever and somehow a wrong business partnership must end. Again this is a time where anything you really need could happen if you trust in yourself. Be patient with someone responding to the Sun's desire for power. It's a good time to meditate by the ocean or the river about the high purpose of your joined fate, your relationship and how it fits in your life. The Sun will make these days particularly romantic and beautiful for some.

Family and Friends: The Sun rules the children and love. Take the kids out to the park, but keep your eyes on them as, sadly enough, combined with other negative stars, some have disappeared under this energy. Unspecified vampires out there regenerate only by dealing with children and they will do all it takes to satisfy their unhealthy hunger. Accept the upcoming transformation with faith, as the changes will promote a better life. You may want to plan a special gathering with someone you are close to. A friend will have to move away soon and this could bring tears. The family circle will also be active these days and mother will be requesting your presence. Enjoy Mom's food at home in the security and safety of your own family if you are in a new area and do not know many people. Expect an element of surprise from friends.

Love Affairs: Romance is on your mind more than ever and a meeting with some playmate can lead to an exciting love affair. You may feel comfortable with the person involved and sense that you can succeed; with the New Moon on your side you may end up with a form of commitment. If you are a Pisces, someone born in July or November may give you the opportunity to experience real love. The stars are on your side, look for it now.

Travel and Communication: Surely an interesting trend full of changes and surprises. Still, be careful in all you do and don't take chances. Visit or call your friends; they need to share interesting news. This is a great time to plan for future trips to Europe; you may also use the creativity of the Sun to start or finish a book. With the Sun (life) in charge, much of the destructive news will be seriously altered. Flying is also under his protective power, unless the doomed pilot was born with an Aquarius Dragon's Tail and was introduced to flying for the first time in his life after the Full Moon. Use a positive approach in all your words and you will attract more luck.

Environment: Much work will be done to further life and security these days and nature will be radiant with life. If you are out in the wilderness and you plan to cook, beware. Some accidental explosions could still occur, as some of the propane gas containers might have been purchased under a vicious energy or under the bad Moon. Mother Nature is still very much alive and may decide to show her power, forcing thousands of people to relocate.

Famous Personalities: On the negative side expect weird news and dramatic ending of relationships. Be ready for good news of births and marriages. Much will be done for the children these days.

Events: This will be an important time for your company or your local government to make decisions about a situation which needs to be dealt with. Thousands of people may be forced to relocate and start life anew, due to new construction plans or previous natural catastrophes. Expect some stubborn conservative groups to make the news about abortion and religion. The light is green, thus many will succeed.

Shopping: This is a perfect time to invest in real estate and expensive items will bring great joy to some people. Great opportunities are to be found also at the swap meets and antique shops. Shop for anything that will further life and happiness. If you need to invest in something dangerous such as gas propane, cookers or sharp and dangerous items to take out to the wilderness, you can do it now. Share my valuable forecast on with others. For someone's birthday obtain accurate guidance in the form of a full life reading, or offer my book or a comparison chart for a newly wed couple.

Welcome to Your
Day - to - Day Guidance

For June 2006

June 3, 2006 — Venus enters Cancer: With this New Moon perfect conditions exist to launch any financial or real estate endeavors. Home improvement, and buying or selling a beautiful house is on the agenda for some. You may also invest in anything beautiful for your home. Souls born now will be soft and emotional in matters related to love and family. They will make money in hotel and restaurant business endeavors. Many of them will strive to find partners who will exchange deep emotions and spiritual research. Some will have to learn to let go of wrong relationships. This position makes for one of the most sensitive signs of the Zodiac. Usually the gift of cooking is present with this position. Those souls are born to feed the world with food and love. This position of Venus is a top position for financial security, communication and success in real estate.

June 4, 2006 — Mars enter Leo: Many thoughts will be geared towards an immense feeling of responsibility and true love for the children of the world. Souls born with Mars or Mercury in Leo will be gifted with a natural managerial disposition. Many of them will be born shrewd to business and attracted to the professions offering fame and fortune. Artistic talents involving music, dancing, and painting, will lead these souls towards the great fame and security they seek. This position makes for one of the most mentally and physically domineering signs of the Zodiac. As with Venus in Leo, this Mercury position will lead the soul towards success in many artistic endeavors. An opportunity to experience mental fame is also offered to the soul. The downfall is the misuse of the creative forces of the Sun, producing egocentrics. Those young souls would do anything to attract attention to themselves, by behaving and dressing eccentrically in public, body piercing, hair coloring, over tattooing etc. This need for attention reflects a subconscious fear of inferiority and turns them into ridiculous disguised shining puppets of the stars.

SAT., SUN., MON., TUE., WED. — JUNE 3, 4, 5, 6, 7:

RULERS — Mercury (Traveling) Venus (Money) Pluto (Drama/Secrets).

Work, Career and Business: be very careful towards the last day of this month. Pluto will punish the ignorant of induce serious dramatic wake up call for the unlucky. Time to reorganize your approach and a few things around you. Use the new Moon to look for a better way to develop your business. The new Moon will make everyone happy and very communicative. Your boss or your employees are going through some changes and you must be patient with them. With the New Moon on us, all will be fine again. Make the most of these days.

Partnerships: Important people are watching you; present an attitude of brightness and courage in front of difficulties. Some of your partners can only admire your inner strengths and will follow your example. Don't let anyone create negative energy with uncontrolled disturbing thoughts. Show others the power of positive thinking.

Family and Friends: Keep busy with the children, as speedy Mercury will give them tons of energy. Let them spend time outside the house. Watch them closely and see yourself as a child doing exactly what kids do best, playing! Use that opportunity to burn some calories if you can keep up with them. Take the time to listen, as one of them may need specific attention.

Love Affairs: Expect interesting surprises coming your way. With Venus around, love may enter your life without much notice; however, this world is a physical one and you must participate in the activities if you have any chance to succeed in finding what you're looking for. Do not stay home now as anything great could happen to you. Use that magnificent New Moon to enjoy nature and the sea. Keep in mind that Venus rules love and romance, and if you are single this is your chance. If you are a Sagittarius, a Leo or an Aries will find you irresistible.

Travel and Communication: We are still in the positive Moon, and a strong desire for change will be felt everywhere. Go on the road and make the most of this lunation. Also with Venus, some may drive to or find the love they are looking for.

Environment: Expect progressive news pertaining to concerned groups warring for the environment. They are after those wealthy executives who make money destroying the earth. Great news is in store for the earth workers.

Famous Personalities: Positive news is ahead with some famous personalities endorsing and supporting great community acts. New and beautiful love partners are in the air for some. A new birth will make many people happy. Moon Power 2003 -12/26/05 -LOS ANGELES, California — Buddy Ebsen, the loose-limbed Broadway dancer who achieved stardom and riches in the television series "The Beverly Hillbillies" and "Barnaby Jones," died. He was 95.

Events: Nature should be quiet during this great trend where love, romance and communication will reign. The only trouble I expect is with Mercury's winds; he may decide to announce himself and create tornadoes in parts of the US. Interesting news from France and England could surprise some scientists.

Shopping: Satisfy Venus' desire for beauty. Invest in a fitness program or a diet; the results will amaze you. If you need a checkup now, the stars are in your favor as your physician will be accurate in his prognostication. Surgery is also fine and you can add anything to your body; cutting is permissible with those stars. Control your imagination as Mercury could get your mind going wild with all sorts of silly fears about your health.

Note: Attention: Pluto is back with us — Expect dramatic happenings all over; control is a must. Do not be one of Pluto's many victims; be aware of Pluto's destructive power. Anything you say or do under his power will follow you for the rest of your life. This is time to use extreme caution especially in time of a waning (negative) Moon.

THU., FRI., SAT. — JUNE 8, 9, 10:

RULERS — Venus (Temptation) and Pluto (Fatal Action).

Work, Career and Business: You may be forced to realize the end of an era and the beginning of a new portion of your financial life. Your wishes for better business may not match your situation; Pluto will see to it and force a rebirth. It is all to your benefit in the long run; be at peace with yourself.

Partnerships: Time to enjoy good food, red wine and real safe sex! If you are in the wrong relationship, Pluto will free you soon. The opportunity to find real love will finally be given to you then. Better use diplomacy in all you say or do; you may end up sorry if you don't. Some secrets may come your way; keep them for yourself and respect Pluto's desire for privacy.

Family and Friends: Expect dramatic news from all over within the next few days; be ready to take care of some friends in trouble, but realize your limits. Everyone will have a short temper; don't let Pluto affect your psyche. Use beautiful Venus' diplomatic power with everyone around you.

Love Affairs: The great planet of love will make you feel good about yourself and will give tons of charm and beauty. Be aware of mysterious Pluto and his sensual magnetism. Accompanying Venus he could transform you into an irresistible sex magnet. Trouble may come your way if you fall for passion in unprotected sex activity. Fight insecurity and jealousy avoid stressing. A love relationship started under this trend will become passionate and will stay (for good or for worse) with you for ever. If you were born in January, a Virgo or a Taurus will get your heart. A friend born in November could prove difficult around you.

Travel and Communication: Pluto tends to choose the weakest or the strongest members of our society and play with their emotions. Whatever you say or do now will have incredible consequences; be diplomatic, stay clear of trouble. Do not stop for anyone on the road and let the police deal with Pluto. If you are with the children, it's time to watch them closely; this celestial mixture is totally against the children and many will fall victims to abusers. Anything you hear about school or drama should be taken with consideration, remember the growing children of the "Death Wish generation, see my book the power of the Dragon". Terrorist's plots and planning for death and destruction are taking place behind a curtain of deception.

Environment: As always, keep in mind that Pluto is very dangerous and could do some serious damage with nature's devastating forces, just to remind us of his power. The police could make drastic news too.

Famous Personalities: Famous people will meet with their death. Under Pluto's power, CNN anchor Don Harrison died after a long battle with cancer. He was 61 years old. Avoid large crowds where emotion and passion reign. Be aware of the destructive power of Pluto; do not take chances. Be patient.

Events: Do not trust strangers and avoid unfamiliar places. Pluto stirs man's animal tendencies. Pluto rules the crooks and the cops, and has the infinite forces of good and evil constantly teasing each other. The crooks will become more active and the police will try hard to cope. 1/8/2005 UNITED NATIONS (CNN) — U.N. peacekeepers in the Democratic Republic of Congo exchanged eggs, bread and a few dollars for sex with girls they were meant to protect, the United Nations watchdog agency has said. CNN 03/29/05 - PATERSON, New Jersey (AP) — A police officer responding to a report of a fight found that the mortally wounded victim was his son. More under Pluto's power in CARMEL, Indiana — A man apparently upset that his loan application had been denied, opened fire on four bank employees and killed a woman who was going to offer him an umbrella to ward off the rain. The shooting was followed less than an hour later by a bank holdup a few miles away in Indianapolis. A suspect in that robbery was critically injured after police shot him. A third bank robbery was reported in Richmond, Indiana, about 65 miles east of Indianapolis, an hour after the second. Two men wearing ski masks, one armed with a pistol, escaped with an undetermined amount of money. If you are a police officer or a security guard on duty now, don't take chances, as the worst could happen to you. Offer Moon power and true guidance to anyone involved in the law agency, you may save their live. Some children will make dramatic news.

Shopping: Invest in your soul and your reason to be on earth. Not the time to visit your psychic friend or ask for direction. If you are into kinky stuff be careful as Pluto children kill with sex. Weird sexual behaviors are often produced by a mixture of Pluto (power/leather/sex) and Venus (sensuality/enticement/beauty), and combined with Uranus (weird/ freedom/original), this could lead to unusual sexual escapades even death. Religious Neptune's vibration (deception/guilt/hidden/drugs) in your chart mixing with these energies will enhance deadly sexual encounters.

Full Moon — June 11, 2006 in Sagittarius: Disturbing news from foreign lands is to be expected. Jupiter, the Lord of law and religion, will impose his righteous, dogmatic views on some lost souls. Dramatic transformations in the world of faith and the church are ahead. The previous wake-up call provided by Pluto's impact will induce a form of financial death for the Vatican and a rebirth for some people psyche where exploitation fear, religious poisoning and ignorance won't prevail for long. Pluto will bring to light the shameful manipulation, sexual and financial secrets deals of organized religions and some of their religious leaders. Pluto is still interacting with Uranus to further the truth and the new Age of Aquarius against the dying Piscean age. There is still a war in heaven while the Middle East and Asia are rebirthing through death, diseases and wars.

Lunation impact on all signs

Aries - Difficult news from a foreign land, a study or a trip gets you worried.

Taurus - Trouble with a contract or corporation don't sign anything now.

Gemini - Stress coming from a business or emotional partner is heavy.

Cancer - Don't worry about your health, stress at work is expected soon.

Leo - Love, romance and children or a new endeavor will start you worrying.

Virgo - A change of residency or a problem with the family is ahead, be patient.

Libra - The mail or telephone may bring you sad news soon, be strong.

Scorpio- Expect a restructure of your self-esteem and finances soon.

Sagittarius - Don't take any chances within the next two weeks, be patient.

Capricorn - Let go of your past, eliminate all guilt to be happy, and no drinking.

Aquarius - Some of your wishes won't be granted for a while, just be cool.

Pisces - Your career may not go as expected, wait for the next new Moon.

SUN., MON., TUE., WED. — JUNE 11, 12, 13, 14:

RULERS — Jupiter (Foreigners/religions) and Saturn (Karma/Demands):

Work, Career and Business: With Pluto's dramatic experiences behind, many will keep low profiles and accept the intense transformation. With benevolent Jupiter, the future has much more to offer, and now you should be more confident in all your dealings. Jupiter, "the Lord of Luck," will make this transition easy and may even decide to throw you some luck; listen to your intuition and keep a positive attitude. A new career or a new beginning is on the horizon. Have faith and pray.

Partnerships: With Saturn's touch you can expect to work harder to organize or rebuild. For the hard-working souls, a promotion of some sort is coming your way. Your career will also be on your mind, and serious decisions will have to be made soon. Nothing comes easily; one must strive and plan if he is to succeed. With the Full Moon upon us, you might have to let go of someone or a portion of your business life soon. Let go.

Family and Friends: You may receive or give presents to the deserving family member or dear friend. Take the time to enjoy the week and the good food offered to you and if you decide to socialize during the night, you should be aware of the waning Moon. A foreigner could make you happy and further an important wish. An older person has something to share with you, listen to the advice.

Love Affairs: Someone you have known for a while, much older or much younger, could surprise you — Don't be shy with life; take a chance with someone you care for; there is plenty to gain in the long run if this person came into your life in a waxing Moon. This endeavor may lead to an opportunity to further your career. If you were born under any of the earth signs, avoid the Full Moon's depressing power. If you are a Gemini, a Libra or an Aquarius will be getting closer to you. Listen to a friend born in April.

Travel and Communication: Expect your telephone to be busy but the messages won't be too good. Don't try to be in so many places at the same time. If you have to drive, take extra time to get there; don't rush, as the police could spoil your day. A brother or a sister needs to talk to you. Keep a positive attitude; positive people attract positive experiences. Remember a magnet won't attract a piece of wood.

Environment: In a Full Moon time, Mother Nature may decide to stretch herself and surprise some. Environmental groups will become active and will receive support from the media to save the earth from uncaring corporations. The earth will be active soon; stay clear of bridges as much as you can. Don't take any chances for a while.

Famous Personalities: The great loss of an old and eminent political, religious or entertainment figure will trouble the media soon. A group of people will work hard to help those starving in an area affected negatively by nature. Life goes on.

Events: Under this energy 80 people were killed in a fire that gutted a shopping center in the West Java town of Bogor and in south-central Alaska a fire engulfed 7,000 acres and destroyed as many as 100 homes. Some terrorists groups could also get really ugly, and surprising destructive explosions are on the way.

Shopping: You may spend money on your pet or invest in anything to be used in nature of for your pet. It is surely a good time to spend with those you know well, as Jupiter will replenish you with fresh air and a new approach to life.

THU., FRI., SAT., SUN. — JUNE 15, 16, 17, 18:

RULERS — Uranus (Explosions/Surprises) and Neptune (Oil/Middle East):

Work, Career and Business: Combined with the Full Moon, Uranus may make you feel erratic and Neptune may make you feel depressed and overemotional at work; this could lead you to think about a new job. Keep your eyes and ears open; with Neptune's "dreamy" nature, you are prone to making serious errors or forgetting something important. Do not sign any contracts now; in the long run, you will be sorry if you do. Be patient and wait until the next New Moon.

Partnerships: Crazy things may happen now; do not make a fool of yourself in public. Things done or words said without forethought might bring trouble later. Use your will; be positive in all you say. Expect disturbing news by mail or telephone but avoid fears, as insecurity could take over your common sense; all will be fine, there is a Divine plan for you. This timing is ideal for meditation and renewing your faith in each other and the universe. You must control negative thoughts, even if many things around you do not seem positive. Have faith in yourself and those you care for during these days.

Family and Friends: Spend some valuable time with your family. Do not expect the affairs of the heart to progress or get better for a while, and teenagers may get themselves in trouble. Watch for the use of drugs, as Neptune will lead them towards wrong friends. Give them solid direction and be ready for some friction. Depressed friends may call you asking for spiritual support or direction. With Neptune, confusion and deception is in the air. If you socialize during the night hours, keep your eyes on your possessions as they may disappear. Don't misplace your keys. Avoid complaining about life's problems to those who care about you.

Love Affairs: Love and romance may suffer as during a waning Moon, Uranus' erratic emotions may preside and disturb your relationship. Be patient with the partner and use diplomacy to save trouble. However don't let someone else's problem get to you and affect your feelings. If you were born in August expect a Gemini friend to give you disturbing news soon. A friend from a foreign land may bring better but surprising news soon. All fire signs will suffer this lunation emotionally, so try not to let it happen to you, use you will. If you are a Leo, Sagittarius or Aries remember the waning Moon and be patient.

Travel and Communication: If you can, avoid flying during this trend unless you made your reservations before the waning Moon. Protect yourself against aeronautic accidents; use "Moon Power" and your knowledge, take no chances. This is the perfect time to pass on the light and talk about Starguide's guidance. Avoid drinking and driving at all costs; many accidents happen under Neptune and Uranus' iniquitous energy. If you have to play or travel be aware of the ocean or the river these days.

Environment: Expect bad news about quakes and the possibilities of sea/air accidents. Many naturalists will be upset and some groups will make dramatic decisions followed by dangerous actions. Nature will start to go berserk and may throw a cluster of negative weather patterns such as tornadoes or earthquakes in the near future. Remember the Florida tornadoes in 1998? Uranus was in charge then.

Famous Personalities: Under Uranus power the British Artist John Michael made weird news in Los Angeles in a public bathroom, again surprising Uranus (weird) and Neptune (kinky sex) was in charge. Remember another British singer O'Connor? She cut up a picture Pope's face on national TV in one of her performances, right in front of the entire audience. Again Uranus (freedom) and Neptune (religion) were in charge. Many unaware famous daredevils will lose their lives because they have no knowledge of the stars' impact on human affairs. Do not take chances after the Full Moon, ever, and all will be fine.

Events: Under Uranus' powers expect anything weird and explosive to take place. Stay clear of strangers and any suspicious packages, especially in airports or dams. Let's hope for the best! Many eruptions have taken place under this energy - 3/8/05 - CNN Mount St. Helens coughs up ash - 3/8/05 - Severe cyclone hits Australia

Shopping: Provide spiritual guidance and support to all in need. Many will fall victim to Neptune's deceiving and Uranus' eccentric wills. Do not invest in alcohol now; you would further a disaster later on. Some people out there are not aware of the stars' impact on their lives and may decide to jump from a bridge or a plane; good luck to them. You may invest in my work for them, mention or offer them 2003 Starguide, this can and will save them trouble. Avoid investing in any form of electronics; a nasty virus may get to your computer.

MON., TUE., WED., THU. — JUNE 19, 20, 21, 22:

RULERS — Mars (danger/Men) and Venus (Docile/Women):

Work, Career and Business: The Moon is still waning (negative), so think twice before committing to an investment program. A powerful hunch might save you trouble if you are unsure about a person or a business scheme. Don't let Mars affect your judgment; be patient with everyone around. Expect upsetting financial news; don't let it get to you, you can only do so much. The future will offer better opportunities. Wait patiently for the next New Moon; right now just clean up and reorganize.

Partnerships: As usual with Mars' aggressive personality, expect all sorts of trouble with partnerships. As always with the Lord of war around these days, you are seriously advised to use discretion in all you do or mention to avoid serious complications. Keep in mind that the Moon is waning (negative) so don't expect progress in any of your endeavors for now. Finish up a project or re-evaluate a situation, but most of all be patient.

Family and Friends: A difficult trend is taking place; do not let it get to you. Use your will and look for happy people. Starguide is preparing you for this type of celestial affliction; take a passive attitude and all will go your way. Use Venus' loving touches with practical advice to provide spiritual help to those you care for, but realize your limits. You need your own spiritual strength to face those tough stars and you can do it.

Love Affairs: Expect some secrets to be divulged, especially the ones related to sex or financial scandals. Venus' gentle nature will reward you if you use her diplomatic, loving powers to smooth things out. Better stay home and enjoy good food during the late hours. A great movie with the one you care about this weekend is your best shot. Many will fall prey to con artists and weird sexual endeavors. If you are a Virgo someone born in March, a Taurus or a Capricorn could be looking for you. A Cancer friend will give you good advice, but do not complain too much if you want to save your friendship. Stay clear of alcohol consumption.

Travel and Communication: The people of your past will soon show up. After the Full Moon always stay clear of suspicious deals. Deal with the people you know and avoid dangerous dark alleys. Keep your eyes open and your personal alarm (intuition) on all the time. Mars rules man's animal instincts and he could stimulate one of his aggressive children (Mars in bad aspect) to hurt you, given the occasion. With any trouble on the highway, stay inside your car with the doors secured. Many violent crimes have been reported during this type of energy, especially when drugs or alcohol are involved; take no chances.

Environment: Soft Venus will try to stop her violent brother Mars and Pluto from stirring the earth's entrails and producing earthquakes, explosions, volcanoes and disasters. In time of a waning Moon and with a Supernova window in action she might not have much influence. Be ready for destruction from both Pluto and the red planet, Mars, "The Lord of War."

Famous Personalities: This same type of energy has taken the lives of many famous people, sometimes dramatically. Drama, sex, and scandals of all sorts will go public and may induce suicidal tendencies in some prominent people. Stay clear of any chemicals and be aware around the water.

Events: Mars is like Pluto in some ways and will stimulate the villains; expect them to be nasty and active during this trend. Again, do not trust strangers and do not put yourself in any situation that could make you a potential victim. The police will make disturbing news and many officers will be dispatched to cool off situations, especially those of domestic violence. If you are in law enforcement, beware; Mars or Pluto could hurt you; don't take any chances.

Shopping: Do not deal with finances these days. Avoid investing in tools or sharp instruments. Some will get bad news from their creditors and bank accounts or credit cards will be a source of trouble. Do not open a bank account now; the negative energy will induce unneeded financial stress in your life.

April 24, 2006 — Venus enters Gemini: The planet of love in the sign of flirtiest Gemini. Souls born with this celestial gift will need mental stimulation at all times. Unless the partner is animated, boredom will bring about a swift break. Great ability is often found in poetry, writing, photography and drawing. A natural zest for diplomacy and learning foreign languages is often found with this position. The soul could also marry and reside in a foreign land during the course of this reincarnation. Expect lots of great news, and to spend money on anything that writes, reads, rolls and speaks.

FRI., SAT., SUN., MON. — JUNE 23, 24, 25, 26:

RULERS — Mercury (Information) and the Moon (New Beginnings).

Work, Career and Business: Great news is to be expected soon in the work and career scenes, and progressive changes are on the way. Make the most of Mercury's intellectual powers to review your business life and do some financial planning. Concentrate on everything important, and then go for it with faith. Lots of progress is ahead, make the most of this positive trend. As always drive with caution, don't let speedy Mercury ruin your day with the police.

Partnerships: The Moon is up and happy for the next few days; do all you can to further your partnerships and if you have to, let go of your past and look for someone else. There are plenty of great souls walking this earth; just ask for your happiness and let go of the past. Use Mercury's strength to take a trip with your partner.

Family and Friends: Your maternal instinct will show itself to your children. Share your knowledge with friends; help them to understand some of the secrets of life and make them understand their emotions, which are regulated by the Moon's passage through each and every sign of the zodiac. The subconscious response to the moon's fluctuations upon humans is referred as "lunatic behavior or moodiness" and right now she will make you and others feeling happy. Expect the beginning or ending of important parts of your or others' life. Expect some surprising news from the children. A close friend needs your attention to deal with an emotional situation. Give help.

Love Affairs: Realize your limits with the wrong people, be honest with your feelings and make the needed changes. Your own future, positive or negative, is mostly based upon your decisions, and is the reincarnation of your thoughts. An old friend who lives far away may need to communicate with you, use Mercury and write those letters. The mail could bring you great news and everyone will want to talk to you. If you are a Virgo a Capricorn or a Pisces will want you. Someone born in July needs to spend some time with you very soon.

Travel and Communication: If you have to travel for business purposes, do it now and always use the two weeks following a New Moon to do so. Don't let insecurity stop your progress, and promote important business now. Expect the mail and your telephone to bring you interesting news. Many will be going back home while others will have to go away.

Environment: The Moon's waxing energy could induce stress on the faults, so that many people will be forced to relocate soon following natural disasters. It's time for her to stretch herself and restructure her inside. Mars is still in Scorpio; be aware of fires and destructive emotional behaviors.

Famous Personalities: The rich and famous will be investing or planning reunions to feed the children of the world. Their artistic gifts will benefit many generous organizations. Some other crazy famous people may make surprising news trying to use Mercury's (the press) power to gain free publicity.

Events: Expect the military to make the news or perform deeds that will aid the general public and provide relief from disasters or war areas. Nature will begin to feel agitated and under this celestial manifestation — Wildfires that had burned nearly a quarter-million acres in the Western United States remained out of control Thursday in at least six states. The same energy was active in SIDON, Lebanon — Five people died and 15 were wounded when explosions sparked by an electrical fire ripped through a house used as an arms depot, Lebanese security sources said. Seven other houses were also destroyed.

Shopping: Buy anything that your home or garden needs. You are under the protection of the New Moon, thus signing anything related to real estate, hotels or restaurants is OK. Share my valuable forecast on www.drturi.com or offer my Starguide and its accurate guidance for someone's birthday, or offer a comparison chart for a newly wed couple.

New Moon — June 25, 2006 in Cancer: With the Moon so close to the earth, this specific lunation will have an important effect on many of us. Expect the beginning or ending of important phases of your and other people's lives. This lunation could represent a very significant part of your destiny even the United States of America. You may be forced by the universe to let go of your past and forge into your new future. Whatever the changes are, go with confidence. Many will be affected and forced to move on due to war and/or natural catastrophes or simply to further specific wishes. Dr. Turi needs your help to promote his Astropsychology schools and help the children of the world. Help us to pass on his very important star message to the world. See www.drturi.com or call 602-265-7667 to help us to set a crash course in your area on Astropsychology, Kabalistic Healing or the Astro-Tarot).

Lunation impact on all signs:

Aries - New home and good news from the family are ahead of you. Be happy.

Taurus - A trip or a study will pay off, great news by mail or the telephone soon.

Gemini - Opportunity to invest in a home and a great financial deal is on the way.

Cancer - This new Moon is on you, be ready for super progressive changes.

Leo - The past is about to show itself, you can fix some financial situations.

Virgo - A friend may bring your past alive and with it good wishes.

Libra - Great news about your career, changes are needed.

Scorpio - A far away trip and a study will pay off in the long run.

Sagittarius - A legacy or business will bring a partner with the money you need.

Capricorn - A great business or emotional partner is ahead of you go out more.

Aquarius - Your health and your work will undergo very progressive changes.

Pisces - Good news about love, romance and children is due to you.

June 29, 2006 — Mercury enters Leo: This next trend's promise is a rich mixture of love, romance, creativity and children. Many thoughts will be geared towards immense feelings of both hope and true love. Souls born with Mercury in Leo will be gifted with natural managerial dispositions. Many of them will be shrewd in business, and attracted to professions offering fame and fortune. Artistic talents involving music, dancing, and painting will lead these souls toward the great fame and security they seek. This position makes for one of the most mentally domineering signs of the Zodiac where the soul will be forced to learn humility and service to others. This Mercury position will lead the soul toward success in many artistic endeavors. An opportunity to experience mental fame is also offered to the soul. The parent educated in Astropsychology will realize the child's gift and promote the new soul towards communication, acting or writing. Dr. Turi needs your help to pass on his very important star message to the world call 602-265-7667 to set a crash course on Astropsychology, Kabalistic Healing or the Astro-Tarot in your city.

TUE., WED., THU., FRI. — JUNE 27, 28, 29, 30:

RULERS — The Sun (Children/Light and life) and Mercury (Traveling):

Work, Career and Business: Don't let the egotistic power of the Sun take over your management skills. Keep in mind that we are still human and have egos that sometimes get out of hand. Make the most of the Sun and Mercury's revitalizing energy to further your business life. Interesting progress and surprises are on the way. You've been waiting for this New Moon long enough; push now.

Partnerships: We are under the white power of the Moon and you can also feel the valiant Sun's strength light up your life and your relationships. This is the time to offer presents or flowers to those for whom you care. You should nurture happiness and feel rejuvenated; your spirit is free and happy. Use this long-awaited New Moon to your advantage; get active with life. You may hear about a birth soon.

Family and Friends: Remembrance of the he past will activate for many, and great time is ahead. Let the golden protective Sun's rays further everything related to children, love and creativity these days. A trip to the wild or the zoo would be rejuvenating for the entire family; get your camera as those laughs and sincere smiles are priceless. With Mercury's speed affecting the kids, and dangerous Mars in Scorpio watch over them carefully around the water. If you feel confused about a situation, Mercury will help you find the perfect words to fix the situation. Expect interesting surprises coming your way via telephone, mail or social activities. Use this powerful lunation to your advantage; get yourself in shape and do something different this weekend.

Love Affairs: Time to get active as love can be found practically anywhere, especially if you set your mind to it and participate in all events. Throwing a party will pay off for some people and love may just enter your own home. Again don't stay home if you are invited to a gathering; the Sun may reward your heart's desire. One of your important wishes is in the hands of a friend; don't miss the party. If you were born in May, a Scorpio or a Virgo will be strongly attracted to you. A friend born in March or January may need your help.

Travel and Communication: Use all the beautiful words you can come up with. Everyone will sparkle with the Sun's power. Make plans now for a trip close to the water. Let your loved ones know that you miss them and that you'll be there soon. Travel is under the protection of the Sun but please remember the Supernova window and dangerous Mars in the deadly sign of Scorpio.

Environment: The Moon is near Saturn these days, and this aspect could remind us of our vulnerability to the shocking destructive forces of nature. With the new Moon upon us, let's hope no earthquakes will come to remind us that the earth is still very much alive. Trouble may be coming from an accident involving children. Again, keep your eyes open, especially close to the water.

Famous Personalities: Many new figures will show up on the entertainment field and much work will be done to produce the finest in the arts. Great movies are being made and expected to appear in the fall. Some famous actors will get in or out of business and love relationships. A famous personality will make weird news.

Events: Are you into the extraordinary? If so, go to the desert now; bring your camera, as this energy activates UFOs sightings. The Sun's light brings the undiluted truth to whoever wants to see or experience the incredible power of the divine. Nature may do things of her own and disturb power and electronics in some areas. Be aware of Mars in Leo with children as explosions, earthquakes, tornadoes and volcanic eruptions are high on the list.

Shopping: Buy anything expensive: gold, cars, electronics for the children. Presents bought now will bring luck to both of you. Invest in all that shows true love and you will win the heart of that person later. Now is the perfect time to invest in the light and my Astropsychology course and learn all about the stars.

Note: A happy 4th of July to all readers. Just be aware that it falls after a negative Full Moon and could be quite memorable even negative for some. Remember last year, it was just a day before the full moon! Regardless how much I tried to get close to the action, the police, the madness, and the people walking all over, made the situation unsafe and caused me to turn back a few minutes before the fireworks show. Please make a good use of my work, watch the children with fireworks and if you spend some time by the water, be aware of Neptune's tricks. Share the knowledge with others, recommend my book and help them to understand the will of God throughout the cosmos. Have a great time but be careful please.

Welcome to Your
Day - to - Day Guidance

For July 2006

SAT., SUN., MON., TUE. — JULY 1, 2, 3, 4:

RULERS — Venus (Coherence) and Mercury (Babble).

Work, Career and Business: The worse of both of these planets is to be expected mainly due to the waning Moon (negative) and the pessimistic trend of the Dragon's Tail in Scorpio. Do not fall for depression or self-defeating attitudes. You may communicate your feelings but avoid uncontrolled imagination. The stars have a specific role to play in your life and you are the actor. Go with the trend, do not force issue, be patient and further your business life after the next New Moon. At work keep a low profile, your co-workers or your boss may not be aware of the work of the Moon on their psyches, and may become "lunatic" towards you. Keep busy and rearrange your desk or your paper work.

Partnerships: If you want to save a difficult business relationship, now is the time to use full diplomacy and understanding. And with affairs of the heart, use Venus' loving touch; you could apologize with some flowers or a romantic dinner. Take serious precautions if you happen to be in the road as Mercury could mean impatience and speed.

Family and Friends: Expect disturbing news involving friends, brothers or sisters and take the time to reply to the mail. If you get caught on the telephone, steer the discussion towards a positive tone. Mercury rules communication and will help you pass on your thoughts deeply and correctly. Again, provide a helping hand, but do not let abusive or depressing friends take the best of your own spirit.

Love Affairs: Many will feel the disheartening energy of the waning moon. Secret love affairs may be started. However, do not expect this undercover relationship to stay a secret for long. A love affair started now could have a dramatic impact in your life. Many unsuited couples will also be forced out of their unhealthy relationships and realize the end of a section of their lives. With the tail in Libra stress may come from the partner, and the emphasis these days will be on destructive behavior and violence. If you were born in November, a Cancer or a Pisces could be difficult just now. Listen to a Virgo friend for good advice.

Travel and Communication: Mercury will pass on all sorts of news including some of a secret nature. Improve your cosmic consciousness and do some "deep" reading concerning life and death or metaphysics. Finish your book if you are into writing. Drive slowly and be ready for obstacles on the road. Be ready for the approaching Supernova window.

Environment: Tornadoes, hurricanes, earthquakes, and chain-reaction accidents due to bad weather are high on the list. Stay safe and be aware of Mother Nature's destructive forces. She is alive and she needs to stretch herself now and then.

Famous personalities: A famous individual from a foreign country will see the end of his life. Many will miss his message and his great spirit.

Events: With the Tail of the Dragon in Libra at home in the US, acts of terrorism could produce devastating explosions. Stay clear of crowds, and listen to your intuition at all times. Avoid crowded places and beware of suspicious foreigners.

Shopping: Electronic equipment, cars, telephones, computers, etc., may decide to give you trouble. The purpose behind this disturbing energy is to re-evaluate your existence and life's mission and restructure your opportunities to make progress. Fix it or rent it but do not buy anything new now. Take care of your car as the machine may decide to let you down at the wrong time and in the wrong place. Be cautious and be patient.

There will be three major negative SUPERNOVA windows in the year 2006. Each destructive "window" is operational for three to four weeks, thus caution is strongly advised during this period. Heavy loss of lives due to nature's devastating forces, aeronautical disasters and structural damage is to be expected. Once more realize that I do not use traditional dates found in popular ephemera. Years of practical observation lead me to extend the Mercury retrograde motion and period of time.

July / August: Second SUPERNOVA window - From Saturday July 1st through Wednesday August 2nd 2006.

October / November: Third SUPERNOVA window - From Saturday October 21st through Tuesday October 21st 2006.

EXPLANATION OF A SUPERNOVA WINDOW

There is a celestial concentration of negative celestial energy bombarding the earth for a few weeks. Be extremely prudent in driving, and expect chain-reaction accidents. Be prepared for delays, strikes, and nature producing awful weather, including hurricanes and tornadoes. The same energy that produced the Titanic disaster, the Northridge, Los Angeles, and Kobe, Japan, earthquakes is approaching again. Double-check all your appointments, and if you can, postpone traveling and flying during this Supernova "window".

Communication and electricity will be cut off, and a general loss of power is to be expected. Appliances, computers, telephones, planes, trains, cars, all of these "tools" will be affected by this energy. They will be stopped in one way or another. The people of the past will make the news and will reenter your life. Expect trouble with the post office, education, students, strikes, prisoners' escape, newspapers, broadcasting industries and computer viruses may bother us again.

Many a failed mission and expensive electronic equipment (Mars probe etc.) and our tax dollars have been wasted because of the scientist's lack of knowledge of the stars. As usual NASA, which is not aware of the science of astrology, will waste our tax money with failed missions due to bad weather and electronic malfunctions. In the name of ignorance a few years ago, in the Challenger explosion seven astronauts lost their lives when NASA launched the shuttle under a "Supernova Window".

Note: Regardless of Dr. Turi's expectations posted on his website for the second time and his desperate attempts over the years to make NASA officials aware of dangerous Super Nova Windows, the Columbia was also launched during this window and re-entered the last night of it producing the death of all courageous astronauts.

Again in July 2005 NASA repeated the same error regardless of many failed attempts to launch the space vehicle. As expect foam from the fuel tanker damager the shuttle forcing astronauts to take an historic unplanned space walk costing millions of dollars for the tax payers once more and risking another disaster. When will NASA learn?

Marine life sharks, whales etc may also beach themselves due to Mercury retrograde affecting their natural inborn navigational systems. All these malevolent predictions and waste of lives and equipment do not have to occur. Those predictions do not have to affect you directly as they unfold. Instead, they are printed to prepare you for setbacks and frustrations, thus advising you to be patient and prudent during this trend. There is no room for ignorance, and those who are not aware of the celestial order, including the NASA space-program management team, will continue to pay a heavy price. In all mankind's affairs, ignorance is true evil. Why any scientists who are against my research do not honor the word science, which is based upon solid investigation, is solid proof of mental snobbery. By omitting any physical or spiritual laws can only bring penalty; for science's purpose is to explore all possibilities, even those laws written in light via the stars.

July 7, 2006 - The anniversary of 7/05 and the memory of what took place on these days will affect many people all over the world. All the memorable activities will take place just before the New Moon at the lowest time of the month, thus many souls will suffer this depressive lunation. Just be ready to provide as much help as needed and do not lose faith in the future.

Memo of 2005 Moon Power: KEY WORDS for those dates are "The beginning and ending of people's lives". This energy produced the Asia Tsunami and usually produces also natural disasters including large quakes/tornadoes, bad weather and force thousands of people to relocate or evacuate. Many people will see the end of an important part of their lives and every one of us to a certain degree will be touched personally. This is the same energy that produced the Asia tsunami. The US is under this celestial energy and will be also be touched directly. The dates are: July 6/7/8, 2005.

Note: Attention: Pluto is back with us for a few days — Expect dramatic happenings all over; control is a must. Don't be one of his victim; be aware of Pluto's destructive power. Anything you say or do under his power will follow you for the rest of your life. This is the time to use extreme caution, even in the time of a waxing (positive) Moon.

WED., THU., FRI., SAT. — JULY 5, 6, 7, 8:

RULERS — Venus (Passion/Love) and Pluto (Drama/Sex/Secrets):

Work, Career and Business: The Moon is waxing (positive) and much can happen as long as you understand how to use Pluto and Venus' energies positively. Promote your business life now: advertise and reach the people, travel. Do that and soon your telephone will be busy and the mail will bring awakening news. You will be soon being forced to realize what is wrong in your career, and the needed changes are on the way.

Partnerships: A new plan is needed to succeed in your endeavor; use this trend to get rid of whatever or whoever is bothering you. Expect some secret to resurface soon. Nothing can really go wrong if you use Venus' diplomatic gifts to deal with others and aim high. Diplomacy with others will pay off.

Family and Friends: Expect shocking news from people around you; you might get in touch with some of your friends for a good chat. Do not fall for gossip; you may end up sandwiched between two friends. Use the positive Moon and Venus kind-hearted natures to promote your life. Surely a good time to appreciate your loved ones or plan a dinner at home, or maybe just see a great movie. Avoid Pluto's sarcastic remarks or you might be sorry later. Many will experience drama in their own homes, keep the police away.

Love Affairs: Combined with Venus' sensuality, Pluto will give you the power to "stimulate" your partner in many ways. Candlelight, soft music and words of love will pay off considerably if you are in a solid relationship. This is a trend loaded with powerful emotions and good energy, where nothing can go wrong if you play your cards right. A foreigner could play an important part in this trend and later in your future. If you were born under a water sign you are advised to keep your emotions in control. If you are a Gemini, a person born under the sign of Libra or Sagittarius will be strongly attracted to you.

Travel and Communication: The call of nature will be strong for many. Enjoy the wild and water and make plans for fishing trips. The river and the sea have lots of fish to give away and for some magical reason they will all bite the bait. Drive slowly; don't spoil your day with a speeding ticket. Watch over Pluto's destructive communication and use Venus' diplomatic manner instead.

Environment: Many mother earth supporters will march to be heard by government officials and they will succeed in their requests to save the environment. Pluto is about to show mankind the awful power of destruction. Dramatic news for some unlucky souls is to be expected.

Famous Personalities: Legal action in the news from a famous entertainer. Another famous figure may have to leave this world. News from similar past energies produced the story of "Arab world's longest-serving monarch dead at 70." Large corporations will find strength in their new associations. Moon Power 2003 - 12/26/05 –DENVER (AP) — , one of basketball's brightest stars, was arrested after a woman accused the ' guard of sexual misconduct at a hotel near Vail.

Events: This energy will touch the police force so don't take any chances now. The police will make disturbing news, as Pluto will induce drama and death. Expect nature to get out of hand, and accidents to plague the media. Under Pluto's power a mother's hysterical reaction after a gunman brings a lesson in terror to a buffalo school. Police arrest an Eerie county sheriff's deputy accused of gunning down his estranged wife... and wounding a bystander right inside school. 18 were terrified after a man opened fire inside the elementary school right after the morning bell. Police say 37 year old Juan Roman, an Eerie county sheriff's deputy, chased his estranged wife into the school in a domestic dispute.

Shopping: Cameras bought now will take dramatic pictures or will be used against criminals. Invest in anything that will be used to clean up your environment. Good metaphysical books can also be bought and used for your own mental progression. Spruce yourself up by brightening your wardrobe. Purchase or wear black or red garments; they will bring magic to you. Your favorite astrologer or psychic will have great insights for you visit them now.

Full Moon — July 11, 2006 in Capricorn: Expect some serious career or personal developments to take place. Some will be starting a new job, and others dropping one, this could include a business relationship. Promotion or deception, whichever happens, will mark an important part of your life. Just be ready to accept the upcoming changes with faith in your new future. Be ready to provide a supportive shoulder to the victims. Nature can also decide to do nasty tricks in some states, promoting destructive weather or earthquakes in the very near future. The government will have to take serious, crucial steps, to avoid trouble and promote peace in the world. Expect news coming from important political figures in England and India.

Lunation impact on all signs:

Aries - Your career will see some important but needed changes. Have faith.

Taurus - A study or stressful news from foreign lands will start you worrying.

Gemini - Sad news from corporate money, a legacy could reach you soon.

Cancer - Problems with a partner or a business associate are to be expected.

Leo - Don't put stress on your health because your work is tiring.

Virgo - Doubt about a person or an endeavor will upset you, just let go.

Libra - You might need to relocate or deal with a stressful situation at home.

Scorpio - Control your imagination; don't believe in what others say.

Sagittarius - Money setbacks will let down your self -esteem, be patient.

Capricorn - Big changes are needed in your life, have faith in your abilities.

Aquarius - Let go of your past, you belong to the future. Career changes ahead.

Pisces - A friend will become too burdensome. Learn to say no, you need your spirit.

SUN., MON., TUE., WED. — JULY 9, 10, 11, 12:

RULERS: Jupiter (Foreign Affairs) and Saturn (Government):

Work, Career and Business: Jupiter's positive energy will help restore faith and new opportunities in your life. You could use this trend to gather your thoughts and get close to God in your local church or in nature and enjoy the wildness. Keep your notion of life clean; avoid poisoning your future with negative attitudes. Pray for the world, for the children of the future. Many of those restorative thoughts are needed, then slowly but surely a healing process will take place. With the New Moon upon us you may begin to see the light. Signing important documents is OK while the moon is still waxing, and valuable opportunities are on the way. Be ready for the beginning or ending of important parts of your life.

Partnerships: A new business partner wants to share a great plan with you; it probably is! Don't rush. Listen to your intuition before and add your own creative force in the process. A foreigner could also enter the scenery and the meeting could positively affect your future. Avoid tensions this weekend about a specific project or trip. Nothing can really stop you if you mean business. Keep a positive attitude.

Family and Friends: Friends will be active and many will be requesting your presence. Do not refuse invitations. The waxing Moon through your great friends can still grant many of your wishes. You may plan to throw your own party with some good friends this weekend. Keep your eyes open for an older person with good deals or kind words to offer. Kids sense that they are the center of attention, be patient with their demands. If Mom is far away, she may call you; don't dwell on the past and avoid gossip. Be happy. Don't let other people's trouble upset you, and all will be fine.

Love Affairs: Socialize with friends and have faith in the stars. You will feel positive away from home with the people around you. They will enjoy your company and one of your wishes may come true. Avoid impulsive actions where romance is concerned and drive carefully on your way back home during the late hours. Do not fall victim to Saturn's gloomy power; forget about your responsibility, go out, meet new people and expect a lot. If you're born in January or September, your magnetism will be high and you could find love. The future has better to offer, so put a big smile on your face and be confident. Progressive changes are ahead; be patient and participate in life. If you were born in August, someone born in April, or an Aquarius or Gemini could be strongly attracted to you.

Travel and Communication: Saturn rules old people and parts of your past. Take care of the old people you love. Make these days' good ones, as those folks might not be around for the next cycle. Some will plan to travel far this weekend, and some just around town to meet their pasts. Be aware of early celebrations as people could drink too much and drive dangerously. Stay safe and watch the roads. Many will find themselves with car problems or stuck in airports. City workers may also decide to cut off traffic making you late for work.

Events: Jupiter may decide to entertain us with some new from foreign powers. Under Saturn's power, people challenge governmental structure. For instance a few years ago the news reported that many Taliban fighters asserted authority in northern Afghanistan. Warlord Dostum flees to Turkey. Taliban fighters moved swiftly Sunday to assert their authority over this northern stronghold, whose capture nearly completed a three-year campaign to unite Afghanistan under the white flag of the radical Islamic army.

Famous Personalities: The rich and famous will busy themselves to alleviate pain in the world.

Events: A political person may make surprising news. Be ready for startling news from a foreign land soon. The Middle East, Mexico or a Spanish-speaking country needs help.

Shopping: Invest in traveling or learning a foreign language, and you will have a rewarding time ahead of you. Use Jupiter's philosophical values to improve your consciousness, or plan to start an important study. Invest in anything for your pet.

July 2004: Neptune is still in the futuristic sign of Aquarius. Neptune the planet of illusion is presently cruising through the futuristic sign of Aquarius. This advanced sign will help man free him from fears and deceiving religiously doctrines and help him to refuse to advocate or expect apocalyptic disasters. We are the masters of our destiny, and the positive trend of your thoughts will further your and others' lives. The future is nothing other than the reincarnation of your thoughts and we are all responsible for your own reality. Do not join or promote the thought poisoning processes generated by many unaware young souls. Responding to Pluto's position in religious Sagittarius, another wave of re-born evangelists will take to the bullhorn, using the "last days" of the Apocalypse to make fortunes by deceiving the uninformed, God-fearing religious masses. On the positive and artistic side, combined with Uranus' electronic ingeniousness in Aquarius, Neptune (movies) in Aquarius (the future) will promote a serious increase in creativity, involving more electronic sub-realities within the cinematography industry. The "Titanic" and "Jurassic Park" movies are good examples, and represent some incredible electronic advances. On a higher note, real spiritual leaders will begin to transform Neptune's illusive/pious vibrations into a more and rational advanced Uranian oriented generation.

THU., FRI., SAT., SUN. — JULY 13, 14, 15, 16:

RULERS — Uranus (Explosions) Neptune (Deception):

Work, Career and Business: — Do not expect to make much progress for a while; many of your plans will fall apart. Listen to other people's stories; the stars affect everybody and they may come up with interesting, even surprising news. Be ready to invest in some appliances or equipment. Saturn will help you make some great adjustments after careful planning. Wait for the next New Moon for more progress.

Partnerships: With Uranus in charge, anything and everything unusual can happen and with a waning Moon (negative) upon us, do not expect great news. Restaurants will be busy; better make reservations if you don't want to be turned down. However, any changes should be accepted with faith in yourself and the new future. Be patient with everyone, as Uranus may make them eccentric and Saturn depressed. Avoid drinking at night.

Family and Friends: An opportunity to meet with some family members you have not seen for a while will be given to you by this lunation. The past will come alive again and an old friend will reappear soon. A person who owes you money sincerely wants to repay, but may be in such a difficult set of circumstances that he can't. Be patient as he may repay you in a different way. A friend who has invited himself and who has been a house guest for a while may need a little push to get him out of your domicile. Providing help is great, but let people know your limits.

Love Affairs: Be ready for the incredible to happen; if you are in a karmic relationship, changes are needed. Friends may fall in love with other friends or mistake love for friendship. An old love or an old friend long gone will reappear in your life soon. If you were born under any of the water signs expect needed changes. If you are a Libra, a Leo friend needs to talk to you and someone born in April or February needs to understand you. A friend born in June might fall for you.

Travel and Communication: A business trip or an invitation may lead you to many good contacts from the past. However, you might have problems getting to the given address and may get lost a few times. Be patient, as you will still have plenty of time to play and enjoy yourself with various unusual people. For paranormal investigators, now is the time to look for UFOs in secluded places. Don't forget your video camera; you may be sorry if you are not ready when Uranus is willing to display the secret of extraterrestrial intelligence. Stay clear from tall trees and posts to avoid lightning; many people met with their deaths in stormy Uranus trends.

Environment: General electronic failures or viruses could produce aeronautic disasters soon. Expect this type of news to happen: Australian wildlife officials made repeated attempts to prevent up to 300 long-finned pilot whales from beaching themselves on a remote part of Australia's west coast. Mammals', birds' and man's navigational systems are confused when Uranus is in charge and many get lost. Tornadoes are high on the list. See my site www.drturi.com for more information all year round. Your questions and comments are welcome on the forum.

Famous Personalities: Very surprising behavior or news will come from the rich and famous. Disturbing and sad news about a famous child could reach the media. Fire and electrocution are also high on the list; be aware. On July 4th 2003 Velvet-voiced R&B crooner Barry White, renowned for his lush baritone and lyrics that oozed sex appeal on songs such as "Can't Get Enough of Your Love, Babe," died. White, who had suffered kidney failure from years of high blood pressure, died at Cedars-Sinai Medical Center around 9:30 a.m., said manager Ned Shankman. He was 58. Note for my student. Mrs. White was born in September under the sign of Virgo. His 3rd house (communication/singing) is located in the sexy, mystical, hypnotic sign of Scorpio and gave him that deep sensual voice that brought him towards a singing career.

Events: — Uranus loves accidents and explosions; under his power expect surprising and original pieces of news such as: ANCHORAGE, Alaska (AP) — Two people camping along the Hulahula River in the Arctic National Wildlife Refuge were killed by a grizzly bear, officials said. - 6/24/05 STOCKHOLM, Sweden (AP) - A Swedish man who was injured in a helicopter crash on his 100th birthday has died, a hospital statement said Friday. Also on July 5th, 2003 - Two female suicide bombers killed at least 14 people today outside a rock concert in Moscow, Russian authorities said. Russian Interior Minister Boris Gryzlov said he believed Chechen separatists were responsible for the attack.

Expect more shocking news like two teen-agers were killed when a butane pipeline broke and exploded in northeast Texas. Lastly I gave the date of August 18th and asked the readers to be prepared for "electronic failures". On the exact date (printed months earlier) NASA shuttle lost his main computer in space and made international news. The costly loss of the Mars probe took also place under this disturbing Uranian energy.

Shopping: This is not a time to purchase new electronic equipment or plan a long voyage by air to a foreign land. As always, Uranus rules the future, and his psychic powers can be used through your trusted local psychic or astrologer. Second-hand shopping of Hi-tech will pay off for some.

July 19, 2006 — Venus enters Cancer: Perfect conditions exist to launch any financial or real estate endeavors. Home improvement, and buying or selling a

Police stand by the body of a victim of a blast at a giant rock festival in suburban Moscow.

beautiful house is on the agenda for some. You may also invest in anything beautiful for your home. Souls born now will be soft and emotional in matters related to love and family. They will make money in hotel and restaurant business endeavors. Many of them will strive to find partners who will exchange deep emotions and spiritual research. Some will have to learn to let go of wrong relationships. This position makes for one of the most sensitive signs of the Zodiac. Usually the gift of cooking is present with this position. Those souls are born to feed the world with food and love. This position of Venus is a top position for financial security, communication and success in real estate.

MON., TUE., WED., THU., FRI., SAT. — JULY 17, 18, 19, 20, 21, 22:

RULERS — Venus (Love of the Past) and Mercury (Moving Back).

Work, Career and Business: The worst of both of these planets is to be expected mainly due to the waning Moon (negative) and the negative Supernova window in action. Do not fall for depression or self-defeating attitudes. You may communicate your feelings but avoid uncontrolled imagination. The stars have a specific role to play in your life and you are the actor. Go with the trend, do not force issue, be patient and further your business life after the next New Moon. At work keep a low profile, your co-workers or your boss may not be aware of the work of the Moon on their psyches, and may become "lunatic" towards you. Keep busy and rearrange your desk or your paper work.

Partnerships: If you want to save a difficult business relationship, now is the time to use full diplomacy and understanding. And with affairs of the heart, use Venus' loving touch; you could apologize with some flowers or a romantic dinner. Take serious precautions if you happen to be in the road as Mercury could mean impatience and speed.

Family and Friends: Expect disturbing news involving friends, brothers or sisters and take the time to reply to the mail. If you get caught on the telephone, steer the discussion towards a positive tone. Mercury rules communication and will help you pass on your thoughts deeply and correctly. Again, provide a helping hand, but do not let abusive or depressing friends take the best of your own spirit.

Love Affairs: Many will feel the disheartening energy of the waning moon. Secret love affairs may be started. However, do not expect this undercover relationship to stay a secret for long. A love affair started now could have a dramatic impact in your life. Many unsuited couples will also be forced out of their unhealthy relationships and realize the end of a section of their lives. With the tail in Scorpio danger may come from the home, and the emphasis these days will be on destructive behavior and violence. If you were born in November, a Cancer or a Pisces could be difficult just now. Listen to a Virgo friend for good advice.

Travel and Communication: Mercury will pass on all sorts of news including some of a secret nature. Improve your cosmic consciousness and do some "deep" reading concerning life and death or metaphysics. Finish your book if you are into writing. Drive slowly and be ready for obstacles on the road.

Environment: Tornadoes, hurricanes, earthquakes, and chain-reaction accidents due to bad weather are high on the list. Stay safe and be aware of Mother Nature's destructive forces. She is alive and she needs to stretch herself now and then.

Famous personalities: A famous individual from a foreign country will see the end of his life. Many will miss his message and his great spirit.

Events: With the Supernova window in action acts of terrorism could produce devastating explosions. Stay clear of crowds, and listen to your intuition at all times. Avoid crowded places and beware of suspicious foreigners.

Shopping: Electronic equipment, cars, telephones, computers, etc., may decide to give you trouble. The purpose behind this disturbing energy is to re-evaluate your existence and life's mission and restructure your opportunities to make progress. Fix it or rent it but do not buy anything new now. Take care of your car as the machine may decide to let you down at the wrong time and in the wrong place. Be cautious and be patient.

New Moon — August July 25, 2006 in Leo: This sign is ruled by the Sun, thus affairs of love and romance will be on the rise. Expect some surprises this month; the stars are giving you the possibility to reach one of your important wishes if you try hard within the next two weeks. This lunation could play an important part in your love life, with your children, your wishes, and will surely improve your relationships. You may also be forced to let go of a deteriorating love involvement and experience a new one. This month promises to be very interesting for many of us. Make the most of this incredible time; don't waste it but keep an eye on the children as this lunation may take some of them away especially around the water. Expect important news about technology, nuclear endeavor and from NASA, France and Japan soon.

Lunation impact on all signs

Aries - Love is on the rise and a project will turn out. Take chances now.

Taurus - Plan to move or improve your surroundings, throw a party and find love.

Gemini - Great news from foreign lands, take a trip or a study on photography.

Cancer - Great news about money; you may invest in an expensive item.

Leo - A new door for love, light, children and success will open to you.

Virgo - A possibility to do something with love or children is ahead for you.

Libra - A friend will bring you good wishes socialize to get it.

Scorpio - Your career will see important and constructive changes soon.

Sagittarius - Traveling, speaking and publishing is on the agenda for you.

Capricorn - Others fortune will touch you financially, study deep matters.

Aquarius - You will be in demand for love and for fame, travel now.

Pisces - A great opportunity to improve your health and your work is given to you.

July 23, 2006 — Mars enters Virgo: Virgo rules health, paperwork, details and general organization. Mars in Virgo produces a strong desire towards perfection in all areas of the subject's life. Mars in the sign of Virgo breed's workaholics, due to the 'service principle' found in this sign. The strong desire for perfection and accuracy can also bring stress and disagreement with co-workers. On a more positive note, Mars in Virgo will gear the soul towards health and organizational endeavors. Remember Mars is the desire principle. On the medical aspect of Astropsychology Virgo rules the cleansing process and the digestive tract. Virgo rules anything to do with elimination and cleansing. Mars also rules sharp instruments used in surgical procedures. This position produces detail-oriented and precise surgeons. On a negative note Mars in Virgo generates problems on the lower abdomen or intestines, which could require surgery. The digestive tract might be sensitive to changes in diet, especially by becoming a vegetarian or when certain foods are omitted such as red meat. In some extreme cases Mars accentuates a strong desire for virginity (Virgo is the Virgin Mary). The desire for sexual abstinence brings about chastity and translates into the idea of a nun marrying a deity such as Jesus. By doing so the subconscious Martian desire for purity is then established.

SAT., SUN., MON., TUE., WED. — JULY 22, 23, 24, 25, 26.

RULERS — Mercury (Your car) the Sun (Children) and the Moon (Endings).

Work, Career and Business: We are on New Moon timing, but you may find it difficult to concentrate on your duties as your mind will wander over everything you must accomplish. The deserving hard-working souls will benefit from bonuses or new opportunities to promote their careers. Some may face the ultimate end of a portion of their business lives. Whatever happens, you must accept the changes with faith. Your desires or dreams may not fit your present situation and the stars may decide to shut you down. It's for your best interest.

Partnerships: Some of the people you know will have to move away from you, or you yourself may decide to relocate. Expect the beginning or ending of an important phase of your life. Watch the drama of life taking place, as the old must be replaced in many aspects of the human experience.

Family and Friends: You may receive an invitation to socialize with some faraway dear friends or family members; use this opportunity to get closer to them. This New Moon trend may prove to be both sad and great for many. You and some friends get together to socialize; you may be the one doing the entertaining. A family member or a child needs your advice. Be willing to consider the issue from their point of view; avoid emotional involvement or forcing your opinion on others. Most of all provide spiritual support.

Love Affairs: With a waxing Moon upon us expect much progress in the area of love. But some people from the past may become heavy in your heart and could produce stress in your life. If they bring good memories, have fun, but don't get too caught up in the nostalgia. If they were negative in the first place, stay far away from their charms the second time around unless the hard lesson has been learnt from both side. If you were born on one of these days happy birthday to you and count on some really good time ahead. If you were born in December, a Leo or an Aries may find you too depressing lately. Listen to a friend born in October; you may learn something. Don't let guilt drag you down; life must go on. Many will enjoy a trip to Europe, France and Italy.

Travel and Communication: Local errands keep you busy and bring you in contact with interesting people. This trend will bring surprising news and reminds us of our responsibility. Mostly, be cautious and prudent in driving, as people may not see you. Drive slowly and enjoy the trip.

Environment: Nature may also go berserk and news could be significantly large and destructive. TEHRAN, Iran — A powerful earthquake jolted Iran's rugged Khorasan province, killing nearly 2,400 people and injuring an estimated 6,000. The U.S. Geological Survey told CNN the quake had a magnitude of 7.3. Nature may also show her power with shocking weather. Thousands of people may be forced to relocate. Many unaware daredevils or unlucky souls will lose their lives because they have no knowledge of the stars' impact on human affairs. You may suggest or offer them a copy of Starguide; a little information is better than none, and that is the purpose of this publication. They will probably love you forever because of this practical, thoughtful gesture.

Famous Personalities: A famous person or his child could make dramatic news. Expect interesting news about many famous people. The church could also make sad news such as in FAISALABAD, Pakistan. A 67-year-old Pakistani Roman Catholic bishop shot himself to death outside a court to protest against a death sentence on a fellow Christian for blasphemy. Some will work hard providing housing or clothing to the world at large.

Events: Under the same celestial energy in LIMA, Peru — Twelve people survived and 75 were killed when a Peruvian air force Boeing 737, chartered by the Occidental Petroleum Corp., crashed in a northern Amazon jungle. Blackout, tornadoes, volcanic eruptions, including rough weather is high on the list

Shopping: Don't overspend, no matter how glittery the gift in question is. You can find a good deal on a big-ticket item by comparison shopping. Some will want to use the waxing Moon and visit Las Vegas' casinos and may strike luck. Better make all your plans now and go with the New Moon. Don't stress; understand and use the stars; they are there to be used and make life easier. Share my valuable forecast from www.drturi.com with accurate guidance or offer a reading for someone's birthday or offer a comparison chart for a newly wed couple.

THU., FRI., SAT., SUN., MON. — JULY 27, 28, 29, 30, 31:

RULERS — Mercury (Transportation) and Venus (Affection).

Work, Career and Business: The Moon is finally waxing (positive) and much can happen as long as you understand how to use her energy constructively. Promote your business life now, advertise, reach the people, travel and participate in universal growth. If you do, soon your telephone will be busy and the mail will bring promising news. Get going in all your communications; use Mercury's wit to find a solution to your problems.

Partnerships: A plan is needed to succeed in your endeavor; use this trend to acquire new equipment for your office and reorganize your environment. Nothing can go wrong if you aim high and do something about it. Use Venus' "tact" to get what you need from others. Enjoy the evening with a romantic dinner talking about a potential business venture.

Family and Friends: Expect news from your brother or sister; you might get in touch with some of your friends for a good chat. Don't let Mercury get out of hand; avoid gossip; you may end up sandwiched between two friends. Use the positive Moon to promote your life and try to excel in all your wishes. Appreciate your loved ones, plan a dinner at home, or maybe rent a great movie. Kids need attention; give them some time especially if they ask for help.

Love Affairs: With Venus in the air these days, candlelight, soft music and words of love are pretty much on your mind. This is a trend loaded with good energy where nothing wrong can happen if you know how to play your cards right. A foreign person will play a considerable part in your future. If you were born in

January, a Virgo or a Taurus wants to know you. Listen to a Scorpio friend's advice.

Travel and Communication: Driving away from the city would be a good idea. The call of nature will be strong and the fresh smell of the out-of-doors, the river or sea, but keep an eye on the young ones. Drive slowly; don't spoil your day with trouble.

Environment: Many mother earth supporters will march to be heard by government officials and they will succeed in their request to save the environment. Nature may surprise some of us with a volcanic eruption.

Famous Personalities: A famous entertainer will take an important legal action. Large corporations will find strength in their new associations. Concerned groups will do much work for the welfare of children.

Events: Parts of the US, France or Japan may make interesting, even surprising news soon. The government will make important decisions to change or establish laws that will benefit children or the arts.

Shopping: You may invest in anything that will further your education or the arts. Cameras bought now will last long and take incredible pictures. Good books can also be bought and used positively for your own progression and mental exploration. Spruce yourself up by brightening your wardrobe or, if you can afford to, invest in expensive jewelry.

Welcome to Your
Day - to - Day Guidance

For August 2006

Note: Attention: Pluto doesn't care much for the waxing Moon, he is back with us — Expect dramatic happenings all over; control is a must. Don't be victims: be aware of Pluto's destructive power.

TUE., WED., THU., FRI., SAT. — AUGUST 1, 2, 3, 4, 5:

RULERS — Pluto (Drama/Death) and Jupiter (Religion/Foreigners):

Work, Career and Business: Hopefully the New Moon energy will make all of those changes positive in the long run. Push forward for the next few days; make the most of this lunation. At last the negative Supernova trend that has plagued many of us is over. You may also find out why you had to go through so much stress. Be ready for a form of rebirth and accept your limits. A new business proposition may further your entire business life. This is the time to review all your accomplishments and the reasons for your failures. Meditate on improving your future and if you feel you need to educate yourself in some area, do it now; there is no time like the present!

Partnerships: Money will play an important part in your life now, and you are advised to keep a close eye on your bank account. You may inherit a few expensive items, and this will help relieve a form of stress you had to experience. Commitments made now could become very fruitful in the long run. You may also make a commitment on paper as we are still under the blessing of the New Moon. You may decide to spend some time in nature or to visit an old Church in response to Jupiter's religious nature. Some may decide to go to the desert and "see" the creator display his face of lightening to the universe. We will all receive God's full support from the stars.

Family and Friends: Many will be enjoying foreign places and the different cultures of these people. Expect news from brothers and sisters from afar and let yourself be immersed in this great summer season. The circle of friends will be extremely busy as we are all enjoying the best of what life has to offer. Children are very excited and will be enjoying the festivities. Uranus may make them restless, and a trip out of the house is in order. Watch over them, especially close to the water. Use diplomacy at all costs; Pluto will make everyone around very susceptible to your comments. Control emotions and watch what's going on in the house, especially if there are children around. A great time is ahead of you if you listen to your intuition. A friend may bring a stranger in your house; watch the young ones closely. Be aware of Pluto and don't let him upset your life. Enjoy it all.

Love Affairs: Expect secrets of a sexual nature to surface to light and new secret affairs to be born. The planet of passion will make you feel good about yourself and will give tons of charm. Be aware of mysterious Pluto and his sensual magnetism. Do not drink too much during the evenings. Accompanying Jupiter could transform you into an irresistible sex magnet with a passionate foreigner. The Moon is still waxing, but trouble may come your way if you let your passion express itself with unprotected sex. If you're born in August be aware at home and avoid drama, an Aquarius or a Sagittarius could mean love to you.

Travel and Communication: Pluto rules ultimate power, the Mafia and the police force. News pertaining to the police force will always appear during his ruling days. I can hear Police Executives of the future, in the training Academy warning their officers of the impact of the power of Pluto and how vulnerable they all are under his destructive jurisdiction. Once the system catches up to my advanced perception of the human psyche outside of the limited field of today's research, I can foresee the use of Astrology in the police force. They so desperately need this knowledge to pinpoint suspects by using the natal profiles. The impact of Pluto to a sensitive house may predispose the suspect for murder. Most of all, in the name of ignorance, many brave public servants won't have to waste their precious lives. Time will tell.

Environment: Keep in mind that Pluto does not care much about the New Moon and could disturb the earth's belly, producing a bad earthquake. On my newsgroup weeks before the following events, I had posted this note and quatrain. "Please make a note and save this post and explore my predictions on the given dates: May 11th, 18th, 24th, and 30th, 1998. 'The tenth day and when the moon will shine in her fullest, in the month of the Bull. A digit of one's hand of destruction will rule upon the human race. Water, wind and dirt will blind many with the smell of death. Rage and destruction is the legacy, nature will speak to the mortals.' Result: - May 8, 1998- Tornadoes, windstorms sock U.S. South again- EDGEFIELD, South Carolina — In four Southern states, thousands of people began a task Friday that has become somewhat routine during this year's severe storm season. As usual with Pluto in charge, be ready for many interesting secrets to surface and remember to use these secrets to your own advantage.

Famous Personalities: A famous personality will be called to God and many will miss the soul. It will be a reminder of our own mortality and the real power of Pluto's impact upon the earth and humans below.

Events: October 7th, 1970 - Pluto will take many people away; expect this type of news again. Gene, Marshall's sports information director and play-by-play broadcaster, was among the 43 players and coaches and 32 administrators, fans and crew who died in a plane crash 25 years ago. To survive their Plutonic awful deal, the victims had to eat raw human flesh and walk through the mountains in a pure cold hell. Pluto rules death, drama and does not usually spare anyone's life. In this case the sheer will for life did the horrible trick. The Moon was New when the plane crashed and is the only reason why a few "lucky" people survived Pluto's deadly will. Do NOT TRUST any strangers now, as Pluto stirs man's animal tendencies. Pluto rules the crooks and the cops, or the infinite forces of good and evil constantly teasing each other. Thus the villains will become more active and the police will be busy trying to stop them. Of course if you are a Police officer and on duty now, don't take chances and let your fellow officers know about Pluto's jurisdiction of the police force. Make good use of my knowledge and realize that your "bosses" regardless of their high position and accomplishments are NOT aware of this fact. Many lives have been wasted in the name of ignorance; you can make a difference and even save your life by being aware of my work.

Shopping: Invest in anything that can kill pests. Use Jupiter to find a great traveling bargain or start a spiritual course in metaphysical.

SUN., MON., TUE., WED. — AUGUST 6, 7, 8, 9:

RULERS — Uranus (Extraordinary News) and Saturn (Uncle Sam Decisions):

Work, Career and Business: Expect this trend to promote surprising changes pertaining to your career. The lucky ones will benefit all the way with this ending New Moon. Make the most of the last day of the waxing Moon while you can and go after your wishes. Saturn may force you to realize what needs to be done to further your career.

Partnerships: Time to socialize this weekend as Saturn's children (CEOs) will be out in public places and many of them can further your career wishes. This trend will induce serious changes and interesting surprises in your partnerships. A business trip or an invitation may lead you to many good contacts that could prove to be rewarding in the long run. You must take the time to play and enjoy yourself with unusual people.

Family and Friends: A friend may request some money from you or another one who owes you money sincerely wants to repay, but may be in a difficult set of circumstances. Be patient; they may repay you in a better way. A friend may surprise you and may decide to get closer. Providing help is great, but let some of your friends understand their limits. Keep in mind that Uranus rules friends and wishes; do not turn down an invitation during a new Moon. With Uranus, anything great can happen and you have until the Full Moon to do so. After the full moon the surprises will be negative.

Love Affairs: As usual with Uranus be ready for nice surprises brought by friends bringing new people into your life. The Moon is still up for a short while, so those surprises should be of a positive nature. Many lucky souls will find love, and this new relationship may lead you to a rewarding future. Remember, serious Saturn is also part of the festivities and you must not overindulge. If you were born under the sign of Pisces, a Virgo, a Cancer, even a Scorpio will find you irresistible.

Travel and Communication: Your telephone and your mail will bring you all sorts of news and invitations. The lucky ones will enjoy or plan faraway trips close to those they love. Expect news from many people around and get in touch with some of your friends for a good chat. However, do not fall for gossip about other friends, as sooner or later you will have some explaining to do. Use what's left of the positive Moon to promote your life and excel in your mental capacity.

Environment: As always when Uranus is with us, a volcano could erupt soon, be ready for surprising news about the weather. Stay clear of lightning. If you're into UFOs, anything extraordinary from the heavens could happen now.

Famous Personalities: Famous people will behave in a weird way while others will offer the best of their performance and the money will be presented to organizations supporting the very old or the very young.

Events: Saturn (structure) still resides in the sign of Leo (love/children) and could induce some worries about your security. Don't let him get the best of your spirit, have faith. Financial affairs will be a concern for many, as the government will make very important decisions about other countries and wars in the world. With this very last day of the New Moon trend be careful in all you do. Uranus rules the incredible. Paranormal investigators, now is the time to carry your camera and look for UFOs in secluded places. Blackouts, explosions or bad weather could plague some parts of the US. Expect news about nuclear endeavors and electronic devices soon. (6/24/05) - Jail over Ukraine air show disaster (06.24.2005) A military court has jailed for up to 14 years pilots and organizers connected with an air show disaster in 2002 in which a fighter jet ploughed into a crowd in western Ukraine and killed 77 people. 06/28/05-(CNN) — Wal-Mart heir John Walton died Monday when his ultra light aircraft crashed after taking off from an airport in Jackson, Wyoming, the company announced.

Shopping: Purchase electronic equipment or plan a long voyage in foreign lands before the Full Moon. As always, Uranus rules the future, and his psychic powers can be used. Don't waste these days; do something original as your wishes depend on your interaction with others. Visit your favorite astrologer or psychic now. Share my valuable forecast from www.drturi.com with accurate guidance for someone's birthday, or offer a comparison chart for a newly wed couple.

Full Moon — August 9, 2006 in the explosive sign of Aquarius: — Expect some serious surprising or shocking developments to take place in the near future. NASA could make shocking news again soon, especially if they avoid using the value of the stars. This is the same energy that produced many mishaps with expense electronic equipments and the death of many courageous astronauts. Also under Uranus power the Middle East suffered the "US surprise bomb attacks" on Saddam Hussein's forces in Iraq. This energy can affect sophisticated electronic equipment and could produce bad aeronautic accidents. Unlucky children could suffer this disturbing dramatic lunation; keep an eye on all of them. They are accident-prone for a while. Just be ready to accept the upcoming changes with faith in God's desire to restructure the earth's crust. Be ready for nature's devastating forces, producing destructive weather, tornadoes, earthquakes and volcanic eruptions. Expect anything surprising, even incredible including out space manifestation to take place soon. Be ready to see the real power of Uranus, the planet of sudden releases of energy, in action. Explosions are also expected and the US, Japan or France may make disturbing news soon.

Lunation impact on all signs:

Aries - One of your wishes may take time to manifest. Simply be patient.

Taurus - Your career will see needed changes soon, be strong.

Gemini - Difficult news from far away is expected; a trip is ahead.

Cancer - Stress from your investments, a metaphysical study is needed.

Leo – Change with a partner is ahead, sign important papers.

Virgo - Change at work is ahead, concentrate on communication and hi-tech.

Libra – God created the heavens and the stars, not man-made book study.

Scorpio - You might have to review a move or a deal about your home soon.

Sagittarius - Learn about your relationship with nature, the stars, and the Indians.

Capricorn – Difficult news with money, just improve your computer skills.

Aquarius – Stress with friends, and be patient with some of your wishes.

Pisces - Move on to the future. An astrology study would do you good.

August 11, 2006 — Mercury enters Leo: This next trend's promise is a rich mixture of love, romance, creativity and children. Many thoughts will be geared towards immense feelings of both hope and true love. Souls born with Mercury in Leo will be gifted with natural managerial dispositions. Many of them will be shrewd in business, and attracted to professions offering fame and fortune. Artistic talents involving music, dancing, and painting will lead these souls toward the great fame and security they seek. This position makes for one of the most mentally domineering signs of the Zodiac where the soul will be forced to learn humility and service to others. This Mercury position will lead the soul toward success in many artistic endeavors. An opportunity to experience mental fame is also offered to the soul. The parent educated in Astropsychology will realize the child's gift and promote the new soul towards communication, acting or writing. Dr. Turi needs your help to pass on his very important star message to the world. (And get a super deal too! - see www.drturi.com or call 602-999-3010 to set a crash course on Astropsychology, Kabalistic Healing or the Astro-Tarot in your city.

August 13, 2006 - Venus enter Leo: Perfect time to contemplate launching any artistic endeavor. Giving and receiving expensive items is on the agenda for some. You may also think of traveling or investing in a car or expensive items. Souls born now will be very magnetic and dramatic in matters related to love. They will make good livings, and will attract money in artistic endeavors. Many of them will strive to find beautiful, rich and famous partners willing to experience the best of life. Some will have to learn to let go of Mr. Pride and Mrs. Ego to save true love. This position makes for one of the most dramatic but lucky signs of the Zodiac. Usually a gift in acting or other great talents is present with this position. Those souls are born to experience a flamboyant and busy love life. This is a good position of Venus promoting fame and fortune.

THU., FRI., SAT., SUN., MON. — AUGUST 10, 11, 12, 13, 14:

RULERS — Uranus (Explosions) Neptune (Deception) and Mars (War):

Work, Career and Business: We are now into the Full Moon. Listen to intangible impulses from a different plane than the physical before making important decisions. Avoid insecurity and imagination blurring your vision or your faith during this trend. Neurotic tendencies and depression come from a heavy Neptune in anyone's chart; use your will and see the bright side of your business life. You may find it hard to concentrate at work, but everything will be clear again in a couple of days. Keep emotions in control; use plenty of patience and diplomacy with co-workers or the boss at work. Try to concentrate on the future.

Partnerships: Mars is called the "Lord of war" for good reasons. Do not let him aggravate a situation, as this could hurt a friend or a loved one. The purpose of Starguide is to teach you firm control over the stars and to manage positively the outcome of any situation. If you know someone who needs help, offer this book as a birthday present. Mars also rules cars and machinery, and with deceiving Neptune around you should avoid drinking and driving (you should never do this but right now, even a little could hurt you). Danger could enter the lives of those ignorant of the celestial rules just now; beware. You will be given energy from the red planet; make good use of it by channeling the power constructively. Still, Mars' energy can help you start a new project, new business, even a new relationship. Keep a positive attitude.

Family and Friends: Help some family members see through the veil of self-deceit. Some of your friends may need spiritual support; work with them without getting emotionally involved in their problems. Again, keep away from alcohol after dark if you decide to meet them. A trip close to the water or Sea World will be rewarding. Keep a vigilant eye on the kids and your pet, as impatient drivers could hurt them. Be prudent; be patient but firm and confident. Spend some time with the children, teach them love and harmony as Mars may make them play rough. Be aware around water. Remember my prediction about children playing rough with Mars. (Moon Power 1997 page 116) Memo: Water slide collapses kills one, injures 32 — An amusement park water slide collapsed Monday June 2nd, 1997 after a group of high school seniors on a graduation outing ignored a lifeguard's warning and went down together. One student was killed and 32 were injured, six critically. Be aware; watch the kids around water.

Love Affairs: Come right out with what you feel and don't be vague in love matters. Secret love affairs will start under Neptune's deceiving power and many will end up deceived; beware whom you tell! Avoid drinking heavily and enjoy a great walk by the sea or any watery area. If you were born in April, a Leo or a Sagittarius will be strongly attracted to you. At any rate do not expect much with love now; you'd better wait for better auspices.

Travel and Communication: Some of us may experience strange things in unfamiliar places or find themselves with weird people. Keep an eye on your personal belongings and learn to rely on your gut feelings. Nevertheless, you can expect heavenly intervention in a dangerous situation. For those at sea, take all precautions as the weather could turn nasty without much notice. Plan a trip to Hawaii or any exotic islands now and try to go after the new Moon.

Environment: Disturbing news from the sea, oil and flooding is a possibility. News about medicine and chemical explosions and broken dams can also be expected. Neptune rules poisoning and infectious diseases and news from the ocean: CNN) — A 14-year-old girl died Saturday in a shark attack while swimming in the Gulf of Mexico, authorities said. Alcohol poisoning kills 41 Kenyans NAIROBI, Kenya (AP) — The number of people killed after drinking an illegal brew laced with industrial alcohol has risen to 49, police said.

Famous Personalities: Sad news regarding alcoholism, drugs and incarceration will come about the rich and famous. Some famous souls might have to learn the law and may find themselves in trouble. The release of a new movie will make some of them very happy. Certain famous people will suffer incarceration or hospitalization

Events: Depressing and explosive news will come from the Middle East. — Oil prices may rise due to another oil spill. Expect water, tornadoes, typhoons, hurricanes and earthquakes such as; August 31, 1999 - — At least one person was killed Tuesday when a strong earthquake and an aftershock shook northwestern Turkey, just two weeks after a deadly 7.4 magnitude quake left more than 14,000 dead. About oil spills, look to September 8, 1999 - EUREKA, California (AP) — Coast Guard officials have managed to clean up only a small portion of about 2,000 gallons of oil that has leaked into Humboldt Bay from a dredging vessel. The oil leak from the ruptured fuel tank of The Stuyvesant occurred Monday night after rough seas apparently tossed part of the dredging apparatus against the vessel. Part of the equipment sliced through the hull, cutting a 6-inch to 8-inch-wide hole in the tank.

Shopping: This is not a great time to invest in anything related to the spiritual arts. As a rule, musical instruments, painting and spiritual materials should be bought before the upcoming Full Moon. Invest in cleansing tools only.

TUE., WED., THU., FRI. — AUGUST 15, 16, 17, 18:

RULERS — Venus (Diplomacy) and Mercury (Dialogue):

Work, Career and Business: Fight the depressing mood you may find yourself in; you need to reach out to new people and expand the various social networks in your life. The moon might be against you, but you can still make significant progress; reorganize it all. Business started now won't bring much financial security to all parties involved. Not a time to ask for a loan from your bank or a financial favor from a friend or family member. Money and security will play an important part of this trend and you might find yourself investing in a good deal from the past that you missed earlier. You should be confident no matter what, as your will (the part of God in you) is still stronger than the Moon.

Partnerships: Candlelight, soft music, courtship and social gatherings for the upcoming weekend are on the agenda for some. The soft Venus energy will tone down the aggressiveness of many people around you. The time is upon you to make peace and apologize for your mistakes. You need to reach out to the people you know, but avoid expanding the various social networks in your life. Use finesse in all you do, you can't miss. Under Venus' blessings, you must keep in mind that whatever is offered with true love will bring luck to the giver. Abusing her kindness will bring back heavy karma and will be paid in full. Let your partner know about your deep feelings and see the good side of life.

Family and Friends: Do not turn down an invitation or a chance to socialize with old friends; weird new people will be also there waiting for you. Communication is on the fore; don't hesitate to participate in it; everybody will listen to your comments. However, avoid falling into useless gossip over the telephone —

only "Ma Bell" will benefit from that! You may hear distressing news about brothers or sisters. Use Mercury's power of expression to write those long overdue letters.

Love Affairs: Some will happily give; some will gladly receive, presents that will last forever in their hearts. Promote words of love and be aware of the feelings of others; lovely Venus will change uneasiness into love, attention and respect. You and a long-standing friend may discover that your relationship is growing towards romance and both are surprised. A dual situation may force some to make a decision, use your intuition, and keep a cool head. The lessons of the past should be remembered. If you were born in February, a Leo or a Gemini may make your life a misery. Be patient with all the people around you.

Travel and Communication: Do not expect interesting news, as your telephone might be full of distressing messages. Not a time for traveling, however, avoid the impulsive Mercurial need for speed. You might have to deal with high winds or water. It's time to express yourself, write letters and start (or finish) a book.

Environment: With the waning Moon upon us, nature may get out of hand with a bad earthquake. A monetary scandal could also make the news. A famous personality may pay a heavy price for a stupid and selfish act.

Events: A financial scandals or some secrets may reach you. Foreign affairs could be distressing for many governments, forcing some dramatic interaction soon.

Shopping: Take care of your wheels and shop around for things for the office. If you decide to purchase a second-hand car, you could strike a good bargain; don't be afraid to barter aggressively. Mercury loves mental stimulation and your wit will help you to save money. Be happy and alert — don't be afraid to use your powers of communication.

SAT., SUN., MON., TUE., WED. — AUGUST 19, 20, 21, 22, 23:

RULERS — The Moon (Ending parts of life) and the Sun (Children Matters):

Work, Career and Business: You may find yourself discussing goals for the future with someone close to you. Some will even sell their homes or move to better locations. Life is a process of constant change and this lunation will touch you or someone close to you. Make the most out of this change and trust the upcoming future. Not exactly a time to promote any endeavors, sign contracts or travel; wait for the upcoming New Moon to move or deal with important matters.

Partnerships: Time to promote only faith and confidence in all you do. This type of energy will be difficult for some as they might be forced in or out important situations. Accept those changes you may not be able to control. You might be going through a hard time now, but the Universe will pay you back in spades if you learn from your experiences and keep faith in yourself.

Family and Friends: Listen to your friends' stories and be ready for the beginning or ending of an important part of their lives. Keep in mind that the Moon is waning (negative) and those unexpected changes must be faced with courage no matter what. Give special attention to the children these days and provide them guidance if needed. Their young and fragile spirits need constant reassurance and appreciation. Also, with the Sun in charge you might stimulate their creativity and enjoy their youth and boundless energy. This energy could also work against them, and some may be accident-prone, so watch them carefully.

Love Affairs: Some people might surprise you; however, don't dream or hope for finding a lost love now. Be ready for the beginning or ending of an important part of your life. If you are stuck in the wrong relationship, this lunation will force you out of this stressful situation very soon. Accept the upcoming changes with grace and have faith in the future. Those changes will bring someone worthy of your feelings. Wait for the next upcoming New Moon to get active in your social circle again. Your friends possess all your wishes and you should spend more time with them, especially if you are single and looking for love. For those born in May, a Pisces or a Virgo will be strongly attracted to you. Enjoy a great show when possible; you need to forget a few things in your own life.

Travel and Communication: With the waning Moon affecting our psyches, tears and depression might be a problem. Keep busy, avoid negative thoughts of the past and look for positive endeavors. Free yourself from pessimistic people or stressful situations; use your will and surprise others with a formidable optimistic attitude. Be a defensive driver ever ready to give way to the crazies of the freeway. Plans to travel far may be imposed upon your life by Uncle Sam.

Environment: The weather will turn very nasty in some states, and many will lose their lives and possessions. Thousands may be forced to relocate due to dramatic experiences with nature. A loss of power is part of this trend; don't take any chances, stay safe. April 9, 1998 — 39 die in Southeast storms - At least 39 people were killed in tornadoes and thunderstorms that raked the Southeast overnight. Most of the deaths were in Alabama.

Famous Personalities: An important figure could suffer a heart attack or surgery! A naughty love affair may dramatically end. Some unlucky children could be involved in awful accidents.

Events: On a large scale, many governments may also make news that will affect all of us. Disturbing news may be coming from The US, France or Japan. Read the headlines of the past under similar stars; in NAHA, Japan — A powerful undersea earthquake rumbled through Okinawa, Taiwan and the Philippines Monday, setting off a tidal wave. The earthquake struck at 8:30 a.m. Japan time (7:30 p.m. Sunday EDT/2330 GMT Sunday) and had a preliminary magnitude of 7.7, according to Japan's Central Meteorological Agency. ATHENS — At least 27 people were killed Tuesday when a powerful earthquake struck just north of Athens, trapping dozens beneath the rubble of collapsed buildings.

Shopping: It's the perfect time to give old toys or clothes to unlucky children. Avoid spending money on expensive items for your own children. Now is not the time to find good deals in your local flea market. Spend time doing something creative; it doesn't have to be a masterpiece, just something to ease your spirit. We are getting closer to the New Moon and all will be much better soon.

New Moon — August 25, 2006 in Leo: This sign is ruled by the Sun, thus affairs of love and romance will be on the rise. Expect some surprises this month; the stars are giving you the possibility to reach one of your important wishes if you try hard within the next two weeks. This lunation could play an important part in your love life, with your children, your wishes, and will surely improve your relationships. You may also be forced to let go of a deteriorating love involvement and experience a new one. This month promises to be very interesting for many of us. Make the most of this incredible time; don't waste it. Leo rules France and Italy; expect news from those countries soon.

Lunation impact on all signs

Aries - Love is on the rise and a project will turn out. Take chances now.

Taurus - Plan to move or improve your surroundings, throw a party and find love.

Gemini - Great news from foreign lands, take a trip or a study on photography.

Cancer - Great news about money; you may invest in an expensive item.

Leo - A new door for love, light, children and success will open to you.

Virgo - A possibility to do something with love or children is ahead for you.

Libra - A friend will bring you good wishes socialize to get it.

Scorpio - Your career will see important and constructive changes soon.

Sagittarius - Traveling, speaking and publishing is on the agenda for you.

Capricorn - Others fortune will touch you financially, study deep matters.

Aquarius - You will be in demand for love and for fame, travel now.

Pisces - A great opportunity to improve your health and your work is given to you.

THU., FRI., SAT., SUN. — AUGUST 24, 25, 26, 27:

RULERS — Mercury (Traveling /Siblings) and Venus (Love/Promise):

Work, Career and Business: You may find yourself in an awkward or difficult situation with a co-worker, and something must be done soon. Don't let this stressful situation in your working life become a major problem for you and others; handle your affairs with discretion and dignity. Meditate for insight; use your intuition and be patient; the right opportunity is on the way. Use the new Moon to push forward.

Partnerships: With the new Moon upon you, much transformation will take place soon. However, avoid getting into a heated argument with a friend or an acquaintance who will challenge you about politics at work or your personal philosophy of life. Be patient and tolerant.

Family and Friends: Expect interesting news from close friends or family members and provide them with some spiritual support. Avoid gossip, and make sure that what you say is actually what you mean, as others could interpret it the wrong way. Nothing really can happen to you now; have faith in the stars and your new future.

Love Affairs: Romance is on your mind and therefore you may consider a trip with your special someone. An important person close to you may be a challenge to understand; just realize that none of us is perfect. A desire for a permanent commitment from a lover or the chance to find love this weekend has a good possibility of working out. You may find yourself focusing on personal relationships; you feel better with others' approval. Don't be tempted to let sadness or depression or the ending of a situation get the best of you. This emotional approach to decision-making can be the source of strife; use diplomacy and coordinate your efforts with your mate's. If you were born in June, a Libra or an Aquarius could denote love to you. Make the most of this New Moon; with Venus' touch you can't go wrong.

Travel and Communication: Take extra time in explaining yourself, as the possibility of miscommunication is high and ill will could ensue. Venus will see to it that there is harmony these days. Also, emotions may run high and could affect your words; make sure they are well thought out and supportive. Remember, Mercury rules transportation, and impatient drivers could promote accidents. Time to take care of your car's brakes, oil or anything else it may need, as you might have to take a journey soon.

Environment: Expect difficult news about the ocean or a chemical accident. News of medicine and hospitals may also come your way. The weather will not be too cooperative and many thousands of people might have to relocate due to nature's devastating forces.

Famous Personalities: News of hospitalization, drugs or alcohol may plague the media as the rich and famous won't be able to hide their dependency.

Events: Leaders of the Middle East may surprise some of their neighbors. Religion and many difficult topics such as abortion or chemical warfare will trouble the world.

Shopping: This is surely a great time to invest in anything you need to make your home a better or safer place to live. You may also invest money in shopping for clothes, plants, food and little surprises for your loved ones.

Note: We may be in a new Moon period, but be alert of Pluto's power upon us for a few days. As always with the Lord of Hades, expect dramatic happenings all over; control is a must. Anything you say or do now will have serious repercussions in your and other's future. Be aware of Pluto's emotional and dramatic nature.

MON., TUE., WED., THU. — AUGUST 28, 29, 30, 31:

RULERS — Pluto (drama) and Jupiter (law enforcement):

Work, Career and Business: Don't be Pluto's victim; avoid all confrontations. Emotion, destruction, hate and crime are all part of Pluto's signature. You are aware of Pluto; many others are not! Compromise in the office and don't let the stinger of the beast get to you. Sarcasm is the last thing you need to use just now. You will be forced to recognize many of your errors and your limits. A wake-up call for some dreamers is ahead.

Partnerships: The crooks and the police are going to be busy; avoid the unsafe or unknown. Pluto's power is not for unity but discord and will affect the masses, including your very own relationships. Do not participate in large gatherings, as death may strike anytime, anywhere, against the unaware. Secrets like Whitewater, RTC's allegations, sex scandals, police, CIA, and FBI's wrong doings will be divulged to the public. Expect news pertaining to AIDS, abortion and religious groups to make the news once more. I fully predicted the Rodney King dilemma the WA sniper attacks and the awful Rancho Santa Fe mass suicide in my Moon Power and this type of dilemma will always take place under a Plutonic trend. Both Chiefs of police Burgreen (San Diego) and Daryl Gate (Los Angeles) received my mail and predictions but never took notice of my guidance. When will the police authorities wake up to true knowledge and save lives?

Family and Friends: The influence of benevolent Jupiter should tone down Pluto's desire for drama. Participate in promoting cosmic consciousness among friends and family, and share your knowledge about Pluto's destructive energy. Build up good karma for yourself and let them know about the energies that control them — share your knowledge. The good thing about Pluto is that you, your friends and family members will all be forced to realize their limits and do something about any and all aggravated situations. Stay alert! Be patient and practice super diplomacy during this trend. Use the secrets you hear to your advantage and don't repeat them to others!

Love Affairs: The real you, the raw you, and the plain truth around you and its impact in your life, will force you to mutate or transform with your newly acquired knowledge. Expect secrets pertaining to sex and money, but most of all stay calm in your dealings. Take smart precautions if you are going to be sexually active. If you were born under water or an earth sign, a Cancer, a Scorpio or a Pisces can either go crazy for you or against you.

Travel and Communication: You had better stay and enjoy your home, read a good book or watch a movie! Observe and listen to your intuition. The less you talk the less chance of being hurt. Control your own thoughts; don't fall for jealousy or depression. If you must take the road, be extremely prudent and don't trust any strangers. Watch the children; the vampires are out. Mention my work to your friend by suggesting www.drturi.com and let them learn about real astrology. You may also offer him a copy of the current Starguide Moon Power for his birthday.

Environment: We are still in a waxing moon period, but let's hope that Pluto won't stir a tragedy with nature's devastating forces like an earthquake or a series of floods. Anything dramatic can happen now; let's pray for the victims of the planet of death. If you are a law enforcement officer or a security guard, be extremely cautious, as violent and dangerous karmic souls will roam the streets. Remember, the Rodney King beating also took place under Pluto, and those who lost control over their emotions will have forever to pay the ultimate price. The legacy of this action that took place on that night transformed later on into the Los Angeles riots where disorder and fires ruled the nights. Be ready for news such as Sept.14, 1999 - - Hurricane Floyd tore through the Bahamas on Tuesday, uprooting trees, shearing off roofs and hurling debris into buildings as frightened tourists and residents hunkered down in shelters or barricaded houses to wait out the monstrous storm.

Famous Personalities: Lots of people die under Pluto's rule and those who had a significant life will also have a significant departure from this world. The same energy may also remove a famous public figure in a secret way where drugs, sex, and rock and roll are never far away. Eldridge Cleaver, the 1960s Black Panther activist and fugitive who later swung to the other side of the political spectrum to become a Republican, died at the age of 62 under a Plutonic trend. Pluto rules the police force and brings the hidden facts to life. There can be a form of rebirth, a new part of life for the parties involved and for some, million-dollar lawsuits!

Events: This is a particularly destructive time, even in a good Moon, and I want you to be aware of everything around you and your loved ones. Under Pluto's power, May 1997, a brutal slaying follows a beer drinking in Central Park, New York. Two teenagers stabbed a real estate agent at least 30 times and tried to chop off his hands so police couldn't use fingerprints to identify him before dumping him in a lake in Central Park. The perpetrators, Daphne Abdela, 15, and her boyfriend, 15-year-old Christopher Vasquez, "gutted the body so it would sink." Both of those young souls were born in the dramatic Pluto "Death Wish Generation." See Pluto's impact upon generations or order any of my two new books "And God Created the Stars" and "The Power of the Dragon" to learn more about this phenomenon. On 12/26/05 Pluto was stopped just in time.

Some unlucky souls will have to undergo sorrow and loss such as those 3 kids mentioned above. Be ready to help those in need as the favor may hit close to home. Expect the weather to be harsh and crime to be high such as 'Calm' gunman walks into church, kills 7 before committing suicide on September 16, 1999 - — Police on Thursday sought a motive for the nation's latest killing rampage, a shooting spree that began when a man spewing anti-Baptist rhetoric burst into a church service for teen-agers and opened fire.

Shopping: A great time to purchase anything related to metaphysics or look for a good attorney. Anything related to checkups, investigations or cleansing is under good stars. Do not invest in dangerous tools or weapons just now.

Welcome to Your
Day - to - Day Guidance

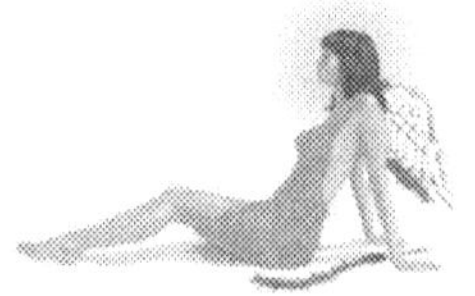

For September 2006

September 6, 2006 — Venus enters Virgo: A perfect time to concentrate on your health and launch an exercise program or a diet. Giving and receiving plants or flowers are on the agenda for some. You may also decide to invest in some good deals with clothing. Souls born now will be quite critical in matters related to love. They will concentrate and achieve perfection in many of their artistic endeavors. Many of them will strive to find a "perfect" and hard working partner willing to exchange a love/career relationship in their lives. Some will have to learn to be less critical of the world around them in order to avoid loneliness. This position makes for one of the most practical and enjoyable business or emotional partners. Usually a gift in dealing with details and an interest in health matters are present with this position. These souls are born to experience love on a practical level. This is a great Venus position producing success in the medical or clothing fields. Plants or gardens are needed around these souls.

FRI., SAT., SUN., MON., TUE., WED. — SEPTEMBER 1, 2, 3, 4, 5, 6:

RULERS — Saturn (Politics/Boss) and Uranus (Explosions/Surprises):

Work, Career and Business: Better keep an eye on your attitude as eccentric Uranus could jeopardize your job or image. With the waxing Moon, some of your wishes may take place. Keep in mind that sometimes a full breakdown is needed if you hope for restoration. Be ready for anything to happen these days and accept the challenges with a sunny disposition. A beginning and ending of an important phase of your life is about to take place. Many ingenious ideas of rebuilding or investing will come to fruition during this trend.

Partnerships: Like Pluto, Uranus is a rebel and he likes to destroy relationships, so caution is also advised in all you do or say to others. Be patient or suffer the consequences of impetuosity. The light is green for friendship and hope, and so much can happen if you participate in life. Try something different this weekend; you'll be surprised by the payoff. Throw a party; you may bring a wish to you or a dear friend.

Family and Friends: Help a friend in trouble and meditate on the world around you. The more positive people think, the more definite things will happen in this world. Don't turn down any opportunity to socialize, but be responsible with children. Some of them need to burn off some energy and will be begging for a boisterous outdoor romp. A trip close to nature or to the nearest electronic attraction will do wonders for the entire family. Make the most of what is left of this New Moon trend.

Love Affairs: Absolutely anything can happen this weekend; stay alert and participate with the best of your social life. A chance to find love or reach a dream will be given to you if you try hard enough. You may encounter funny people or be involved in strange situations; make the most of it. If you were born in June, a Libra or a Sagittarius will want to know you.

Travel and Communication: Your desire to travel will become intense. Some will plan a very long trip by airplane. As always, make your plans and try to travel after the New Moon. Be gentle with words and realize your inner mental power; promote your future. Remember, the future is the reincarnation of all your thoughts and you may use the universal mind to influence your fate. Knowledge is power.

Environment: I have noticed also that the sudden release of Uranus' energy has in the past produced serious explosions and terrible accidents such as the US shuttle explosion, so be aware of his discharging power. Both US attacks on Iraq happened under his command and I wonder if our Presidents were just lucky or if they follow the advice of wise astrologers! Remember, Uranus rules the future; computers, avionics, atomic and aeronautics, and both wars were very much "electronics-oriented with the introduction of the Patriot missiles." Keep in mind that Uranus also rules earthquakes and volcanoes; many surprising things take place on these particular days. Be ready for the ending of important phases of your life and expect the government to make serious decisions pertaining to other countries. Japan, France and China will be on the news soon. Expect news such as September 20, 1999 - 6:01 p.m. ET when a powerful earthquake rocketed Taiwan, toppling buildings and knocking out power across the island. The U.S. Geological Survey measured this quake at a preliminary magnitude of 7.6. A series of aftershocks added to the chaos.

Famous Personalities: Many "crazy" souls will fall for Uranus' desire for originality and some will do all they can to make weird news. Famous people will be caught doing silly things, such as a movie star slapping a police officer, or a well-known actor caught having sex in a car with a prostitute, not to mention a famed British singer caught doing weird things in a public restroom. Japanese and French personalities may also make the news. Some scientists will gain fame for their accomplishments.

Events: During a Saturn (traditions) and Uranus (changes) trend, Iranian voters stunned the experts and their country's conservative rulers by choosing as president a man who is considered open-minded, intellectual and tolerant. If you are into UFOs, now is the time to look for them. Uranus nuclear devices and rules the incredible. Extraterrestrials may need this sophisticated Uranian energy to manifest themselves in our dense physical world. Don't forget your video camera! Uranus also helps produce explosions, volcanoes, earthquakes, tornadoes etc., so be prepared to hear about these kinds of situations.

Shopping: The futuristic spirit of Uranus rejects anything religious or traditional and promotes the new age. Uranus hates dogma and needs to deals with the future only. Use his advanced energy to tap into your own subconscious or visit your local psychic or astrologer. Remember that you get what you pay for, so not to give your psyche to unprofessional that may need more help than you do. Others may just decide to update their stereo equipment or buy some of those flashy trendy fashions as seen on those famous Paris runways.

September 8, 2006 — Mercury enters Libra: A trend loaded with communication related to peace, treaties, justice, partners, contracts, legal activity, marriage and divorce. Many thoughts will be geared towards finding a better working environment or a new business partner. Souls born now will be gifted with a natural ability for diplomacy and "savoir faire." The opportunity to learn everything under the sun is offered to the soul. Many of them will be born with aptitudes for judicial investigation and psychology. Some will be attracted to the professions that offer artistic skills, such as interior designing. Fame and fortune will come to the writers and teachers. Artistic talents in harmony and mental health will lead these souls toward the balance they seek. This position makes for one of the most well balanced signs of the Zodiac. The soul must avoid being too diplomatic with others and may be suffering a lack of expression and direction. However, an opportunity to experience justice, real love and harmony is offered to the advanced souls.

Full Moon – September 7, 2006 in Pisces: Expect serious news coming from the Middle East oil and religion. Don't let this depressive moon get the best of you. Learn how to read Moon Power and be aware of the power of Neptune. Read "SOS To The World" from my home page.

Memo: The same Neptunian energy produced the terrorists WTC destruction of September 11 in New York. Two years prior to the attack read what I wrote in Moon Power. This exact portion of Moon Power and my message was posted on my site two weeks prior to the destruction of both towers.

Pisces rules the Middle East, religion, drugs, alcohol, deception, the difficult abortion dilemma, the Pope, the church, oil, etc. This could also mean bad news for denominations where religious figures will "pass over." Deception, illusion and secret affairs are on the agenda. This lunation marks a significant point involving the US and the Middle East conflict and will negatively affect the young generation. Many souls will suffer this disturbing lunation. Just be ready to provide as much help as needed and do not lose faith in the future. More devastating forces producing destructive weather and floods will make themselves known in the very near future. Expect a general feeling of hopelessness to plague the media and church authorities. Deceiving news will take place and affect many of us; some desperate souls will fall for Neptune's suicidal tendencies, and some will end up in jail or mental institutions. This trend will be very difficult for some, but do not lose faith in yourself and trust the Universe; get all the help you can to fight Neptune's depressing tendencies. Amuse yourself, keep busy and let go of the past. Life must go on. Anticipate shocking news about volcanoes, earthquakes, tornadoes, etc. Expect anything surprising, even incredible to happen soon; see in action the real power of both Uranus ruling sudden releases of energy, and Saturn forcing the government to take drastic action.

Lunation impact on all signs:

Aries - Forget the past and build new confidence. Many love you.

Taurus - A friend could become a problem stay clear of deceiving people.

Gemini - More challenges involving your position in the world, be patient.

Cancer - Some foreigners could prove to be burdensome, learn their differences.

Leo - Don't get sued, do the right thing, drama is ahead but you'll do fine.

Virgo - Use your head, let go of your heart, wrong people are around you.

Libra - Don't put stress on your health because of your work. Relax your feet.

Scorpio - Love, romance and children need serious attention, if not-you're history.

Sagittarius - Stress coming from home, family or real estate is ahead.

Capricorn - Avoid depression and stay clear of Prozac, sad mail is ahead.

Aquarius - You'll experience financial stress, be more practical with money.

Pisces - The stars are against you for a while, swim upstream, have faith. Don't drink.

THU., FRI., SAT., SUN. SEPTEMBER 7, 8, 9, 10:

RULERS — Neptune (Deception/Religion) and Mars (War/Army):

Work, Career and Business: Make the most of what is left of this waxing Moon. Be practical at work and clean around the office and don't challenge authority. Don't initiate actions these days and slow down. With Neptune in charge, many of your wishes to further your career may just be a deceiving dream and you should be practical in your expectations of all the promises made.

Partnerships: The Full Moon's energy will induce depression to some sensitive souls. Hope and activity will once again show the way to a better future after the New Moon, just be patient. Neptune will sharpen your intuition and your creativity; many will ask you for direction in their personal lives. Support your partner and build self-confidence. Peace of mind can be found close to the water.

Family and Friends: Give spiritual support to those you care for, but don't get emotionally involved in their personal problems. Don't let them waste too much of your time talking or complaining over the telephone. If you feel blue yourself, know that it is Neptune's deceiving power and use your will to fight him. At home, stimulate love and attention to the ones around you and be careful of fire (Mars) or water (Neptune). As always, don't overindulge in alcohol, as it will only make things worse. Narcotics will only further those gloomy thoughts of your past and promote accidents. A trip to the local playhouse or a Movie Theater may be just what your soul needs for inspiration. For those with a laid-back attitude, some good tunes and a walk by the ocean will do the trick. Get close to God and meditate about your life in general; Neptune may reward you magically.

Love Affairs: Under Neptune's auspices, secret love affairs flourish. Whatever you choose to do, make a solid decision about your own relationship and be aware of deception. Aggressive Mars may stimulate your desire for action; dancing and music would be a good outlet. Mars is far from being diplomatic; use gentleness if you intend to have a smooth evening. If you were born under the sign of Virgo, a Pisces or a Taurus needs your help.

Travel and Communication: Use Neptune's dreamy nature, and consider spending time by the water away from the city's stressful activities. If you have to drive a long way, remember to take plenty of rest beforehand, because dreamy Neptune could make you sleepy. Some will have to take a trip to the hospital to visit a person. Others may hear deceiving news about a legal decision pertaining to arrest and imprisonment. Come clear with what you mean these days and control your imagination. Watch your possessions.

Environment: Mars is an aggressive planet. Like Pluto he could put stress on some of the earth's faults, producing tremors and terrifying the inhabitants above. This negative trend of calamities will be with us for a while, and caution is advised in all you do. Let's hope that Mars will be tolerant for the people living on this earth and play somewhere else in those worlds above and below us.

Famous Personalities: The cinematography industry will prepare many great movies, and numerous actors and actresses will parade all over. Some will be caught doing the wrong thing at the wrong time and others will pay a visit to an "alcoholics anonymous" organization. The unlucky ones will be caught doing something nasty and will pay a heavy price for it.

Events: With this powerful duo, Neptune (oceans) and Mars (explosions) the worst that could happen is another devastating oil spill or chemical explosion. Mars is a warrior and favors accidents on the road. Be extremely careful when driving. Boating is something you should forget about, especially after the Full Moon. Bad news from the Middle East and terrorist activities will trouble the media.

Shopping: Use Neptune's sensitivity to further artistic talents and become more creative. Finishing a metaphysical study will favor this lunation. Visit your spiritual friend but avoid a trip into your future; Neptune will blur his intuition. Neptune will offer bargains on alcohol and paint, and by Mars sharp tools, but invest in those items before the Full Moon. Do not invest in any chemicals or dangerous tools during this lunation.

September 13, 2006 — Mercury enters Libra: A trend loaded with communication related to peace, treaties, justice, partners, contracts, legal activity, marriage and divorce. Many thoughts will be geared towards finding a better working environment or a new business partner. Souls born now will be gifted with a natural ability for diplomacy and "savoir faire." The opportunity to learn everything under the sun is offered to the soul. Many of them will be born with aptitudes for judicial investigation and psychology. Some will be attracted to the professions that offer artistic skills, such as interior designing. Fame and fortune will come to the writers and teachers. Artistic talents in harmony and mental health will lead these souls toward the balance they seek. This position makes for one of the most well balanced signs of the Zodiac. The soul must avoid being too diplomatic with others and may be suffering a lack of expression and direction. However, an opportunity to experience justice, real love and harmony is offered to the advanced souls.

September 11, 2006 - The anniversary of 9/11 and the memory of what took place on these days will affect many people all over the world. All the memorable activities will take place just before the New Moon at the lowest time of the month, thus many souls will suffer this depressive lunation. Just be ready to provide as much help as needed and do not lose faith in the future.

MON., TUE., WED., THU. — SEPTEMBER: 11, 12, 13, 14:

RULERS — Mars (War News) Venus (Diplomats) and Mercury (Talks).

Work, Career and Business: The most evil of all these planets is to be expected due to the pessimistic trend of the Full Moon. Do not fall for depression and self-defeating attitudes. The stars have a specific role to play and you are an actor on the big stage of life. Go with the trend; do not force issues, be patient for a few days. At work keep a low profile; your co-workers and your boss may not be aware of the work of the Moon on their own psyches, and could become "lunatic." Keep busy on Wednesday and rearrange your desk or your paperwork. Use patience.

Partnerships: If you want to save trouble in your relationship, now is the time to use full diplomacy and understanding. Don't let the waning Moon make you feel down or "moody." If you experienced trouble with the one you care about, you could make up with a romantic dinner at home. With Pluto in Sagittarius much of your thoughts will be spiritually oriented. Use Venus as much as you can to uplift any difficult situation.

Family and friends: Disturbing situations involving friends or family members will come to the fore. Take the time to review all the reasons and find a way to make peace with the party involved. Mercury rules communication and will help you pass on your thoughts deeply and correctly. Provide a helping hand, but do not let disrespectful friends take the best of your spirit. Emotions will run high these days; keep a cool head.

Love Affairs: Many will feel the desire to further romance at home. However, new love affairs started now will need much work to survive. Many unsuited couples will also be forced out of their unhealthy relationships. Mars (the desire principle) may induce attractive foreigners into your life. Because of the waning Moon, the general feeling will be geared towards destructive behavior, even violence. Many young souls will find themselves fighting with someone about an ideal love. They will be forced to realize the limits of their actions and Mars will destroy the old degrading relationship. You cannot build a new house under weak or unsuitable foundations, so the stars may decide to free you soon. If you were born in October, a Gemini or a Sagittarius will drive you nuts.

Travel and Communication: Mercury will pass on all sorts of news. Use his power to convey your ideas to those willing to listen. Work on improving your cosmic consciousness and do some "deep" reading concerning life and death or metaphysics. You should finish or a start a book if you are into writing. Be aware on the road and take care of your wheels.

Environment: Following the Full Moon, tornadoes, high winds, earthquakes, and aeronautical accidents due to bad weather are very high on the list. The earth is alive and she needs to stretch herself now and then. Stay safe and be prudent on the road. Expect difficult news about the ocean or a chemical accident. News of medicine and hospitals may also come your way. The weather will not be too co-

operative and many thousands of people might have to relocate due to nature's devastating forces.
CNN)8/10/05 — An explosion at a hazardous waste plant rocked suburban Detroit late Tuesday, sending fireballs and billowing smoke hundreds of feet in the air.
CNN - 08/06/05: BEIJING, China (Reuters) — Typhoon Matsa battered China's eastern coast with strong winds and heavy rain on Saturday morning, killing one and forcing more than a million people to flee their homes, state media reported.

Famous Personalities: A famous personality will see the end of his life. Many will miss the Great Spirit. Rumors from a powerful politician in the Middle East could vex the media soon.

Events: As usual after the Full Moon, stay clear of the crazy crowd and listen to your intuition at all times.

Shopping: Rent anything; do not buy anything new now. Take care of your car as she may decide to let you down at the wrong time and in the wrong place. Be cautious and be patient.

FRI., SAT., SUN., MON., TUE. — SEPTEMBER 15, 16, 17, 18, 19:

RULERS: The Moon (New Starts/Moving) and the Sun (Love/Children).

Work, Career and Business: The general mood will be depressing. You can expect a serious beginning or ending of important parts of your (and others') life. Be ready for those upcoming progressive variations. Keep in mind that life is a constant process of change and even if you don't realize it, the stars are working for your benefit. With Mercury (communication) in Scorpio (directness), avoid sarcasm with others. Be patient with everyone around the office.

Partnerships: You will be forced to let go of negative people in your life and disturbing situations. You must take a chance on the new future with faith. Many will experience the closing of a destructive relationship and others may see the new beginning. Under these stars any new relationship is doomed to fail in the long run. Further the positive only and don't fall for the waning Moon.

Family and Friends: The Sun rules love, romance and children, but we are still under a difficult trend, so this energy won't bring you good news. The Sun gives life to children, but watch over them especially close to the water. On a more positive note he will put his undiscriminating light on many secrets. Friends will need spiritual support; give love and attention and build good karma for yourself.

Love Affairs: Be ready for new starts in love matters and provide a solid shoulder for the victims suffering a broken heart. The right partner might not be the one you were with; use the newfound freedom to look (after the New Moon) for someone who really deserves your love. Under the Sun's command, the lucky ones will find great happiness with true love relationships. A new arrival is to be expected by a young couple. If you are a Scorpio, a Cancer or a Taurus, this lunation could induce serious stress in your life. A Virgo friend has a good discernment for you; you must listen.

Travel and Communication: You may be asked to go home and see mom. Be aware on the road; WE are under a Supernova window trend! Do not trust any driver and be ready for sudden action. Under the same destructive stars in LIMA, Peru — A Peruvian air force plane carrying civilians fleeing El Niño-driven floods crashed into a canal that cuts through a shantytown in the northern city of Piura Sunday morning, killing at least 28 people. Surprises are on the way and the people from your past will come into the picture soon. Expect this type of news again and again - Death toll jumps in London commuter train crash - A shattering train collision near Paddington Station during rush hour Tuesday morning killed at least 26 people and injured scores. Police said more bodies were still trapped in the tangled wreckage of the crash, which happened in Ladbroke Grove in west London, about a mile (1.2 km) from the Notting Hill neighborhood.

Environment: What was once built by man (cities/homes) or nature must be destroyed; what was once born must eventually die, and this is the grand cycle of life. Recycling is the key word in nature and not anything is really wasted. There is nothing one can do other than accept the ultimate changes imposed by God, and usually the future offers better.

Famous personalities: Expect interesting but not necessarily positive surprises with the rich and famous. Be ready for the unexpected in their words and actions. Don't take chances unless you know what you're in for and be prudent.

Events: Large quakes and nature forces may force thousands of victims to relocate to rebuild a new life. Terrible tragedies such as the Kobe, Japan earthquake and many volcanic eruptions have happened under this configuration and thousands of people were forced out of their homes because of nature's destructive forces. Expect news such as -. The Mexican government declared a state of emergency Tuesday in four states where rampant flooding has caused seven rivers to overflow, killing at least 15 people and forcing the evacuation of more than 100,000. . Swollen rivers and mudslides have killed at least 83 people throughout Mexico, officials said Thursday. - The rains that flooded 10 states in eastern and southern Mexico have driven more than 157,000 people from their homes. Several hurt as quake rattles southwest Turkey.

Shopping: Buy anything for children as long as it is not new. This is a great time to get rid of the extra stuff clogging the house or the garage, and a garage sale would not be a bad idea. Do not invest in silver, gold or expensive items. Anything to clean the house will do you well.

****

New Moon — September 22, 2006 in the practical, health-oriented sign of Virgo: Much progress is ahead of you in terms of employment and foreign affairs. Mercury rules this critical sign, so the affairs of work and health will be on the rise. Expect an overwhelming feeling of perfection and an unusual worry about health and working on foreign grounds; do not let this lunation pressure you. This trend will play an important part in your health and working life and in some ways will affect your environment. You may be forced to let go of a deteriorating working situation and forced into a new one. The emphasis is on the body (perfect health) and the mind (education) to perform efficiently in serving the world at large. All the changes you may be forced to experience are positive in nature, and will in the long run further your deep desire for a better state of affairs.

Lunation impact on all signs:

Aries - A great opportunity will be offered for your health or your work.

Taurus - Your love life will improve, you may hear about a birth soon.

Gemini - You may have to consider doing something from home or relocate soon.

Cancer - A great study or a new health program will appeal to you, talk to your siblings.

Leo - Great news involving your finances and your self-esteem is ahead.

Virgo - The stars shine on you, you can't loose, make the most of them.

Libra - A secret will bring light to your world. Let go of the past.

Scorpio - A friend has a wish for you, socialize more these days.

Sagittarius - Your career is moving on the right direction, if not study computers.

Capricorn - News from far away or a trip will make you happy, study and rewards.

Aquarius - Some unexpected financial help will bring joy to your life.

Pisces - A chance to face the world with a new emotional or business partner is ahead.

WED., THU., FRI., SAT. — SEPTEMBER 20, 21, 22, 23:

RULERS — The Sun (Hope) Mercury (Important Talks) and Venus (Peace Talks).

Work, Career and Business: You are close to a new fresh breath of life; this New Moon will make your life much easier. Wait for her upcoming white light, and then take your opportunities. Do not try to push your business until she lights up. Advertisements, important calls, traveling, and meetings will pay off if you learn to wait for the green light. Use "Moon power" wisely and respect the Universal Law. Knowledge is power; have faith in your abilities.

Partnerships: Mercury rules the mail, telephone and communications in general; expect disturbing mail to reach you. Deal with it now and clean up the situation before the New Moon. A get-together after work could also be a great idea; Mercury will have everyone "gossiping."

Family and Friends: The very last days of the waning moon will sap your spiritual and physical energy. Help those in need to clean up their mess generated by karmic experiences. Let no one exhaust your spirit, and show no frustration to loved ones. Some of your friends need spiritual regeneration, even a helping hand; as usual do so but realize your limits. Use Venus' generosity and show your love to everyone. Avoid spending too much time on the telephone with a depressing person.

Love Affairs: Your spiritual life will expand with Uranus (future) crossing its own Aquarius (astrology) sign. Don't be too picky or demanding with those for whom you care; no one is perfect. However, use your head not your heart with someone who drinks too much, and realize your limits if you are in a deceiving relationship. With Venus around, the opportunity to find love will be given to you after the New Moon. If you were born in September you may decide to work harder on your diet or your looks. A friend born in July has a few thoughts for you. You may also use Uranus in Aquarius to learn all about your partner with comparison chart for the two of you. Now is the perfect time to apply your will and start a spiritual Astropsychology, Kabalistic Healing or Astro-Tarot course (see www.drturi.com or call 602-957-1617 to help us to set a crash course in your area and get a super deal on the full tuition).

Travel and Communication: You may feel like traveling either physically or spiritually, make the most of an upcoming opportunity. Get your wheels in action; prepare for traveling under the protection of the upcoming New Moon.

Environment: Recharge your batteries; a trip to the mountains is strongly recommended. Both Mercury and Venus will make you appreciate the beauty of Mother Nature. Many environmentalists will make serious progress and get the attention they deserve. Sad news from the ocean or the Middle East may reach the media soon.

Famous Personalities: A famous person will promote a new product pertaining to health. News of water management is also on the horizon. A notorious religious person could make depressing news soon.

Events: We are not yet out of trouble as the Moon is still waning for a few more days. Thus, Mother Nature may decide to disturb us with bad weather. Negative news may come from the ocean or the water. Be aware of abductors; this type of energy has swiftly taken many children away and also a plane away from its initial course. Expect this type of news soon — Rescuers desperately searched for survivors of mudslides in eastern Mexico on Saturday, digging into collapsed hillsides in hope of finding signs of life from a disaster that killed nearly 300 by Friday night.

Shopping: Do not poison your mind with imagination and fears of the apocalyptic end times. Use your own positive thinking to avoid negativity entering your life or your body. Some may decide to join spiritual groups or invest in far away trips. Anything to clean can only be a good thing to buy now.

Note: Even though it is a New Moon, Pluto is back and caution is a necessity. As always with the Lord of hell in charge of this trend, better think twice before saying or acting on impulse. Expect secrets to be divulged, affairs of sex, and nature's devastating forces to be at work. The police and blackguards will make the news. More than ever, use diplomacy, as whatever you do now will have very serious repercussions in your life.

SUN., MON., TUE., WED. — SEPTEMBER 24, 25, 26, 27:

RULERS —Pluto (Death /Secrets) Venus (Passionate Love) and Jupiter (Law).

Work, Career and Business: You are now walking on a fine razor blade and it's windy. You know what I mean! You'd better use all the "savoir faire" you know. A serious wake-up call will come to many unaware skeptics of predictive Divine Astrology's powers. The possibility to lose it all (and rebuild it) will be a serious matter for some karmic souls. You will be able to see exactly what's wrong in your business life soon. The new Moon will help you make all the changes needed. Have faith in yourself.

Partnerships: Many ugly secrets may surface now. You could learn something sexual or financial about a partner. Keep his trust; do not divulge the secret. Money will play an important part of this trend; listen to your intuition in all you do. Venus will help tone down the stress induced by Pluto.

Family and Friends: Be patient with all. Do not expect anyone you care about to be diplomatic to you during this trend if Venus (diplomacy) is weak in his or her chart. Again, do not fall for Pluto's destructive or sarcastic remarks; words of love will pay off in the long run. Be ready for some dramatic news from someone close to you. Whatever happens, be strong; life must go on. Pluto will work to your benefit.

Love Affairs: Passion is in the air. Secret affairs involving sex and passion may be publicly divulged, forcing people to take stands to destroy and rebuild relationships. This might happen to you too. In any case, use tons of diplomacy to save unwanted trouble in your love life. If you are a water sign such as Scorpio, Pisces or Cancer, this lunation will touch you directly. Leos must take it easy at home and avoid traumatic experiences involving the police force.

Travel and Communication: Expect news pertaining to the police force and crooks. Nature's destructive forces will be obvious in some parts of the world. Be careful of what you do or say during this trend. Drive carefully, and stay clear of weird strangers and strange places. Again, if you learn about someone else's secret, do not tell, you may be asking for trouble. Your intuition will be accurate; listen to the little voice within.

Environment: Pluto belongs to the Divine family and has specific regenerative work to accomplish, and his impact on earth and its people is needed. As Pluto destroys it all, he also gives the opportunity to rebuild stronger and better. Be ready for all sorts of dramatic news everywhere. Stay safe; don't try the devil. Many people will lose their precious lives. Expect such news COLLEGE STATION, Texas — Had Brandon Kallmeyer dozed off and let his truck slide onto the shoulder almost anywhere else, he might have simply awakened and steered back onto the highway. But police said Kallmeyer tragically veered off a straight, flat four-lane road at precisely the place where a group of college students had gathered en route to a fraternity party, leaving six dead. GABORONE, Botswana (AP) — A disgruntled airline pilot today commandeered an Air Botswana plane at the country's main airport, circled above and crashed it into two planes on the ground in a suicide mission. More ACALAMA, Mexico — The danger of new erosion forced rescuers to abandon their search for victims of another landslide in southeastern Mexico that has left as many as 170 dead.

Famous Personalities: Some famous people will be called back to God. A famous person's secrets will be made available to the media. Expect news such as Death of a legend: NBA great Wilt Chamberlain found dead at his home in LOS ANGELES — Wilt Chamberlain, a center so big, agile and dominant that he forced basketball to change its rules and the only player to score 100 points in an NBA game, died Tuesday at 63. Secrets comes to light under Pluto jurisdiction such as October 12, 1999 - MIAMI— O.J. Simpson called 911, saying he was trying to get help for a woman he said had been on a two-day cocaine binge with a former baseball player. Simpson, 52, placed the call Sunday night from the townhouse of his 26-year-old girlfriend, Christie Prody, in southwest Miami-Dade County.

Events: Hopefully with the New Moon, lovely Venus and knowledgeable Jupiter, we can only hope they will stop Pluto from damaging us by way of dramatic happenings. With the Lord of Hades in Sagittarius (religion/foreigners) we can only expect drama in these areas. If you are a Police officer or a security guard, be very careful during this trend. The wildest crooks may be facing you soon. Don't take any chance and stay alert. Often the police make dramatic news and kill people.

Union 12/26/05: Nigerian police kill 10. AJUBA, Nigeria (CNN) — Ten protesting strikers have been shot dead by police in Lagos, a top union official said. If you know someone involved with the police or dealing with death on a daily basis, offer him a copy of my book. He may well avoid serious trouble and perhaps save his life. CNN 08/05 — A Bernalillo County Sheriff's Department helicopter that crashed Saturday in the yard of an Albuquerque home was brought down by a bullet, Sheriff Darren White said

Shopping: As Jupiter is with us, a visit to your local church for God's guidance or your favorite psychic/astrologer will do you well. Anything bought now that can be used for metaphysics will bring unusual power to you. Alarms bought now will stop the crooks.

THU., FRI., SAT. SEPTEMBER 28, 29, 30:

RULERS — Jupiter (Foreigners/Religion) Saturn (Politicians/Rules).

Work, Career and Business: Following the last few days of destructive Pluto in our lives, Jupiter and Saturn's restructuring powers will be a blessing for some organizations and your own business. Expect a new beginning offered to you. Uranus might also throw great surprising developments your way. With the New Moon, get active and get what you need; the timing is now right. If the work that you are doing is inappropriate or stressful, with Uranus in charge you can only happily look for the needed changes. Resolve to find a new career soon and for the lucky ones expect a well-deserved promotion.

Partnerships: Be original; don't let others pressure you into following them instead of your own heart. You will not build anything until you break new ground. Stressful situations stimulate you to become more independent. Meditate on where you are going in your life and don't be afraid of tomorrow. There is no better time for new and progressive change. Be nice to others and get active on the social scenery.

Family and Friends: Expect interesting surprises during these days as many will be back with the people of their past. Uranus also makes the children very active and they will drive you a little crazy. Don't be afraid of computers; a study in this area will open many new opportunities. Watch the children carefully this weekend, especially close to bodies of water.

Love Affairs: Friends will call you and with Uranus' touch (surprises) try-doing things you would not usually do and go to unusual places on a whim. Visit your future and invest in astrology or the psychic phenomena. Time for catching UFOs on film, and see them materializing in this dense physical world. If you want to see something astonishing go for it now! Uranus may decide to grant one of your important wishes. Love can be found now; get active, do not turn down any invitations. If you are an Aries, a Libra or a Leo may fall for you. An Aquarius friend will surprise you.

Travel and Communication: You may be thinking to visit your past. Do not turn down an invitation, as a professional contact could bring people who will positively influence your career. For this occasion, you may feel like spending some money on your car. Some may get stuck in airports as Uranus may disturb electronic equipment. If some of your plans get canceled; don't be mad, be patient.

Environment: On a sad note, keep in mind that Uranus rules earthquakes. Thus volcanoes, earthquakes, explosions, are high on the list. Let's hope that he won't do anything silly now, but he usually does. Flying is fine but the weather will make the trip bumpy. A blackout or trouble with electronics is high on the list too.

Famous Personalities: Many famous people will be really active in helping those less fortunate. Beautiful music, great movies and great actors of the past will come alive.

Events: Saturn rules politics, so expect surprising announcements from foreign governments. Under his power in 1997 in Africa, many armed men staged a coup attempt in Sierra Leone. President reportedly flees to Guinea. Armed men launched a coup attempt and said they had taken power in this West African nation. A spokesman, who identified himself as Cpl. Gborie, went on national radio and said that junior army ranks had ousted President Ahmed Tejan Kabbah.

Shopping: Electronic components will fail; you may be forced to invest in new equipment. You may want to pay a visit to your future and meet with your favorite "spiritual guide." Any electronic tools bought now will bring you luck in your business.

Welcome to Your
Day - to - Day Guidance

For October 2006

October 2, 2006 — Mercury enters Scorpio: A trend loaded with communication related to finance, sex, legacy, death and metaphysics for the advanced souls. Much thought will be geared towards finding the meaning of life for some, and for others finding the weakest part and reviving an unproductive business. Children born now will be gifted with incredible staying power, and natural abilities for investigation. The opportunity to learn anything hidden is offered to the soul. Many will be born with an aptitude for deep medical investigations or financial endeavors. Some will be attracted to the professions of danger such as the police force, or emergency service where quick thinking and courage can make a difference between life and death. Fame and fortune will come to the ones involved in writing and teaching, or to those deeply involved in science, research, and the medical or metaphysical fields. This position makes for one of the most intense researchers of the Zodiac. The soul must learn to use diplomacy in times of confrontation and may suffer a lack of communication skills. However, an opportunity to experience cosmic consciousness and spiritual peace is offered to the advanced soul.

SUN., MON., TUE., WED. OCTOBER 1, 2, 3, 4:

RULERS — Saturn (Politics) Uranus (Explosions) and Neptune (Suicide, Religion).

Work, Career and Business: This busy trio will be with us for the next few days and a few surprises will bring about progressive changes. Do not turn down an invitation, as a professional contact could bring people who will positively influence your career. Expect a new beginning concerning your service to the world or your career. Work that you are doing leaves you unsatisfied and is a source of stress; you might be forced to change direction. Many souls are late starters in life and no one should feel depressed about it. Resolve to find a new career that fits your natural talent. The lucky ones can expect a well-deserved promotion. Use Neptune's intuitive power to find your way through the clouds.

Partnerships: Stand strong against opposition; don't let others pressure you into pursuing their opinion instead of your own. Meditate on the possibility of improving and understanding where your partnership is going. Did you make the right choices and can you live with them? If not, there won't be a better time to deal with those questions; Uranus' desire for change and freedom will help you to transform it all. With the waxing Moon upon the world, nothing can really go wrong if you act scrupulously.

Family and Friends: Make the most of this great trend. Some friends may invite you to a gathering or a party soon. Enjoy this opportunity and be ready for lovely surprises. Uranus also makes the children very active and accident-prone. They will lean heavy on you; so be patient with their young demanding spirits. No one but yourself can bring about joy in your life; just participate with an open heart. Let the children enjoy Uranus' world of miracles, maybe by going to Disneyland or the zoo. Keep your eyes on everything they do and everywhere they go. Saturn will make it hard to forget your responsibilities. You should enjoy your life while you can tomorrow is another day.

Love Affairs: Expect interesting surprises during these days, many friends will bring some of your dearest wishes. With Uranus' touch (surprises) try doing things you would usually not do and go to places you have never been. Love is around the corner for some willing to go out and get it. If you are a Taurus, a Capricorn or a Virgo may enter your life. Leo, Sagittarius and Aries, your magnetism will be very high and you will also be in demand for love.

Travel and Communication: Some lucky souls will travel far and fast or make great plans to visit the past soon. Uranus rules electronics, the future, astrology, psychic phenomena, and UFOs. If you want to see something unusual, talk about it and do it now! Who knows, Uranus may decide to grant one of your important wishes. Keep an eye on your possessions and avoid drinking too much in public places.

Environment: On a sad note, keep in mind that Uranus rules earthquakes and volcanoes. He may also decide to disturb the weather or produce a violent explosion. Let's hope the positive Moon will stop him from getting close to you and those you care about. A magnitude 7.0 earthquake rumbled under the Mojave Desert east of Los Angeles before dawn derailing an Amtrak train passing near the epicenter. North Carolina Gov. Jim Hunt declared a state of emergency Saturday as Hurricane Irene threatened to let loose a new round of serious flooding in the already flood weary state. With Uranus around expect this type of news soon - Evacuations ordered as Ecuadorian volcano threatens. Clouds of gas and ashes rise from the Tungurahua volcano, 120 kilometers (75 miles) south of Quito, Ecuador, on Sunday— The Ecuadorian government has ordered the evacuation of some 25,000 people from a popular tourist town as a nearby volcano continues to spew ash and appears on the verge of a major eruption. NUEVO LAREDO, Mexico (AP) — In what was Mexico's second fatal fireworks accident in a month, an explosion in a candy store illegally selling fireworks killed at least five people in the border city of Nuevo Laredo.

Famous Personalities: Be ready as usual for strange types of news coming from some extroverted celebrities. Much will be done for children during this trend but this type of energy can also be surprisingly dramatic. Uranus took the life of British singer Eric Clapton's baby son in New York a few years ago. The unattended child felt to his death from a high building. Be aware, be prudent and watch the children closely.

Events: Under Uranus' surprising power anything weird could happen. The news will be somehow original. Avoid playing in the rain; many people have lost their lives under Uranus' lightning power. The government will make important decisions pertaining to the younger generation, computers, and education.

Shopping: For this occasion, you may feel like spending time and money on your appearance; it's a great time to shop for new wardrobe items or consult a beautician. This is the time to pay a visit to your future and your favorite "spiritual guide." A sense of freedom and brotherhood will be felt all over. Uranus rules astrology and Dr. Turi needs your help to pass on his very important star message to the world. See www.drturi.com or call 602-999-3010 to help us to set a crash course in your area on Astropsychology, Kabalistic Healing or the Astro-Tarot).

Full Moon — October 7, 2006 in the warlike sign of Aries. This upcoming trend will be tough for many. With Mars in Libra (justice/war/foreigners) expect serious confrontations, explosions, fires, and the possibility of war. Be ready for serious even fatalistic news in the near future. With fanatic Pluto (death) in the pious sign of Sagittarius (foreigners), a new and disturbing development with Asia and the Middle East is to be expected. Anticipate a negative development pertaining to oil spills or explosions, even terrorist activity, to take place in the near future in the US or supporting countries. Sad news from Germany is ahead of us too. Be ready for devastating forces producing destructive weather and flooding in different parts of the world. Do not lose faith in the future; we all must go on. The stars are a reflection of God and his Divine plan for all of us and we must go through with it. Do not lose faith, but expect news of explosions and wars.

Lunation impact on all signs:

Aries - The Full Moon in your sign means lots of painful restructures for you.

Taurus - Do not let this full Moon depress you, let go of the past.

Gemini - A friend will deceive you and a wish won't come true.

Cancer - Career setbacks are ahead, just be patient and all will be fine.

Leo - Stress from foreign affairs or a difficult study, perseverance is the key.

Virgo - A legacy won't go well and a person close to you may have to go.

Libra - A secret will bring light to your world. Let go of the past.

Scorpio - Problems at work might get to your health just take it easy.

Sagittarius - Stress with love, gambling and children is on the agenda for you.

Capricorn - Be aware of fire and avoid fighting in the home, real estate stress.

Aquarius - Slow down your brain if you can and learn to listen to others.

Pisces - Money matters won't go too well for a while, just be patient.

THU., FRI., SAT., SUN. — OCTOBER 5, 6,7, 8:

RULERS — Neptune (Belief/Religion) and Mars (Danger/War).

Work, Career and Business: You still have a few days in front of you to push forward, but then be ready for the impact of the Full Moon. An important decision involving a business situation will have to be made. Wait patiently for the next New Moon (positive) to restructure or sign important documents. Don't let Mars show his aggressive face to those close to you. Try to be nice to others.

Partnerships: Just before the Full Moon, expect interesting news coming your way via your telephone or mailbox. It's time to realize the truth about yourself, a situation or a person whom you trusted. Make the most of what is left of the waxing Moon, get out of the gloom and do something interesting this weekend. The Dragon's Tail will bring consternation and needed changes to you soon.

Family and Friends: The family circle could be quite the dramatic place for a while. Again do not let aggressive Mars and the Full Moon take over your words or your attitude. Keep emotions in control and be ready for secrets to surface. You can still have a good time, enjoy life and friends, but be aware of what you say or do. Do not lend money to anyone.

Love Affairs: Mars' and Neptune's captivating personalities will stimulate sexual activity; your magnetism will improve dramatically. As always with Neptune take precautions if you are sexually active. If you're married, plan a romantic dinner with a great French wine and soft music. You have a few more days to enjoy what's left of the good celestial energy; make the most of it. If you are an air sign such as Aquarius, Libra or Gemini, you may feel a strong sense of independence and freedom enveloping you. If you're a Cancer expect some stress in your relationships soon. You may be in for a long over-due change where you could experience real love.

Travel and Communication: You may uncover a clandestine relationship or a secret about someone who travels a lot. You may be forced to look inside yourself and see your own strengths or weaknesses. Don't take any chances on the road and avoid flying after the Full Moon. You'd better stay away from anything that moves, as this lunation will take many lives. Always plan your trips before the Full Moon and you will save yourself much unwanted trouble. Use the power of Starguide and help those in trouble with life.

Environment: In time of a Full Moon and with ruinous Mars around we can only expect nature's destructive forces. Drama and demise are around the corner; protect your self at all times. Do a candle ritual if you feel down or if you want to protect someone you care for. Email me from and order a Cabalistic Candle Ritual for $15.00 and learn how to burn white, green, and blue candles for full protection the use your Guardian Angel protection.

Famous Personalities: A serious wake-up call is in for some. More secrets, more drama, more doom is on the way for famous people. This upcoming Full Moon will be nasty for some well-known people. Germany will make some stressing news and a famous Army figure will be called close to God, having terminated his work on earth.

Events: Religious fanatics will get out of hand. Their own hell making could come loose; pray for the safety of your loved ones, as this lunation will be extremely difficult. Stay home and watch a good movie is my best advice; let the drama reach the unaware souls. You will see and appreciate the power of Starguide and the importance of letting others know about my work. Expect news such as preliminary radar data shows that an Egypt Air 767 jet made a rapid plunge before crashing into the Atlantic Ocean about 60 miles (96 kilometers) off the coast of Nantucket early Sunday morning. And in (CNN) — All 18 people aboard a Mexican DC-9 jetliner were killed Tuesday when it crashed shortly after takeoff in a mountainous region of central Mexico.

Shopping: Now is the time to buy pesticides and things of this nature. If you want to get rid of something, now is definitely the time. Make absolutely no investment in weapons, sharp tools, or anything that could explode. Let this nasty energy dissipate; stay safe.

MON., TUE., WED., THU., FRI., SAT. — OCTOBER 9, 10, 11, 12, 13, 14:

RULERS — Mercury (Serious Talks) Moon (Endings) and Mars (Explosions):

Work, Career and Business: This long trend will be quite dramatic, emotionally stressful, and depression and difficulties are ahead for many of us. Work and career matters won't please you much. Serious changes are on the way. Make the most of Mercury's revitalizing energy to plan a form of rebirth in your working life. Be patient; anything weak or insincere must give way.

Partnerships: A long-standing partnership could be coming to an end, possibly because you sense that you may do better by yourself, or maybe your partner lost his enterprising spirit. Avoid nurturing depressing thoughts and provide spiritual help for those who have been touched by these difficult changes. Mercury will help you to pass on the right words to those in need. Avoid complaining and hold back your negative words and thoughts.

Family and Friends: Your maternal instincts will show and will be needed for your children. Share your knowledge with them. A friend needs help, reflecting the full impact of this difficult Full Moon. The subconscious response to the moon's fluctuations upon humans is referred as "lunatic behavior or moodiness," and right now you may realize this yourself. Expect the beginning or ending of important parts of your life. Anticipate some surprising news from children; some people close to you need serious attention and plenty of love. Help a close friend deal with a departure.

Love Affairs: Ask yourself about your deep feelings for a person who seems to be moving away from you. An old lover from your past may surprise you soon. An old friend who lives far away may need to communicate with you. Don't expect great news, and provide the help required, as long as you are not being used. Another person from your past will bring you relief but could also mean more trouble than anything else. If you were born under a fire sign, such as Leo, Sagittarius or Aries, don't let the Full Moon depress you. If you are a Scorpio you will be forced to deal with some drama at work.

Travel and Communication: A business deal that would have required you to travel may be postponed or canceled without much notice. Don't let it get to you and avoid promoting important business just yet. Expect the mail and your telephone to bring you difficult news. Keep a strong spirit and face life's difficulties with faith and courage. Remember if there is a hell, its right here on this dense physical world. Have faith in your abilities and face all that comes your way with courage.

Environment: The Moon's energy could also make the human race aware of its vulnerability against the shocking destructive forces of nature. It's time for her to stretch herself and restructure her insides.

Famous Personalities: The rich and famous will be planning an event for the well being of many children of the world. Their artistic gifts will benefit numerous organizations. Some others may make surprising news trying to use Mercury for free publicity. An accident on the road could take a prominent person.

Events: You will hear about the military performing deeds that will aid the general community and save lives from a disaster area. Thousands of people will be forced to relocate to start new lives. War and destruction is a part of this lunation.

Shopping: Anything that needs to be replaced in the home or the garden may be bought now. Avoid signing anything related to real estate endeavors. Do not invest in appliances or a car just yet.

SUN., MON., TUE., WED., THU. — OCTOBER 15, 16, 17, 18, 19:

RULERS — The Sun (Children) Mercury (News) and Venus (Friendship).

Work, Career and Business: The waning Moon is being felt by many. Keep a low profile at work; all the people around you are not exactly aware of the impact of the Moon upon their psyches and could become "lunatic." Keep busy on Monday and Tuesday; use the waning Moon to shuffle a few things around. Not much progress can be made just now. Be patient and endure this tough trend with diligence. Don't get mad with others and be ready for setbacks.

Partnerships: Do not poison your mind with fears; use your own positive thinking to keep negativity from entering your spirit and your body. The future is based upon the creation of positive thoughts and lots of actions. You may feel like joining your local gym or enrolling in a weight loss program. Use Venus' gentleness and Mercury's power of articulation to communicate your feeling to someone you cherish.

Family and Friends: Family matters will demand much of your attention and could make you feel tired or depressed. Use your will; do not to let her deplete your spirits or show your frustration with loved ones. A child may need some direction and could be impatient with you. A depressed friend also needs spiritual regeneration; as usual, provide help but do not let their problems affect your own spirit. You need to get away and retire from all the activity in the home. Have an early night and enjoy a great book; tomorrow may bring a surprise.

Love Affairs: Use the sensitive touch of Venus and the light of the Sun to save yourself from a difficult situation. People are very sensitive and will be easily hurt. If you were born under a water sign a Scorpio, a Pisces or a Taurus may induce stress in your life. One of the fire signs has better to offer and may present you with an opportunity to develop your inner talents. Venus' diplomatic nature will help to heal the wounded heart of an old lover. A secret love relationship may be found close to the water, and a great trip to Hawaii is in store for some.

Travel and Communication: Mercury rules the mail, telephone and communication in general. During this difficult trend don't expect anything great. Get rid of the extra stuff clogging the house or the garage. Your car may decide to give you trouble and may upset your trip. Take care of it before taking a long journey. Get up a little early as the waning Moon may throw some obstacles your way.

Environment: Do not expect much from nature; bad news may be coming from the sea or the fishing industry. Water, ice, wind all is there to bother you. All the elements are there trying to stop you; be careful on the road.

Famous Personalities: Many prominent people will be involved in a lawsuit that could seriously harm their emotional and social standings. Serious drama is ahead for some.

Events: News involving children is ahead. Under the same celestial energy, in September 1996, 1997 and 1998, President Clinton approved federal regulations that declare nicotine an addictive drug; this was a dramatic gesture aimed at curbing teen-age smoking. Expect more important regulations and signing to take place soon.

Shopping: This is a great time to do a medical checkup, as the stars will make your physician very detail-oriented, helping him detect possible trouble. Stay clear from any psychics for now; unknowingly they could hurt your psyche. A practical approach to life will pay off for some.

New Moon — October 22, 2006 in the diplomatic oriented sign of Libra: Venus rules this sign, thus affairs of love, money, the law and politics will be on the rise. Expect an overwhelming feeling for peace and diplomacy instead of war to take over the world and your psyche. Many famous politicians will work hard to avoid dangerous conflicts during this trend. Stand firm on your decisions and do not let this lunation stress you, as balance and harmony must prevail. This trend will play an important part in the equilibrium of your physical and spiritual lives. This trend will affect some of your business and emotional relationships. The upcoming changes must be accepted as the New Moon (positive) has a great plan that you may not understand just yet. Some will be involved in the signing of very important documents, contracts or the legal system. You may be forced to realize the importance of evaluating a serious situation and making painful decisions. The emphasis is on balance and harmony in all, if we are to perform efficiently and live in peace with the rest of the world. Diplomats will be requested and busy in many parts of this crazy world to prevent future wars.

Lunation impact on all signs:

Aries - The New Moon will fall in your partnerships area, as changes are needed.

Taurus - Important changes at work are eminent, and legal matters are on the way.

Gemini - Love and romance will improve; a new deal is ahead of you.

Cancer - Important decisions about home, real estate and the family soon.

Leo - A new trip or a study is ahead of you, good news soon.

Virgo - Great opportunities to improve your finances and your self-esteem is ahead.

Libra - Try anything and everything. The stars shine on you, a new start.

Scorpio - A secret relationship will start or finish, a secret will come to light.

Sagittarius - A friend will bring about a good wish, a marriage or a contract.

Capricorn - A great opportunity to further your career and make a new commitment.

Aquarius - A far away trip or a publishing promotion is a blessing for you.

Pisces - People in power will want to help you in your affairs, go out more.

There will be three major negative SUPERNOVA windows in the year 2006. Each destructive "window" is operational for three to four weeks, thus caution is strongly advised during this period. Heavy loss of lives due to nature's devastating forces, aeronautical disasters and structural damage is to be expected. Once more realize that I do not use traditional dates found in popular ephemera. Years of practical observation lead me to extend the Mercury retrograde motion and period of time.

October / November: Third SUPERNOVA window - From Saturday October 21st through Tuesday October 21st 2006.

EXPLANATION OF A SUPERNOVA WINDOW

There is a celestial concentration of negative celestial energy bombarding the earth for a few weeks. Be extremely prudent in driving, and expect chain-reaction accidents. Be prepared for delays, strikes, and nature producing awful weather, including hurricanes and tornadoes. The same energy that produced the Titanic disaster, the Northridge, Los Angeles, and Kobe, Japan, earthquakes is approaching again. Double-check all your appointments, and if you can, postpone traveling and flying during this Supernova "window".

Communication and electricity will be cut off, and a general loss of power is to be expected. Appliances, computers, telephones, planes, trains, cars, all of these "tools" will be affected by this energy. They will be stopped in one way or another. The people of the past will make the news and will reenter your life. Expect trouble with the post office, education, students, strikes, prisoners' escape, newspapers, broadcasting industries and computer viruses may bother us again.

Many a failed mission and expensive electronic equipment (Mars probe etc.) and our tax dollars have been wasted because of the scientist's lack of knowledge of the stars. As usual NASA, which is not aware of the science of astrology, will waste our tax money with failed missions due to bad weather and electronic malfunctions. In the name of ignorance a few years ago, in the Challenger explosion seven astronauts lost their lives when NASA launched the shuttle under a "Supernova Window".

Note: Regardless of Dr. Turi's expectations posted on his website for the second time and his desperate attempts over the years to make NASA officials aware of dangerous Super Nova Windows, the Columbia was also launched during this window and re-entered the last night of it producing the death of all courageous astronauts.

Again in July 2005 NASA repeated the same error regardless of many failed attempts to launch the space vehicle. As expect foam from the fuel tanker damager the shuttle forcing astronauts to take an historic unplanned space walk costing millions of dollars for the tax payers once more and risking another disaster. When will NASA learn?

Marine life sharks, whales etc may also beach themselves due to Mercury retrograde affecting their natural inborn navigational systems. All these malevolent predictions and waste of lives and equipment do not have to occur. Those predictions do not have to affect you directly as they unfold. Instead, they are printed to prepare you for setbacks and frustrations, thus advising you to be patient and prudent during this trend. There is no room for ignorance, and those who are not aware of the celestial order, including the NASA space-program management team, will continue to pay a heavy price. In all mankind's affairs, ignorance is true evil. Why any scientists who are against my research do not honor the word science, which is based upon solid investigation, is solid proof of mental snobbery. By omitting any physical or spiritual laws can only bring penalty; for science's purpose is to explore all possibilities, even those laws written in light via the stars.

October 24, 2006 — Venus enters Scorpio: With the love planet in the dramatic sign of Scorpio secrets will come to light and if you are in a weak situation Pluto may force you to rebuild your partnerships. This trend will allow many souls to see clearly and do serious cleanup in the near future. The lucky ones will start lifetime commitments blessed with love and happiness. If your natal Venus is in a good aspect to Pluto, your sensuality will be extreme, and sexual relationships will be for the better. Souls born now will be given the opportunity to experience love on the emotional level, and much drama is to be experienced there. If Venus is badly afflicted, "La Femme Fatale" or the "Black Widow" will suffer many disturbing relationships (Elizabeth Taylor is a good example). A full commitment is needed with this position, and the soul will have to use its head in affairs of the heart. Blessed with such a powerful location, Venus in Scorpio will endow the soul with incredible magnetism. Some karmic souls will have to learn to be less emotional and more critical in their natural jealousy. This position makes for one of the most emotional but beautiful and loving partners. Usually artistic talent is present with this position. Those souls are born to experience love on an emotional and dramatic level. Due to the emotional Scorpionic intensity, this is a top position for those involved with the arts.

October 24, 2006 — Mars enters Scorpio: With the war planet going through the sign of death and drama expect serious news about plots, secrets, sex, money laundering and nature devastative forces to unleash her power soon. This trend will allow affect the secret service and the police. Many police officers and secret service agents will lose their lives in the name of ignorance. If your natal Mars is in a good aspect to Pluto, your sensuality and magnetism will be extreme. Souls born now will be given the opportunity to experience power in all its forms and much drama is to be experienced by the soul. If Mars is badly afflicted the soul could suffer a violent death due to his involvement with drugs, sex and crimes. Blessed with such a powerful location, Mars in Scorpio will endow the soul with incredible strengths where the soul will have to learn the hard way and suffer the ultimate consequences. This position makes for one of the most powerful and dangerous partners. Those souls are born to experience death and drama and rebirth themselves to a more productive element of society. Due to the investigative Scorpionic power this is a top position for those involved with secret services.

Note: As always with the Lord of hell in charge of this trend, better think twice before saying or acting on impulse. Expect secrets to be divulged, affairs of sex, and nature's destructive forces at work. The police and blackguards will make the news. More than ever use diplomacy, as whatever you do now will have very serious repercussions in your life. If you know people working in the police force or involved in any dangerous profession, share my work and advise them accordingly.

FRI., SAT., SUN., MON., TUE — OCTOBER 20, 21, 22, 23, 24:

RULERS — Venus (Love) Pluto (Death/Drama) and Jupiter (Credulity).

Work, Career and Business: Even in this good Moon phase, Pluto's deadly touch is upon us, so keep a low profile and be aware of all you do or say. Some won't be able to stop the upcoming changes and drama. Your intuition about situations will be quite accurate. The future has much better to offer and you should be confident in your dealings. Jupiter, "the Lord of Luck," will make the transition easy and may decide to throw you some luck; listen to your intuition. There will be a serious wake-up call for some people where limitations must be accepted. Avoid dealing with money now.

Partnerships: Money will also be on your mind and serious decisions will have to be made soon. Wait for the upcoming New Moon to share new ideas with others. You may take calculated chances now, but you'd better know your limits. As always with Pluto around you can only expect to dig into other people's financial or sexual secrets. Become involved with the world of investigation, metaphysics or astrology and promote your own cosmic consciousness. The Lord of mysteries may reward you with ultimate light if you take a chance to find answers in the "forbidden" world. Use diplomacy in all your deals and stay on the right side of the law.

Family and Friends: Emotions and passion are running high these days and Pluto may induce sexual encounters with magnetic strangers. Keep an eye on strangers that may be brought into your home and watch over your children.

Love Affairs: Do not take chances and listen to your intuition wherever you happen to be. If you are in a relationship, this is a great trend to stimulate your spouse or lover for some good lovemaking. Good wine, candlelight, soft music and your imagination are all you need with sexual Pluto involved. Jupiter may decide to send you news from a faraway friend. Any new relationship started now will be full of sex and passion. Better take precautions if you are a single person and be ready for that "new" relationship to be full of drama. Spend some time in the wild; Jupiter will replenish you with fresh air, fresh spirits and a new approach to life. All the water signs will feel Pluto's allure and will become walking magnets.

Travel and Communication: You may receive news from far away or give presents to a deserving family member or dear friend. You can also expect your telephone to be busy and interesting mail to come your way. Don't try to be in too many places at the same time and if you have to drive, take a little take extra time to get there; don't rush as the police could spoil your day. People from the past will get in touch with you. Be aware if you travel with Pluto absolutely anything nasty can happen to you now. 08/14/05 - ATHENS, Greece (CNN) — A Cypriot plane with "no sign of life" in its cockpit while approaching Athens crashed into a mountain on Sunday, killing all 121 people on board, Greek officials said.

Environment: Pluto will surely trigger the earth's entrails somewhere in the world and produce dramatic news with the weather. Many human and animal lives have been lost during his dramatic reign. As usual, be ready for negative news such as Air Botswana pilot crashes his plane in suicide mission at airport. 08/14/05: WRIGHT, Wyoming (AP) — A tornado struck a mobile home park with little warning, killing two people and injuring about a dozen others in Wright, Wyoming, authorities said.

Famous Personalities: Pluto will reward those whose lives undergo a metamorphosis, and Jupiter will extend their minds and horizons. Many secrets and hidden dramas will come to light. A very famous public person may go to the other side. CNN 08/13/05 - Sri Lanka has declared a state of emergency after Foreign Minister Lakshman Kadirgamar was gunned down outside his home by sniper fire. Police have sealed off the capital Colombo and are searching house-to-house for the killers.

Events: If you are a police officer or a security guard, beware of Pluto. The crooks will be active and deadly. Passion may ensnare a lost spirit, and Pluto will lead the unwise young spirit to kill innocent people. The worst of Pluto's choleric thunders and lightning are about to strike the earth. Under his power, April 30, 1998 in CARMEL, Indiana — - Two people died and four were wounded in three Indiana bank robberies, while a third bank robbery was reported in Richmond, Indiana, about 65 miles east of Indianapolis, an hour after the second. Two men wearing ski masks, one armed with a pistol, escaped with an undetermined amount of money. Also, in April 1998, Pluto took the lives of 28 people who died in a Peru plane crash. Don't take chances now.

Shopping: Invest in anything that can clean or kill pests. Do not invest in anything that could bring danger to those for whom you care.

WED., THU., FRI., SAT — OCTOBER 25, 26, 27, 28:

RULERS — Jupiter (Religion) and Saturn (Karma):

Work, Career and Business: With Pluto's dramatic experiences behind, many will keep low profiles and accept the intense transformation. With benevolent Jupiter, the future has much more to offer, and now you should be more confident in all your dealings. Jupiter, "the Lord of Luck," will make this transition easy and may even decide to throw you some luck; listen to your intuition and keep a positive attitude. A new career or a new beginning is on the horizon. Have faith and pray.

Partnerships: With Saturn's touch you can expect to work harder to organize or rebuild. For the hard-working souls, a promotion of some sort is coming your way. Your career will also be on your mind, and serious decisions will have to be made soon. Nothing comes easily; one must strive and plan if he is to succeed. With the New Moon upon us, you might have to rebuild with someone new.

Family and Friends: You may receive or give presents to the deserving family member or dear friend. Take the time to enjoy the week and the good food offered to you and if you decide to socialize during the night look for powerful people. A foreigner could make you happy and further an important wish. An older person has something to share with you, listen to the advice.

Love Affairs: Someone you have known for a while, much older or much younger, could surprise you — Don't be shy with life; take a chance with someone you care for; there is plenty to gain in the long run if this person came into your life in a waxing Moon. This endeavor may lead to an opportunity to further your career. If you were born under any of the earth signs, avoid the New Moon's positive power should be use wisely. If you are a Gemini, a Libra or an Aquarius will be getting closer to you. Listen to a friend born in April.

Travel and Communication: Expect your telephone to be busy with surprising messages. Don't try to be in so many places at the same time. If you have to drive, take extra time to get there and enjoy it all. A brother or a sister needs to talk to you. Keep a positive attitude; positive people attract positive experiences. Remember a magnet won't attract a piece of wood.

Environment: Mother Nature may decide to stretch herself and surprise some. Environmental groups will become active and will receive support from the media to save the earth from uncaring corporations.

Famous Personalities: The surprising loss of an old and eminent political, religious or entertainment figure will trouble the media soon. Life goes on.

Events: Under this energy 80 people were killed in a fire that gutted a shopping center in the West Java town of Bogor and in south-central Alaska a fire engulfed 7,000 acres and destroyed as many as 100 homes. Some terrorists groups could also get really ugly, and surprising destructive explosions soon.

Shopping: You may spend money on your pet or invest in anything to be used in nature of for your pet. It is surely a good time to spend with those you know well, as Jupiter will replenish you with fresh air and a new approach to life.

SUN., MON., TUE. — OCTOBER 29, 30, 31:

RULERS — Uranus (Explosions/Surprises) Neptune (Deception) Mars (Conflicts).

Work, Career and Business: Following the last few days of destructive Pluto in our lives, Saturn and Jupiter restructuring power will be a blessing for some organizations and your own business. Expect a new beginning offered to you. Uranus might also throw great surprising developments your way. With the New Moon, get active and get what you need; the timing is now right. If the work that you are doing is inappropriate or stressful, with Uranus in charge you can only happily look for the needed changes. Resolve to find a new career soon and for the lucky ones expect a well-deserved promotion.

Partnerships: Be original; don't let others pressure you into following them instead of your own heart. You will not build anything until you break new ground. Stressful situations stimulate you to become more independent. Meditate on where you are going in your life and don't be afraid of tomorrow. There is no better time for new and progressive change. Be nice to others and get active on the social scenery.

Family and Friends: Expect interesting surprises during these days as many will be back with the people of their past. Uranus also makes the children very active and they will drive you a little crazy. Don't be afraid of computers; a study in this area will open many new opportunities. Watch the children carefully this weekend, especially close to bodies of water.

Love Affairs: Friends will call you and with Uranus' touch (surprises) try-doing things you would not usually do and go to unusual places on a whim. Visit your future and invest in astrology or the psychic phenomena. Time for catching UFOs on film, and see them materializing in this dense physical world. If you want to see something astonishing go for it now! Uranus may decide to grant one of your important wishes. Love can be found now; get active, do not turn down any invitations. If you are an Aries, a Libra or a Leo may fall for you. An Aquarius friend will surprise you.

Travel and Communication: You may be thinking to visit your past. Do not turn down an invitation, as a professional contact could bring people who will positively influence your career. For this occasion, you may feel like spending some money on your car. Some may get stuck in airports as Uranus may disturb electronic equipment. If some of your plans get canceled; don't be mad, be patient.

Environment: On a sad note, keep in mind that Uranus rules earthquakes. Thus volcanoes, earthquakes, explosions, are high on the list. Let's hope that he won't do anything silly now, but he usually does. Flying is fine but the weather will make the trip bumpy. A blackout or trouble with electronics is high on the list too.

Famous Personalities: Many famous people will be really active in helping those less fortunate. Beautiful music, great movies and great actors of the past will come alive while other will behave weird. 06/25/05 - Tom Cruise, Lauer argue on 'Today'- 'Worlds' star: 'You don't know the history of psychiatry. I do'. NEW YORK (AP) Let the cynics talk. Tom Cruise is in love — and he just can't restrain himself.

Events: Uranus rules flying and surprising news and Saturn rules politics, so expect surprising announcements from foreign governments. CNN - 05/30/05 - BAGHDAD, Iraq (CNN) — An Iraqi military plane crashed Monday and four Americans and an Iraqi aboard were presumed killed, CNN Pentagon correspondent Barbara Starr reported. CAMDEN, New Jersey (CNN) — 6/25/2005 Three young boys missing for two days were found dead in the trunk of a car by one child's father, who jumped away screaming and sobbing after his grim discovery.

Shopping: Electronic components will fail; you may be forced to invest in new equipment. You may want to pay a visit to your future and meet with your favorite "spiritual guide." Any electronic tools bought now will bring you luck in your business.

Welcome to Your
Day - to - Day Guidance

For November 2006

WED, THU., FRI., SAT. — NOVEMBER 1, 2, 3, 4:

RULERS — Uranus (Explosions) Neptune (Deception) and Mars (Conflicts).

Work, Career and Business: This trio's impact will make life quite interesting for the next few days. Neptune's blurring nature may affect your judgment. Uranus will certainly bring some spice and surprise to your life soon. Be practical in all your expectations. If a business is not going well, you might be going in the wrong direction. Use all those above-mentioned planets to look for the right one. With the good Moon around, the opportunity might be in your local newspaper; take the time to cruise through it. Communicate your desires to whoever can help.

Partnerships: Come clear with what you mean. Some people could be deceiving; ask pertinent questions and watch their reaction. Be ready to support depressed partners, but don't let their problems affect your judgment and feelings. A trip related to your business life could prove beneficial. A contract or a deal may be offered to you; sign it before the Full Moon.

Family and Friends: Expect tons of action around you, and with Mars cruising above use patience and diplomacy with others. Uranus will bring new friends and the elements of love and joy this weekend. Mercury will join in and make us very communicative. Much of your time will be spent organizing trips, or getting in touch with your past. This trend will be an interesting one where friends and family members will try to get in touch with you all at the same time. This trio may drive you crazy and you will have your hands full of projects and not enough time to deal with them.

Love Affairs: Affairs of the heart will progress these days and the weekend could prove to be very interesting. Some teenagers need your attention; if you don't provide it, they could get themselves in trouble. Offer guidance and support to all in need, as they are not aware of the stars' impact on their lives. Some will be caught in love affairs of their past and may be deceiving themselves. Neptune will make you feel low of both mental and physical energy. If you are an air sign, expect much with love now.

Travel and Communication: The strength of Mars combined with the speed of Mercury may bring trouble on the road. Be safe; take the time to go places and give yourself plenty time to deal with everybody you care for. Use precautions and take your time if you have to travel far; don't let Mars or Neptune stop you. Most of all DON'T DRINK AND DRIVE! Neptune could get you into serious trouble. The past will become alive; deal with it and enjoy all the planning ahead.

Environment: Keep in mind that Mars is with us and many people will become aggressive, be patient with them. Uranus and Mars may decide to throw an earthquake or produce disturbing weather all around. Be patient with everyone.

Famous Personalities: This timing is ideal for meditation and renewing your faith in the universe. Pious rich and famous will prepare all sorts of activities to perform, and will give the checks to charitable organizations. Try your best to participate and provide for those in need.

Events: The last breath of the deceiving Pisces age is in full action. Religions, dogmas, fears, man-made hells, and imaginative stories of the Apocalypse will be soon replaced by more healthy approaches to the future. With Uranus in its own sign, the new Age of Aquarius will completely transform man's cosmic consciousness within the next few years. Before this celestial transformation the worst of Pisces religious fanaticism must be experienced by the world at large by producing terrorist acts, wars and madness all over the world. Have faith in the future and the celestial order imposed by the stars' eternal motions. Man can only grow and eliminate any form of spiritual poisoning through spiritual research.

Shopping: Great deals will be found well before the upcoming festivities in the most unexpected places. However, do not let all the advertisers run away with your pocketbook, as you will feel like buying all the best and most glamorous things right now. Be sure to treat yourself to something nice these days too. The Christmas spirit is already here, but people will be busy, short tempered and impatient. Make sure that you plan a leisurely day to do your shopping where the pull and hurry all around won't affect your mood. Remember, you know better than the others, so just smile and brighten a sad day. Many of you have realized the value of my work; Starguide is a perfect and valuable present to offer. Contribute a solid, true piece of the Universe to your loved ones with my books.

Full Moon — November 5, 2006 in Taurus: Disturbing news from financial corporations and the stock market are to be expected. Venus, the queen of security and love will suffer and bring serious setbacks to your security. Dramatic transformations in the world of finance and the banking industry are ahead. The impact will induce a form of financial death and rebirth for some large corporations, and others will have to merge to survive. Sad news from Switzerland and the arts are on the way. This Full Moon will also shed some light the shameful manipulation, sexual and financial secrets of organized religions and some of their religious leaders.

Lunation impact on all signs:

Aries - Difficult news about your finances and a deal or a trip worries you.

Taurus - Trouble with a contract or corporation, don't sign anything now.

Gemini - Stress coming from your past, a business or emotional partner is weighty.

Cancer - Don't worry about your friends, stress at work is expected soon.

Leo – Career, romance, and new endeavors will get you worrying.

Virgo - A change of residency or a study is a problem, be patient.

Libra - The mail or telephone may bring you sad news about investments, be strong.

Scorpio- Expect a restructure of your self-esteem and partnerships soon.

Sagittarius - Don't take any chances with your health or at work, be patient.

Capricorn - Let go of your past, eliminate all guilt with love or children and no drinking.

Aquarius - Family matters or your home life will stress you for a while, just be cool.

Pisces - Your words can be destructive to you simply wait for the next New Moon.

SUN., MON., TUE., WED. — NOVEMBER 5, 6, 7, 8:

RULERS —Venus (Friendly/Amorous) and Mercury (Travel/Communication).

Work, Career and business: Another week of stress but a new fresh breath of life will be offered to you after the next New Moon. Her blessings will make your life much easier. Wait for her upcoming green light, then go and ask the universe to make it happen. Do not try to push your business just now, instead plan and do some cleaning. Again advertisements, important calls, traveling, and meetings will pay off if you are patient. Use "Moon power" wisely and respect the Universal Law.

Partnerships: Mercury rules the mail. Phone calls and communications in general could be a source of trouble with family members. A get-together after work could also bring stress; Mercury will have everyone sharing new ideas of how to get the job done better.

Family and friends: Don't let the waning Moon get your spirit down. Many will need your support to help them clean up karmic relationships. Again do not let anyone exhaust your spirit and be patient with loved ones. Use Venus' generosity and show your love to everyone. Avoid spending too much time talking about a discouraged person.

Love affairs: Stay clear from someone who drinks too much and realize your limits if you are in a deceiving relationship. This is the perfect time to enjoy a great movie with the one you care for. With Venus around, the opportunity to show true love will be given to you. If you were born in January, someone born in September or May needs to talk to you. A friend born in November will share a secret with you.

Travel and Communication: Take this opportunity to do a check up on your car as the stars will make your mechanic very detail oriented, thus helping him with detecting possible future trouble. Get your wheels in action, but prepare for traveling under the protection of the upcoming New Moon.

Environment: Recharge your spirits; a trip to the wild will do you so good. The energy gained from the earth will recharge your batteries and you could also appreciate the beauty of Mother Nature. Trouble may come from the sea or a plane crash.

Famous personalities: A notorious religious or scientist could make serious news soon.

Events: Be patient and relax while the Moon is still waning, Mother Nature may decide to disturb us with bad weather. This is not a good time to fly, unless you made your reservation during the waxing moon.

Shopping: Some may decide to join the local gym or enroll in a weight loss program. Buy only things to improve the face of your home or cleaning products now.

THU., FRI., SAT., SUN., MON., TUE. — NOVEMBER 9, 10, 11, 12, 13, 14:

RULERS — The Moon (Big Changes) and the Sun (Children/Expectations).

Work, Career and business: The general mood will be depressive. You can expect the serious beginning and ending of important parts of your (and others) life. Be ready for those upcoming progressive variations. Keep in mind that life is a constant process of change and the stars are (even if you don't realize it) working for your benefit. Be patient with everyone around the office.

Partnerships: You will be forced to let go of negative people in your life and disturbing situations. You must take a chance on the new future with faith. Many will experience the closing of a destructive relationship and others may see the new beginning. Under these stars any new relationship will be loaded with challenge and karma. Further positive thoughts only and don't fall for the waning Moon.

Family and friends: The Sun rules love, romance and children but we are still under a difficult trend this energy won't bring you much good news. The Sun gives life to children but watch over them especially with fire and close to the water. On a more positive note he will shine his undiscriminating light on many secrets. Friends will need spiritual support, give love and attention and build good karma for yourself.

Love affairs: Be ready for new starts in love matters and provide a solid shoulder for the victims suffering a broken heart. The right partner might not be the one you were with, use the new found freedom to look (after the New Moon) for someone who really deserves your love. Under the Sun's command, the lucky ones will find great friends and happiness. A new arrival is to be expected by a young couple. If you are a Pisces, a Scorpio, a Virgo or a Taurus could induce serious stress in your life. A Capricorn friend has good advice for you; simply listen.

Travel and Communication: You may be asked to go home and see Mom. Be aware on the road, do not trust any driver and be ready for sudden action. Surprises are on the way and people from your past will come back into the picture soon.

Environment: There is nothing other to do than to accept the ultimate changes imposed by God, and nature will show her powers soon.

Famous personalities: Expect interesting but not necessarily positive surprises with the rich and famous. Be ready for the unexpected in their words and actions.

Events: Nature's forces may compel thousands of victims to relocate and rebuild new lives. Black outs and losses of power are on the way too. Tragedies and many volcanic eruptions have happened under this configuration and thousands of people were forced out of their homes because of nature's destructive forces. Be ready.

Shopping: What ever you do not invest in anything new or dangerous for the children. Get rid of the extra stuff clogging the house and a garage sale would make some lucky buyers happy. Anything to clean the house will also do well.

Note: As always with the Lord of hell in charge of this trend, better think twice before saying or acting on impulse. Expect secrets to be divulged, affairs of sex, and nature's devastating forces to be at work. The police and blackguards will make the news. More than ever use diplomacy, as whatever you do now will have very serious repercussions in your life. As usual if you know someone who is working for the police force or deals with a life and death situations, make this person aware of the power of the stars. You may save this person's life. Just point out Moon Power and the person won't be skeptical for long once the drama unfolds. Time to think of investing and offering the real wisdom and true guidance found in Moon Power to someone for whom you care.

WED., THU., FRI., SAT., SUN. — NOVEMBER 15, 16, 17, 18, 19:

RULERS — Mercury (Words) Venus (Emotions/ Love) and Pluto (Drama/Secrets).

Work, Career and Business: With the waning Moon and Pluto in charge, be ready for dramatic repercussions in your life towards the weekend. Let's hope this trend will not touch you directly, but if it does you will need to be strong and realize the harshness of life. You may also find out your real limits about your life's situation. Now is the time to review all your accomplishments and the reasons for your failures. Accept the upcoming changes with grace. You will be forced out of a situation where you do not belong and you should be thankful for your intuition. Meditate on improving your future.

Partnerships: Finances will play an important part in your life now. Be practical in all your expenses; you are advised not to overspend. The lucky souls will receive very expensive presents; some good-hearted people will offer them. As always with Pluto in charge promises made now could be dramatic. Just wait patiently for the next New Moon to invest in your future. Churches all over will be busy planning to accommodate many pious souls for fast approaching Xmas. Answering to Pluto in Sagittarius, the Christmas spirit is now getting stronger and the world will feel compassionate and loving for all his victims.

Family and Friends: Many will make plans to travel to visit friends and family members. Expect news from all over, as new plans must be set to accommodate visitors. Your family from afar will let you know how much they love and miss you. The circle of friends will be extremely busy as we are making early plans to enjoy the past. With Santa Claus in the mind, children get more excited and will be somehow be difficult to handle. Pluto will make everyone passionate and restless. Don't expect much diplomacy around, as people will become susceptible to your comments. Control emotions and watch the goings on in the house, especially if children are around. A great time is ahead of you if you listen to your intuition. As always, if a stranger is brought to your house, be aware of his motives. Drama is bound to strike a family somewhere, don't be one of Pluto's victims.

Love Affairs: A mixture of Pluto and Venus will transform you into a walking magnet. The potential for secret affairs or sexual intercourse is high on the list of things during the weekend. The planet of love could make you too friendly or trusting while mysterious Pluto and his sensual charisma will bring passion and danger to you. Stay clear of alcohol and use your intuition at all times. The Moon is still waning (negative); avoid trouble. If you are a water or an earth sign, you may be experiencing some stress with love, be patient it will pass soon.

Travel and Communication: As you know, Pluto rules passion, the crooks and the police force. News pertaining to the police will always appear during his ruling days. It is my aspiration with my students and my books, to communicate this knowledge in the future to the police academies. Pluto's impact upon our courageous police officers is lethal; and in the name of ignorance from their superiors, many suffer early and wasteful deaths. In the future, when "ridicule" is cast aside, Police Executives will be forewarning their officers to the influence of the Plutonic impact upon their dangerous careers. Locating the destructive power of Pluto transpiring in the natal profile of a potential murderer can be identified with Astropsychology. Knowledge is power and there is no room for ignorance especially with the police force.

Environment: Pluto will induce drama and could disturb the earth's belly, producing a bad earthquake. As usual with Pluto in charge, be ready for many interesting secrets to surface and remember to keep quiet. CNN 03/29/05 -FORT LAUDERDALE, Florida The police always makes the news under Pluto's power such as (AP) — A police officer who stopped a doctor for speeding on his way to deliver a baby, and then took him to the maternity ward in handcuffs, has agreed to an unpaid suspension for lack of judgment. CNN 03/29/05 - Indonesian officials report 330 people are dead on the islands of Nias and Simeulue off Sumatra from Monday's quake.

Famous Personalities: A famous personality will be called to God and many will miss the soul. A powerful reminder of our own mortality is ahead, this is the signature of Pluto's regular jurisdiction upon our lives. Note when a soul is born with a Dragon's Tail in Aries as was Mr. Kennedy, 39, son of the late U.S. Sen. Robert Kennedy. That soul is prone to experience a violent death. He died New Year's Eve (1997) in a skiing accident in Aspen, Colorado. You may order my book, "Power of the Dragon," from www.drturi.com to find the location of your own natal dragon.

Events: Under Pluto's explosive power, in 1988, at American Pacific's plant near Henderson — Pacific Engineering & Production Co. of Nevada, or PEPCON — a series of colossal explosions left two dead, injured 300 and caused $75 million in damage. Clark County fire investigators blamed the blasts on welders, cramped storage, messy conditions and wind. Company officials disputed those contentions. Shortly after that, the company moved the operation to Iron County, Utah, and renamed it Western Electrochemical. Pluto stirs man's animal tendencies and causes the infinite forces of good and evil to constantly tease each other. Don't trust anyone and be aware of the police. Fact: Controlled by Pluto, the planet of death and drama, the highest suicide rate is to be found within the police force. Expect this type of news soon: (AP) — Five women were found dead of multiple gunshot wounds in a home Sunday night, and police were searching for four suspects, officers said. The shootings capped an unusually violent weekend in the city, where 10 people were killed since Friday. (CNN) — A 13-year-old boy firing a 9 mm semiautomatic handgun wounded four classmates at their rural Oklahoma middle school before being subdued and taken into custody, police said. The victims were taken to hospitals; their injuries did not appear life threatening

Shopping: Only second-hand shopping or well advertised sales will give you the best deals in town. Better wait for the New Moon for super deals. Do not invest in dangerous toys for your children; with Pluto signature, they could get hurt. Give old toys to unfortunate children.

New Moon — November 20, 2006: This lunation in Scorpio promises to be very dramatic for many people. A new moon is usually positive. Thus after any form of death there is always a new life in store for all of us. Pluto is the planet of death and rebirth, and all affairs related to finance, health, sex, secrets, death, war, drama and law enforcement will be on the rise. Expect tragedy of all sorts to take place this month, where all the devil's spirits will be invited to a macabre dance of horror. This will be one of the most difficult lunation this year where one must realize one's limits. The trend will play an important part in your life where impartial judgment from above and below will take place. Health, working life, relationships and the world at large will be affected. Many people and countries may be forced to realize the hard lessons of determination, cruelty, and death. The emphasis is on death and the potential for a rebirth in experiences, strength, and newfound wisdom to perform and live accordingly. Remember knowledge is power and there is no room for ignorance with the stars.

Lunation impact on all signs:

Aries - This lunation will affect your corporate money, take chances but be wise.

Taurus - This new Moon will affect your emotional or business related partners.

Gemini - Improvement in your service to the world, health, good opportunities are ahead.

Cancer - Love, romance, and children; all will shine in these areas for you soon.

Leo - Great news from home and a solid opportunity to buy, sell, or move soon.

Virgo - Results of hard work will pay off, still another great study or a trip is ahead.

Libra - A contract or Legal endeavor will turn to your side. You're happy.

Scorpio - This lunation is on you, you cannot loose if you try hard enough. Go for it.

Sagittarius - Your intuition will become very clear, a deep study is ahead of you.

Capricorn - A younger or older friend will grant one of your dearest wishes. Get it.

Aquarius - Great progress, great changes, and your career, will improve your image.

Pisces - A trip to the past, a deep study, and foreign affairs shine on you.

November 24, 2006 — Jupiter enters Sagittarius: Pluto moved from Scorpio to Sagittarius on November 11th, 1995 and will stay in this sign until January 26, 2008. Constrained to face the horrible consequences of his own destructive power, and pay the heavy consequences of mass destruction, man turns to religion for comfort. In Sagittarius (religion) Pluto (regeneration) did promote a serious disturbing wave of religious fanaticism that plagued the world with many terrorists' attacks. In the US, the impact of Pluto in Sagittarius has already spoken with some religious fanatics, committing serious crimes and many will have to pay the ultimate price for their destructive behavior. With Jupiter (the books/Bible/Koran etc.) some Middle Eastern residents will continue shocking the world, by spawning suicidal bomb attacks on major European and US cities as experienced on the 911 and 07/05 in London. The "contract" they sign with their manipulators, before blowing themselves up surrounded by the highest possible number of innocent victims, promises "the martyrs" twenty or more virgins after an immediate entrance to paradise! After the painful passage of Pluto (expiration) in Sagittarius (codification of thoughts), the world will be ready for wiser, new age and religious leaders. Those well-adjusted souls will teach all the higher expressions of all the religions of the past. They will introduce a new image of a God free of fear, full of love and attention. Those futuristic religious leaders will combine their teachings with a more comprehensive scientific understanding of the manifestation of the Creator throughout the Universe. Expect new laws involving religious rights to take place and let's hope beneficial Jupiter will help mankind to slowly grow outside of its fear and deadly religious convictions and ignorance.

MON., TUE., WED. THU., FRI., SAT. — NOVEMBER 20, 21, 22, 23, 24, 25:

RULERS —Jupiter (Foreigners/Religions) and Saturn (Structure/Governments):

Work, Career and Business: With the waxing Moon upon us opportunities to rebuild the damage inflicted by Pluto will be offered to the valiant. With Jupiter's protection, the finances, resources and expertise of others could provide support this week. All sorts of financial deals will be attainable, especially where foreigners are involved. Be ready for a restructure of a portion of your business, these changes could also affect your emotional life. Take chances, sign contracts, travel and promote your career while the moon is on your side.

Partnerships: Saturn's gloomy attitude may make you feel insecure about life in general. Don't taint those close to you; put a smile on your face; caution in relationships is advised. You may find yourself forced to help someone; if you feel like saying no, don't feel guilty about it. This publication's purpose is to help and guide those who need help on a daily basis. If your partner becomes too heavy, mention my work and release yourself from guilt. Work towards your heart's desire with a practical mind. Saturn wants you to go and find all the answers yourself. Don't be too concerned about doing everything perfectly; you can only do your best. Use or learn computers to make life and your business easier and don't be afraid of technology.

Family and Friends: Share your feelings about a difficult situation with a family member or a trusted friend, but don't be pessimistic about the end. With benevolent Jupiter, a trip close to nature with the children will regenerate your soul. A trip to your local church on Sunday could give you a sense of faith in the creator and in yourself. Some juveniles may ask questions about life. Help them to think differently, inform them outside of religion and take chances on their spiritual natures, they will love it.

Love Affairs: Be particularly attentive to a fascinating foreigner. Being cautious in relationships is always a good thing; be sure to take your time before committing your heart. Expect a significant development with marriage or divorce unfolding with some karmic relationships close to you. If you happen to suffer one at the present time, don't stress yourself and be patient. Sooner or later it will all be gone and you will find a well-deserved peace of mind and true love with a suitable partner. If you were born under the sign of Leo, a Sagittarius or an Aries will be attracted to you.

Travel and Communication: This is the perfect time to make travel arrangements if you have to be away from home after the Full Moon. Be easy on a person who may be quite troublesome; use diplomacy, or the situation could turn nasty, even against you. Your presence may be requested for a gathering, and a wise person may play an important part in a critical decision. Enjoy the road and keep your eyes on the signs.

Environment: Sad news may come from foreign countries experiencing problems with terrorism and emigrations. With benevolent Jupiter with us these days, some "saviors" may become active in respect to their religious convictions or for nature.

Famous Personalities: Your management or some important government figures will impose some new rules. An old person will make his voice heard to the younger generation. The message will bring a new beginning for the children's education.

Events: Saturn always involves Government news such as the terrible explosion directed at an administrative building on April 19th, 1995. — Under the same celestial energy, in Oklahoma City, an explosion felt for miles around rocked a downtown federal office building, blowing away an entire 9-story wall and killing scores of people. Let's hope nothing of this sort will ever happen again. On the negative side, this lunation may activate destructive news pertaining to fanatic foreign groups.

Shopping: Use this trend to find great bargains just before the festivities or in garage sales. You could also enjoy shopping at your local antique store with an exuberant friend. If you have an Indian guide, invest in their works of art to channel spiritual information. Pets bought now will live long and happy lives and give you tons of love.

SUN., MON., TUE., WED., THU. — NOVEMBER 26, 27, 28, 29, 30:

RULERS — Neptune (Oil/Drugs) and Uranus (Explosion/ Shocking):

Work, Career and Business: The New Moon is here, making many of us much happier. Try to accomplish as much as you can even though you may find it hard to concentrate on the tasks. It's time to socialize with co-workers and get to know them better. We are already half way through the month, and accompanying it is a note of serious change and interesting developments. A business trip or an invitation may lead you to many good contacts. You will have time to play and mix business with pleasure.

Family and Friends: Many will be enjoying foreign places and the different cultures of these people. Expect brothers and sisters to contact you from afar and let yourself be immersed in the great Holiday season. Children are getting very excited and will be anticipating the upcoming festivities. With only a few weeks before Xmas, your friends and the family circle will be extremely busy making plans and at the same time enjoying the best of what life has to offer. People will plan to attend church services responding to Neptune's religious power. Many of God's houses will be crowded and you should double check on your plans to get there on time. Combined with the New Moon and Neptune, the Christmas spirit of love and preparations will receive its full support from the stars. Many will participate in volunteer work to provide love and help to the needy.

Love Affairs: As usual with amazing Uranus in charge, avoid impatience and be ready for some surprises. With Neptune here, control your emotions and your imagination. The Moon is waxing (positive), so any surprises ahead of you should be of a positive nature. Many will find love and this new relationship may lead you to a rewarding future.

Travel and Communication: Your telephone and your mail will bring you all sorts of news and invitations. The lucky ones will enjoy a trip close to those they love. Expect news from a brother or sister; get in touch with some of your friends for a good chat. Remember Neptune is also part of the early festivities and you must not overindulge in eating or drinking. A quiet walk by the sea will take your spirit high and stimulate your faith. Many lonely people will feel the depressing power of Neptune and some older souls may call on you for help. With Neptune's stressful imagination, many evangelists will stubbornly spew the gospel, and "re-pent, hell, and the end-times" will be their favorite topics. The only change ahead is in our consciousness and in new faith based upon the understanding of God's celestial tools.

Environment: The weather could prove to be very difficult in some places. Be especially aware around water. Tornadoes, hurricanes, typhoons, and volcanic activity is anticipated, especially close to the last Supernova window.

Famous Personalities: A fantastic time is to be expected by the efforts of many gifted artists to bring love, joy, and faith to the children of the world.

Events: Neptune may bring disturbing news from religion or the Middle East. Let's hope the New Moon will stop anything drastic from happening such as blowing up a church or synagogue somewhere killing innocent people. Some abortion activists will bring their convictions and trouble with them. Explosions and surprises are high on the list, watch for suspicious and suicidal people around you. The children could also be adversely affected, watch them closely.

Shopping: Those days belong to the children and all toys bought now will bring great joy to them on Xmas morning. You may now also invest safely in anything that can be used around water or any survival gear.

Welcome to Your
Day - to - Day Guidance

For December 2006

FRI., SAT., SUN., MON., TUE. — DECEMBER 1, 2, 3, 4, 5:

RULERS — Mars (War/Action) Mercury (Talking/Sales) and Venus (Presents):

Work, Career and business: With the New Moon still here, don't miss opportunities that could be used to improve your business endeavors. The feeling of Xmas will make the general attitude positive and this trend will strengthen your chances of success in the near future. Trust your ability to communicate with Mercury and follow your intuition. The next few days will be vital for launching your business, and Venus' lucky touch will bring additional developments. Use the remaining positive days to maximize your promotions for business.

Partnerships: This timing is perfect for many to participate in all the Xmas festivities. But remember, Mars is around so you should use his strength instead of impatience when shopping. The future promises to bring encouraging results for next year's interviews, employment applications, promotions and other job opportunities. This week is a pivotal turning point for a key relationship. As always consider the long-term implications and respectability of the offer before making up your mind.

Family and friends: With Xmas approaching and with the "Lord" of communication, Mercury in charge these days, expect your telephone to be busy. Everybody will have something to share with you. Use Venus' loving touch in your verbal exchanges and avoid Mars' invective remarks towards an unlucky friend. Don't be shy and pass on your message. Be confident and direct in your approach; your impact on others will surprise you. Enjoy those days with the children but Mars will make them restless.

Love affairs: Currently, the New Moon and kind-hearted touch of Venus are upon us, and you will treat someone you truly love with your best intentions. The timing is perfect to discover what it is you can offer your loved ones. Early gatherings and great times are ahead. With them, your social life and romance is up; a trip is on the way for some. If you were born in June a Sagittarius, a Libra or an Aquarius may fall for you.

Travel and Communication: Anything related to Xmas and general communication will go particularly well and progress is imminent. This week promises to be worthwhile. For the more creative souls, your writing skills will improve dramatically. Under Mercury and Venus' auspices, especially in time of a new moon, great gifts can be found. A trip to Vegas will pay off for some. Don't let Mars make you impatient or accident-prone on the road and be patient.

Environment: Let's hope that Mars' destructive temper will not produce tornadoes, explosions, high winds or flooding.

Famous personalities: Be ready for some good news about famous people's creativity, or great Xmas projects to come to the light.

Events: Do your shopping early; don't get caught in the madness. Remember Mars is around; don't take any chances with confrontations or the police. A positive attitude and diplomacy will keep you out of trouble. Impending breakthroughs with medicine or science is expected soon.

Shopping: The kids rule; Xmas is dedicated to them, to love, to joy and religious faith. This is a great time to buy interesting books, and electronics for your business. As Mercury rules transportation it would be a good idea for you to take care of your wheels or shop for a new car. Toys bought for kids now will bring great happiness later.

Full Moon — December 5, 2006 in Gemini: Disturbing news about transportation and education and the possibility of strikes are to be expected. Mercury, "Lord of Communication and Transportation," will cause serious setbacks to the possibilities of traveling or communicating. Dramatic changes are ahead in the worlds of transportation, finance, traveling, and the postal industries. Sad news involving serious accidents, terrorism and devastating weather is on its way. Many people will find themselves stranded in airports. The impact of these events will bring on a form of financial death and rebirth for some large corporations who will have to merge to survive. The year will end in a destructive Supernova window and could prove to be difficult for government decisions and actions.

Lunation impact on all signs:

Aries - Difficult news from the mail and a deal or a trip gets you worried.

Taurus - Trouble with a contract or corporation, don't sign anything now.

Gemini - Stress coming from your past, a business or emotional partner is burdensome.

Cancer - Don't worry about your past. Stress at home is expected soon.

Leo - A friend and a new endeavor will worry you.

Virgo - A change of career or stress at home is a problem, be patient.

Libra - The mail or telephone may bring you sad news from faraway.

Scorpio - Expect a restructure of your finances and a form of death soon.

Sagittarius - Don't take any chances with your partners or traveling.

Capricorn - Eliminate all guilt to bring about better work and health.

Aquarius - Love and children matters won't go well for a while, just be patient.

Pisces - Your home life brings stress, you may have to move soon.

December 8, 2006 — Mercury enters Sagittarius: A trend loaded with communication about legal activities, traveling, and foreign affairs. Much thought will be geared towards finding better ways of dealing with other countries. Souls born now will be gifted with natural abilities for learning and teaching and many will travel far. Many will also master foreign languages. The opportunity to acquire knowledge of man's laws and religions is offered to the soul. Many of them will be born with an aptitude for judicial investigation, philosophical values, and some will play important parts in passing their knowledge on to the world. Some will be attracted to the professions offering intellectual abilities such as the ministry, teaching and writing, and some will be investing in education for the well being of animals. Spiritual talents involving the new age will lead these souls towards positions of authority and respect. This position makes for either one of the most intellectually advanced or religious dogmatic signs of the Zodiac. The soul must avoid being righteous to others and must often endure the poisoning of an overly religious upbringing. Their challenge will be to take a critical approach to books and collected knowledge. An opportunity to reach cosmic consciousness and the teaching of the creator's celestial manifestation is offered to the advanced souls.

December 6, 2006 — Mars enters Sagittarius: With the war planet going through the sign of philosophy and religion we can only expect death and drama because of the "good books" and man's folly archaic deceiving teachings. This trend will steer more religious fanatics to die for their beliefs and deity and take more innocent people with them. Many religious buildings and/or religious figures will try hard to impose their own spiritual limitation and religious views through the judicial system. If your natal Mars is in a good aspect to Jupiter you will travel far and learn from foreigners. Souls born now will be given the opportunity to experience power in all its forms religious doctrines or the law and much drama will be imposed upon the soul forcing a more advanced perception of spirituality. If Mars is badly afflicted in the chart the soul could suffer a violent death due to his involvement with religion (terrorists). Blessed with such a powerful location, Mars in Sagittarius will endow the advanced soul with incredible mental strengths to teach the true message of God via the universe. This position makes for one of the most powerful self center spiritual religious leader (David Koresh) and its dangerous aims to control weaker god fearing souls. Due to the spiritual values involving Jupiter this is a top position for those involved with mankind' spiritual advancement or on a negative note your local uneducated pious minister. Powerful governmental lawmakers also inherited this celestial position.

WED., THU., FRI. — DECEMBER 6, 7, 8:

RULERS — Venus (Caring), Mercury (Traveling plans) and the Moon (Changes).

Work, Career and Business: Just before Xmas, you may find it difficult to concentrate on your duties. Your mind will wander about the anticipated good times ahead. Deserving hard-working souls will benefit with well-earned bonuses or new opportunities to promote their careers. Mercury will make you think fast, and action will be everywhere. Be aware of the Full Moon's tension and be ready to change your schedule. Wait for the next new Moon to face important deals.

Partnerships: Some of the people you know will have to move away, or you yourself may decide to relocate to a better place within the next few days. Expect the beginning or ending of important phases of your life and others' too. Venus will endorse many gatherings with colleagues you have not seen for a long time. Be ready to control your emotions during the Full Moon.

Family and Friends: Expect a brother or a sister to pleasantly surprise you. A friend might show up uninvited and thus affect some of your plans. You may receive an invitation to socialize with some faraway friends or family members; use this opportunity to grow closer to them if you can. Luckily for all of us, this Christmas season will take place in a positive sign (Aquarius) and we are due for some surprises and extraordinary events to celebrate. Against all odds, endure patiently this Supernova window, and enjoy these good old days. Don't forget that when the Moon becomes full and is waning, things may not go your way. A family member needs your advice. Be willing to consider the issue from his point of view; but avoid emotional involvement or forcing your opinion. Much time will be spent around the children enjoying their Christmas trees. Prepare to enjoy the warmth and the good food of your friends and your family.

Love Affairs: Expect much progress if you are looking for that special person. Some of the people from your past may also become weighty; stand for yourself without guilt. Friends will bring good memories; have fun but don't get caught up in the nostalgia. If you are a fire or water sign many will try to steal your heart. Have fun, but don't make any commitment if the person in question was met for the first time after the Full Moon.

Travel and Communication: You will have to run like mad to keep up with all the things you must accomplish. You will stay busy with all this activity and come in contact with interesting people. Combined with the Full Moon trend and a Supernova window expect all sorts of delays, forcing you to think twice as fast. Slow down; be cautious and prudent in your driving, too. Watch for crazy drivers around the city; they might not have read "Moon Power," so don't let them hurt you (or your car). Many will fly to faraway places early and will get caught in bad weather or find themselves stuck in congested airports. Keep in mind that Mercury may decide to confuse some electronics and bring chaos. Chain-reaction accidents are very high on the list; be careful out there.

Environment: Expect surprises and explosions soon. Be aware of fire and keep an eye on the children. Chances are that nature will go berserk soon, so you don't want to be a victim. She may demonstrate her power with shocking weather. Thousands of people may be forced to relocate, fleeing disasters, flooding or bad earthquakes.

Famous Personalities: A famous person (or his child) will make dramatic news. Expect news about famous or infamous people who have made history. The past will turn alive for a while.

Events: After the Full Moon, electronics may suffer or fail to function properly. This could produce another dramatic air crash. Not a time to take any risks in the air, unless you made reservations during a waxing trend. Expect the beginning or ending of an important portion of your (and other) lives.

Shopping: Use what's left of the New Moon to spend money on expensive gifts. You can still find good deals on big-ticket items by comparison shopping. If you decide to visit Las Vegas' casinos after the Full Moon, you may encounter stress but you could get lucky. Yes, someone will hit the jackpot in a waning Moon in Vegas, but the money will be spent on paying bills or tax and little will be left. Better make all your important plans after the next New Moon for your own sake. Consider offering Starguide to your loved ones for Christmas. It is affordable, valuable, and because it works for you, it will also work for them. They will probably love you for shedding some light of the universe upon their lives. Go to www.drturi.com to order your E-book or hard copy of "Moon Power".

New Moon — December 20, 2006 in Sagittarius. Jupiter, the planet of codification of thought, rules this sign. Affairs of religions, foreigners and the formation of new laws will be on the rise. Expect news coming from foreign powers, forcing many governments to take secret drastic actions. This trend will play an important part on the religious front and could directly affect the Pope. Many people and countries may be forced to realize the hard lessons of religious freedom as dramatic changes are taking place. The emphasis is on abortion rights, foreigners, and religious values. The potential for rebirth is from newfound wisdom to perform and live accordingly with the rest of the world. Don't fall for the apocalyptic preachers' religious poisoning.

Lunation impact on all signs:

Aries - A far away trip or a foreigner will make you happy. Get published.

Taurus - Great financial news and rewards in investments. Study metaphysics.

Gemini - Project yourself to the world with a new partner. Learn photography.

Cancer - A secret will come to light, your siblings needs you. Communications improve.

Leo - An important wish will come true, a new friend brings luck. Run your show.

Virgo - Great opportunities for your career, you deserve it. Learn computers and write.

Libra - A study or a trip will bring you joy. You're a philosopher and a teacher.

Scorpio - A legacy or a business deal will pay off. You're a light worker, power to you.

Sagittarius - The business of a loving partner has good things for you. Don't be too tight.

Capricorn - Great opportunity and better service to the world, master Astropsychology.

Aquarius - Love and light to you, write, talk, shine, be original. Learn metaphysics.

Pisces - An opportunity to do well from home or relocation soon. Be a teacher.

December 11, 2006 — Venus enters Capricorn: The great planet of love and wealth is in the practical sign of Capricorn. On a positive side this position produces high-class musicians and great artists that will work hard to bring their talents to the world. It produces people who will show their love through their work, and give them great patience. On the negative side Venus will make them promiscuous and they will use people with money and power to gain positions of authority or recognition. However Saturn is watching and karma is always repaid.

SAT., SUN., MON., TUE., WED., THU. — DECEMBER 9, 10, 11, 12, 13, 14:

RULERS — The Sun (Children/Light), Mercury (Traveling) and Venus (Caring).

Work, Career and Business: Do not expect much progress these days. The waning Moon (negative) will obstruct any business venture. Don't take yourself too seriously and set a meeting with co-workers to discuss what could be done to improve the business. Why not forget about your responsibility for a while and smell the roses like everyone else? Enjoy a party after work and let your real feelings show.

Partnerships: Old and new friends will be happy to talk and will exchange ideas, hopes and wishes with you. The holiday season is getting close; make sure you don't get stuck at the last minute with heavy shopping yet to do. The year 2004 will start with a Supernova Window so be very careful of what you say or do then. Be aware of what your partner needs and offer him another surprise for the upcoming New Year. A plan to travel close to the water will make some souls very happy.

Family and Friends: Don't be gloomy, and learn to forget whatever dramatic experiences you have had to experience lately. We are on this earth to do a specific work we set for ourselves. Take care of the young, life goes so fast; let them fully enjoy your love and your care. Don't let the waning Moon bother you with guilt or your difficult past. Do something special that will help you fight the melancholic mood. The children have plenty of ideas; listen to them and enjoy life. Friends may request your help in some areas.

Love Affairs: With the Sun (love) in charge, an element of surprise is around. As usual in time of a waning Moon (negative), don't expect long-lasting love if you fall for someone new. If you are an Aquarius, a Gemini or a Leo needs your spiritual help.

Travel and Communication: The police will begin to plan for the upcoming holidays and may stop you if you drive foolishly. Drinking heavily could disturb your plans for the next year and should be completely out of the question. You do not want to ruin your or someone else's family because of depression (or good time). Be safe and if you drink with friends at a gathering, take a cab home.

Environment: Hopefully lovely Venus and the magnanimous Sun will stop any dramas imposed by the waning Moon. The weather will be difficult; stay clear of lightning. An explosion or a fire could hurt some children; watch over them carefully.

Famous Personalities: Many famous people will shine, helping those born with difficult karmic stars. Great shows will be offered to the public. Don't fall for the religious promoters of the Apocalypse; they are after your money and can only survive with your lack of awareness and your fears. GLENDALE, California (CNN) — A man accused of causing a deadly Southern California train crash has been charged with 11 counts of murder, Los Angeles County District Attorney Steve Cooley said. NEW YORK (AP) – Nicole Dufresne, An aspiring actress and playwright whose work explored life's darker sides was shot and killed as she confronted an armed robber during an early-morning street holdup.

Events: We are still in a waning period and some disasters will be happening; be aware and careful in all you do. MIAMI, Florida (CNN) — Passengers aboard a Southwest Airlines flight helped wrestle a fellow passenger to the floor Tuesday night after he tried to force his way into the cockpit, law enforcement officials said.

2/24/2005cnn COLUMBUS, Georgia (AP) — A father fatally stabbed his two young children and seriously wounded three others with a hunting knife before committing suicide by slitting his throat.

Shopping: Use the light of the Sun to regenerate your spirit. Invest in your favorite spiritual healer, psychic or astrologer; this will do you good. Visit your future with faith. Enjoy the fast-approaching festivities. Be aware; those three kings who followed a star to Bethlehem, the birthplace of Jesus Christ, were astrologers! You can only follow a star when it is plotted in a map. Also remember that in the old days there were no astronomers, only astrologers! Wait for the Next New Moon to launch important matters.

Note: Attention Pluto is back with us. So close to a Full Moon trend you can only experience dramatic happenings. Don't be a victim of the Lord of Hell and be aware of Pluto's destructive power. As always, use extreme caution in all you do. Anything you say or do under his power will follow you for the rest of your life. Killers, rapists, psychotics, and the worst of society will become active. While Pluto reigns, you'd better stay home and let the ignorant be killed. This is the time to really pay attention and make good use of my work. If you are a police officer, be very careful out there.

FRI., SAT., SUN., MON., TUE. — DECEMBER 15, 16, 17, 18, 19:

RULERS — Pluto (Death/Drama) and Jupiter (Religion/Foreigners)

Work, Career and Business: You are now walking on fire! You'd better use all the "savoir faire" you know if you are to go through this lunation without trouble. A serious wake-up call will come to many abusers, as the heavy hand of karma will fall on them. Businesses or corporations will be forced into restructures, and those who don't fit the bill will have to go. The possibility to lose (and rebuild) it all will be a serious consideration for some karmic souls. Not a time to deal with money matters; keep a low profile until the next New Moon.

Partnerships: The offensive secret life of a person may surface; you may learn something valuable about a partner. Whatever you find out, do not divulge the secret. Stinky moneymaking schemes will play an important part of this trend;

listen to your intuition in all you do. Stay clear of dark alleys; your life hangs upon your awareness. Many people will learn the hard way these days. Even so close to Xmas, nasty happenings can and will take place under Pluto's power.

Family and Friends: Do not expect relatives to be diplomatic during this trend, especially if the family is experiencing financial stress. Do not fall for Pluto's destructive or sarcastic remarks; words of love and support will pay off in the end. Be ready for dramatic news from someone close to you. Whatever happens, be strong; life must go on as Pluto has important work to do and he is part of a celestial design imposed by God. Time to further my work and offer knowledge to those you care for by letting them read Moon power.

Love Affairs: Secret affairs of sex and passion may be divulged to the public, forcing people to take a stand in destroying and rebuilding relationships. This might happen to you too. In any case use tons of diplomacy to save unwanted trouble in your love life. If you are a water sign or have any planet in Scorpio, be ready for a wake-up call of some form. Stay clear of any new relationship and stick with the old one or refrain from social interaction until the New Moon and you will be safe.

Travel and Communication: Expect news pertaining to secrets, sex, the police force, and medical discoveries. Be careful of what you do or say during this trend. Drive carefully; stay clear of strangers and strange places. Be ready for dramatic news to disturb the media.

Environment: Pluto will have fun destroying it all, remember he belongs to the divine celestial family and has a specific work to do. His dramatic impact on earth (and people) is needed. What Pluto demolishes he also gives the opportunity to rebuild even stronger and better. Be ready for dramatic news with the police and nature's forces soon.

> From: Thu, 1 May1997 23:43:29-0500(CDT)-
> To: drturi@inetworld.net -
> Subject: Earthquakes
>
> Dear Dr. Turi,
>
> I posted a note on alt.astrology that cited the 6.7 quake off the coast of Mexico in the Pacific Ocean. I included it under the rather "nasty" piece of mail that someone sent indicating that they believed your window of probability for April 30 to be invalid. Not that I think you need defending, as I have found your work very compelling. I just thought I'd let you know — in case you didn't — that you were "right again." On the late night of April 30, the 6.7 quakes took place.
>
> — Mary.

Famous Personalities: Some famous people will be called back to God. Many famous spoiled children get involved with the wrong crowd and some are found shot to death along a road. Pluto cares not if he deals with the famous or the commonplace. CNN) — Sen. Hillary Rodham Clinton fainted during a luncheon speech Monday in upstate New York, citing a 24-hour virus, but she recovered and resumed her public schedule. NEW YORK (AP) — Ossie Davis, the actor distinguished for roles dealing with racial injustice on stage, screen and in real life, has died, an aide said Friday. NEW YORK (AP) — Ossie Davis, the actor distinguished for roles dealing with racial injustice on stage, screen and in real life, has died, an aide said Friday. He was 87.

Events: Hopefully knowledgeable Jupiter will slow Pluto's rampage and thirst for blood. Under his power many jealous souls lose control and kill or injure people and the police always make the news. Nature also goes out of order. CNN 03/29/05 -FORT LAUDERDALE, Florida (AP) — A police officer who stopped a doctor for speeding on his way to deliver a baby, and then took him to the maternity ward in handcuffs, has agreed to an unpaid suspension for lack of judgment. CNN 03/29/05 - Indonesian officials report 330 people are dead on the islands of Nias and Simeulue off Sumatra from Monday's quake. SALEM, Oregon (AP) — A man ran into the nearly empty Oregon Senate chamber Monday and sat at the podium for nearly an hour, holding a 12-inch butcher knife to his chest, before police arrested him. FORT WAYNE, Indiana (AP) — — An elephant being loaded onto a truck trampled a circus animal trainer to death at Memorial Coliseum, police said. CNN) — Sen. Hillary Rodham Clinton fainted during a luncheon speech Monday in upstate New York, citing a 24-hour virus, but she recovered and resumed her public schedule.

Shopping: All water and earth signs will see important parts of their businesses or financial lives taking a specific direction within this lunation. In addition, Jupiter is with us too, so the worst might be avoided under his protection. A visit to your local church to pray for Pluto's victims will do you well. Do not invest in weapons; if you do, you might have to use them later. Anything bought now that can be used for metaphysics will bring unusual power to you.

Happy Holidays to all of my readers. Regardless of what you had to go through in 2005 keep a positive attitude; 2006 has so much more to offer. Christmas take place in a waxing moon and will bring about a great time for many of us. Think of offering genuine guidance to your loved ones, visit my site and let me take care of your future you will be happy you did! Please help me to pass on my important message to the world I need your support in all possible ways to educate this world of the true message of God written in light via the stars. I need to build my Astropsychology schools for the children of tomorrow. Please send your suggestions or donations to Dr. Turi 4411 N. 23Rd St, Phoenix AZ 85016.

New Moon — December 20, 2006 in Sagittarius. Jupiter, the planet of codification of thought, rules this sign. Affairs of religions, foreigners and the formation of new laws will be on the rise. Expect news coming from foreign powers, forcing many governments to take secret drastic actions. This trend will play an important part on the religious front and could directly affect the Pope. Many people and countries may be forced to realize the hard lessons of religious freedom as dramatic changes are taking place. The emphasis is on abortion rights, foreigners, and religious values. The potential for rebirth is from newfound wisdom to perform and live accordingly with the rest of the world. Don't fall for the apocalyptic preachers' religious poisoning.

Lunation impact on all signs:

Aries - A far away trip or a foreigner will make you happy. Get published.

Taurus - Great financial news and rewards in investments. Study metaphysics.

Gemini - Project yourself to the world with a new partner. Learn photography.

Cancer - A secret will come to light, your siblings needs you. Communications improve.

Leo - An important wish will come true, a new friend brings luck. Run your show.

Virgo - Great opportunities for your career, you deserve it. Learn computers and write.

Libra - A study or a trip will bring you joy. You're a philosopher and a teacher.

Scorpio - A legacy or a business deal will pay off. You're a light worker, power to you.

Sagittarius - The business of a loving partner has good things for you. Don't be too tight.

Capricorn - Great opportunity and better service to the world. Master Astropsychology.

Aquarius - Love and light to you, write, talk, shine, be original. Learn metaphysics.

Pisces - An opportunity to do well from home or relocation soon. Be a teacher.

WED., THU., FRI., SAT., SUN. — DECEMBER 20, 21, 22, 23, 24:

RULERS —Saturn (Rebuilding/Order) and Uranus (Explosions/Surprises):

Work, Career and Business: With the good moon upon us, expect to make some progress for a while; many of your plans should go forward. Listen to other people's stories; the stars affect everybody and they may come up with interesting deals or surprising news. Be ready to invest in some appliances or equipment. Saturn will help you to make some great adjustments after careful planning.

Partnerships: With Uranus in charge, anything unusual can happen. With a waxing Moon (positive) upon us, those changes should be progressive. Changes should be accepted with faith in yourself and your new future. Be patient with everyone, as Uranus and Saturn may make people eccentric and depressed.

Family and Friends: An opportunity to meet with some family members or friends you have not seen for a while will be given to you by this lunation. The past will come alive again and a great time is offered to all. The children will have a blast on Xmas day enjoying their new toys. Make good use of these days and enjoy the food, security and love of your peers.

Love Affairs: Be ready for the incredible to happen; if you are in a karmic relationship changes may be forced upon you and are needed. Friends may fall in love with other friends or mistake love for friendship. An old love or a past friend will reappear in your life soon and with him the option to start fresh again. If you were born under one of the earth signs, expect good surprises and great changes. If you are a Sagittarius, a Leo friend needs to talk to you and someone born in April or February needs to go places with you. A friend born in June might fall for you.

Travel and Communication: A business trip or an invitation may lead you to many good contacts from the past. However, you might have problems getting to the given address and may get lost a few times due to the Supernova window afflicting the world. Be patient, as you will still have plenty of time to play and enjoy yourself with various and unusual people. For UFO investigators, now is the time to look for UFO's in secluded places. Don't forget your video camera; you may be sorry if you are not ready, as Uranus is now willing to display secrets of extraterrestrial intelligence. Expect things in the sky or NASA to make the news.

Environment: A nasty virus could produce an aeronautic disaster soon. Expect this type of news to happen: Australian wildlife officials made repeated attempts to prevent up to 300 long-finned pilot whales from beaching themselves on a remote part of Australia's west coast. Mammals, birds, and men's navigational systems get confused when Uranus is in charge, and many get lost. Tornadoes are high on the list. Go to and register for my newsletter and get more information all year round.

Famous Personalities: Very surprising news will come from the rich and famous doing great things for the children of the world during Xmas season.

Events: Uranus loves accidents and explosions; under his power expect surprising and original pieces of news to take place. Do not take chances with the children and be safe.

Shopping: Purchase new electronic equipment or plan a long voyage by air to a foreign land. As always, Uranus rules the future, and his psychic powers can be used through your trusted local psychic or astrologer. Invest in your own future and request a taped progressive reading for the upcoming year.

MON., TUE, WED. — DECEMBER 25, 26, 27:

RULERS — Neptune (Christmas), Mars (Religious Wars) and Venus (Affection)

Work, Career and Business: This trio will make life quite interesting for the last few days of the year. Neptune's blurring nature may affect your judgment. Be practical in all of your expectations. If a business is not doing well, you might be going the wrong way. Use all those above-mentioned planets to look for the right one for help. With the good Moon around, the opportunity might be in your local newspaper; take the time to cruise through it. Communicate your desires to whoever can help.

Partnerships: As always with Neptune, come clear with what you mean. Some people could be deceiving; ask pertinent questions and watch their reactions. Be ready to support depressed partners, but don't let their problems affect your judgment and feelings. A trip to Hawaii or an exotic place is in store for the lucky souls. A contract may be offered; sign it before the Full Moon.

Family and Friends: Pisces rules deception, religions and will support the Christmas spirit all over the world. The world id still very young and the God fearing uneducated mass need all sorts of dogmas to face the hard facts of life. Many Christians and Muslims all over the world have died and will continue to die because of their religions but the world is slow to learn. The age of Aquarius is slowly changing mankind consciousness where the realization of Universal love and universal awareness is the only way to bring security peace and respect to this young world and its inhabitants. Expect tons of action around, and with Mars cruising above, use patience and diplomacy with others. Venus will bring an element of love and joy after Xmas. Much of your time will be spent preparing for the future and the New Year. This trend will be an interesting one where friends and family members will try to get in touch with you all at the same time. This trio may drive you crazy with many projects. DON'T DRINK and drive, many unaware souls will end up with a DUI.

Love Affairs: Affairs of the heart will progress these days and the weekend could prove to be very interesting. Some might be caught in a love affair from their past and may be deceiving themselves. Neptune will make you low in mental or physical energy. If you are a water sign you are lucky with love for a while.

Travel and Communication: The strength of Mars combined with the blurring vision of Neptune may bring trouble. Be cautious and take your time if you have to travel, don't let Neptune or Mars stop you.

Environment: Mars may decide to throw an earthquake or produce disturbing weather. Be patient with everyone.

Famous Personalities: This timing is ideal for meditation and renewing your faith in the universe. Try your best to participate and provide for those in need.

Events: The government needs to make lots of decisions about a disturbed area of the world. Let's hope for mankind's desire for peace in the Middle East.

Shopping: Great deals will be found well after the year-end in the most unexpected places. Treat yourself to something nice these days too. Make sure that you plan a leisurely day for yourself to relax your body and spirit. As the year comes to an end, many of you have realized the value of my work; Starguide is a perfect and valuable present to offer for any occasion: a birthday, a wedding, to a friend or child in trouble, for relocation, a comparison chart, etc. Contribute a legitimate piece of the Universe to those you really care for and tell them to visit for their free daily and monthly forecast.

THU., FRI., SAT., SUN. — DECEMBER 28, 29, 30, 31:

RULERS — Mars (Hostility) and Venus (Highly Valued):

Work, Career and Business: The New Moon will exert a revitalizing pull that will be felt in your business affairs. You may use this lunation to perhaps resolve conflicts in a difficult situation with a person of authority or a co-worker. Control Mars' opposing tendencies; don't let him affect your words, your attitude or your emotions. Practice patience during this Martian trend and use diplomacy; if you do so you'll make serious progress. You may also use the tough energy of Mars to do some needed tasks around the office such as removing furniture; in any case, don't get hurt.

Partnerships: Even with the Waxing Moon, learn to keep Mars' impatience under control and use Venus' diplomatic gifts to save difficult situations. Everyone is so intent on having his or her own way and there could be little cooperation around you. It's time to practice tact with the same dedication as a diplomat. Impatience could be detrimental to you and others, so use the knowledge found in this publication accordingly.

Family and Friends: With Venus' blessings upon us, you should try your creativity at home. Your fruitful Venusians imagination will lead you to creations of perfect interior designs. Realize your limits with troubled friends, and don't allow them to rely too heavily on you. As always, give spiritual support but avoid getting emotionally involved with their personal problems. You and your mate or family member can gain through financial endeavors, but discuss all possibilities before making any commitments. You might have an idea yourself that could be used; talk about it. Use what's left of the waxing Moon, so plan to enjoy Christmas this weekend.

Love Affairs: Don't let your relationship becoming shaky because you sense that the person in question may be deceiving in some way. Do not fall for your own insecurity, false information or a wild imagination. Avoid guilt in any of your decisions, and if you feel a change is unavoidable, trust your future. Expect much from Christmas night out on Friday or Saturday if you take a chance on someone. Enjoy social life but don't drink and drive. Mars (action) and Neptune (deception) are not great cohabiters. When alcohol and speed are mixed, it can produce serious accidents. If you are a Gemini, then Aquarius, Sagittarius and Libra will be strongly attracted to you. A friend born in April has a surprise for you.

Travel and Communication: Be vigilant if you must drive, and don't take chances on the road, as Mars' energy could make you careless. Don't let his aggressive nature make you complain about a person, and use your words cautiously. Venus has much more to offer, and it's your choice; so use your will and your knowledge. Many people from your past will be there, have fun make the most of the holiday season.

Environment: Some people will learn about fire the hard way. However, many thoughtful people will use Mars' power to further environmental knowledge on preventing fires in nature. As usual, Mars, the red and violent planet, doesn't seem to care much for the waxing moon or Christmas. He may decide to pull a nasty trick with nature's devastating forces, where all the elements could be invited for a destructive dance. Explosions and fires are common during his reign, be aware.

Famous Personalities: The oblivious rich and famous may be Mar's victims or make sad news involving accidents, drugs or alcohol. On a positive note, Venus will shine and induce love to those often-lonely famous souls. The poor kids will benefit for the season.

Events: The Martian energy is tough and has in the past produced explosions and accidents of all sorts; be prudent. Venus will put up a serious fight against her destructive brother and may save many souls. Violent and dangerous sports will attract many people challenging their respective sides. Some unsuspecting souls may fall victim to Mars, and suffer head injuries.

Shopping: It's your last chance to do late shopping for the festivities. Invest in anything involving love, creativity or the arts. Show for whom you someone you care, the depth of your love. Under Mar's power, dangerous tools and machinery bought now will bring financial opportunities.

The greatness of the Universe is unknown, but the magnetic forces that direct and move all the planets in our galaxy are known; this Divine source of power can be used to guide and bring man a life filled with happiness, peace and harmony.

— Dr. Turi

Closing Thoughts

Today's date is July 7, 2006

Dear Clients and Friends:

I would like to sincerely thank you for your patronage and wish all of you a very successful New Year. It has been my privilege, with "Moon Power" to bring more cosmic consciousness to your life. Please help me promote the cosmic consciousness of everyone you care about. I need both your spiritual and financial help to build many Astropsychology schools for the children of tomorrow. Understand the importance of my mission and be a part of it in the unfolding world karma. Please help me, and invest in the future by promoting the true knowledge of the stars. Your contributions will allow me to spend more time on the air, writing, educating, and publishing my work to those in need. For centuries many resources have been used to discredit the stars and to advance wasteful and dangerous religious dogmas. Times have changed and the stars above do impose a new consciousness for mankind. Be a promoter of light and invest in the true light. The children of tomorrow need to gain cosmic consciousness and use the stars to live more productive and safer lives. Please communicate my work and help those in need to find guidance, comfort, direction and assistance in the celestial order. I hope in "Moon Power," you will find the pathway to the stars and the realization of God's ultimate will throughout the Universe.

Walk in peace with your new knowledge of the stars

God bless you all

— Dr. Turi

Grand Significance

All through the ages there have been spiritual leaders ready to guide man out of his misery. They seem to be saying the same sort of things when you break it all down. This is not to discount those figures at all; only that mankind seems to need reminding of the higher qualities from time to time. But before man, and after man, the cosmos has been above. God created those stars; they are cosmic lights for mankind's destiny. They are reflections of the Divine Will. Yet who

looks above? We all look here on earth for the answers. That is the grand significance of Astrology.

And God said, Let there be lights in the firmament of the heaven to divide the day from the night; and let them be for signs, and for seasons, and for days, and years:

And let them be for lights in the firmament of the heaven to give light upon the earth: and it was so.

And God made two great lights; the greater light to rule the day, and the lesser light to rule the night: he made the stars also.

And God set them in the firmament of the heaven to give light upon the earth,

And to rule over the day and over the night, and to divide the light from the darkness: and God saw that it was good. (OldT:Genesis 1:14-18)

Life Reading $200 – add $10 S&H

NEW - You will also receive over 30 pages of printed information: THIS IS DR. TURI'S TOP SERVICE - Your satisfaction is fully guaranteed. A personalized detailed reading on a 90-minute audio tape that will be used throughout your life. Unarguable facts about your direct relationship with the universe and my guidance that will help you to establish emotional, financial and spiritual stability. An Egyptian Cross Tarot reading is part of this reading and so much more. A must for everybody! This detailed reading will be used throughout your existence. I will explain (using Divine Astrology/Astropsychology) the significance of all the planets in your horoscope and thoroughly clarify, all the vital departments of your life. In addition to adding new insight to your personality, this tape uncovers unique information based on the location of your natal Dragon's Head and Tail and the teaching of the implacable Moon Universal Law. Keep in mind I do not practice the Astrology you know, read, practice or have studied. My work is totally unique and do not resemble any previous psychic readings or astrological work you may have experienced. All readings are taped on top quality cassette tapes. All your questions will be answered and the right direction/guidance for a successful career or specific problem will be offered. The second part of your reading is the psychic cleansing and reading of your own Supraconcious forces in time and space. All areas of your future and past life residue will be covered.

NOTE: You do not have to be present for me to do your Full Life Reading. High quality 90-minute cassette tapes are used and sent daily all around the US and the world. You may call the office at 602-265-7667 for more information!

Progressive Reading $150 – add $10 S&H

If you already have had a Full Life reading with Dr. Turi then you need a progressive reading. This reading is usually done once a year or every two years and allows full regeneration of your spirit while offering solid direction with the current Dragon and stars trend pattern. The 90-minute Audio tape will be mailed to you within 4 to 6 weeks unless you chose the GREEN US postal money order option to save time. Like a Full Life reading, in a progressive reading I will explore the current star trend and explain in great detail what is going on in the 12 specific areas of your life. I will translate the will of the cosmos as it is right now affecting your destiny, your financial situation, your love, your health, your career etc. A full Astro-Tarot spread is always a part of a Progressive reading. The stars are constantly in motion and if you already had a reading with Dr. Turi then a progressive reading is your next step. Great attention is given to the current Dragon's Head and Tail and how it will force the changes in two very specific parts your life. Like a Full Life reading, in a progressive reading I will explore and give more information on what is going on in the twelve specific area of your life. I will translate and emphasize how the Dragon will be affecting your destiny by houses (love/money/career) and by sign so that you can be prepared and make incredible progress almost immediately. I will look into the next two years ahead of you and do very specific prediction and even give you the exact months you can expect the changes to take place. Towards the end of your 90 MN tape I will do '"The Egyptian Cross" Astro-Tarot reading and this process will act as a cleansing of your subconscious in time and space and neutralizes all the negative energy surrounding you. A progressive reading is a "must do" each year so that you can get prepared for the positive or challenging changes are taking place in your life. Note that Dr. Turi readings are a mixture of Astrotherapy and Hypnotherapy and never poison the mind of the client with nonsense, death or negative suggestions and predictions.

Rising Reading $150 add $10 S&H

New service - Exact time of birth is needed for this service. Many people are used to Modern Astrology methodology and this 90 mn taped reading is strongly recommended if you had both A Full Life and a progressive Reading with Dr. Turi. The 90-minute Audio tape will be mailed to you within 4 to 6 weeks unless you chose the GREEN US postal money order option to save time. Like a Full Life reading in a rising reading I will explore your entire life and explain in great detail what is going on in the 12 specific areas of your life from your rising sign. I will translate the will of the cosmos as it is right now affecting your destiny, your financial situation, your love, your health, your career etc. A full Astro-Tarot spread is also a part of a Rising reading. This reading can only be performed if you have your exact date of birth. 602-265-7667 for more information!

Your Personal Lucky Dragon Windows - $150 add $10 S&H

This service request a lot of research but it is highly recommended if you want to be at the right time and at the right place with the right people. Ride the Dragon's Head and see the incredible results in all your endeavors. Note this NEW service has been tested and is very reliable. Be ready for serious changes or experiences to take place on your 12 months Personal Dragon lucky Windows.

Click Here To Order Your Comparison Charts

Marriage/Business Partners Comparison Relationships:

Improve, save or find a quality business or emotional relationship with this service. Your stars have life and like an intriguing painting, colors blend harmoniously. Understand your partner's strengths and weaknesses for a more productive life. Improve, save or find a quality relationship with this service. Discover the differences between you and your partner and learn how to promote only the best stars. Understand how to promote the strengths and eliminate the weakness of the alliance. Realize what the difficulties or opportunities you face together are. While providing a thorough discussion of issues suggested by your charts, I will also give special attention to the fears, weaknesses and karmic residue of both. The location of your respective dragon, by sign and house can seriously promote or alter a relationship. Find out what to do financially or emotionally with that person, remember knowledge is power. Will his stars promote or disintegrate your life? Be aware, save time and money. A must for marriage or business venture's with a new partner.

Astro Carto-Graphy

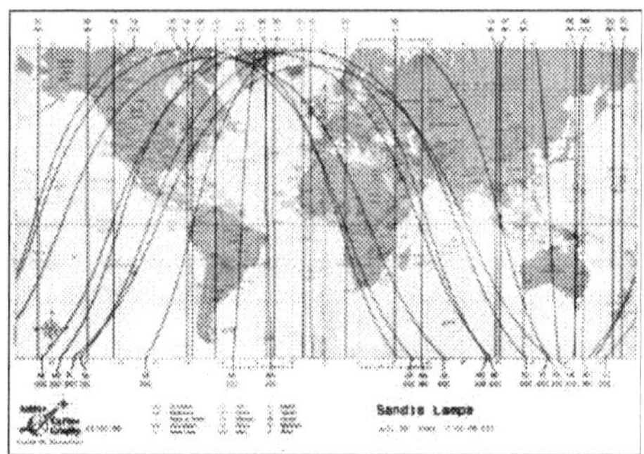

Click Here to Order Your Astro-Carto-Craphy $150 – add $10 S&H

Find the best place in the US and anywhere in the world where the stars above will offer you an easy reach to the best that life has to offer. Don't relocate without it. Map your future. Don't relocate without it! Find out where and what the best of your stars have to offer you. You may be just a few hundred miles from a splendid Venus (love) Sun (fame) Jupiter (study) Mercury (writing) line. You might be, right now living and striving without any hope of success under a nefarious planet like Saturn (depression) or Neptune (drugs) or Mars (war). Take a chance for yourself and make your own reality, learn where those wonderful lines are waiting for you. Astro-Carto-Graphy really works!

Back home in France I was under a nefarious Saturn line and the more I worked the less security or reward I had. Then I relocated under the Sun (fame) to California, in the US and anything that I touched turned out pure gold! The same goes for your home. Don't buy a house without checking it out, as you might not be able to keep it for long. Avoid financial stress (Saturn lines): avoid locations where you are prone to lose your home because nature devastative forces (Uranus lines). Avoid fires (Mars lines) instead let me explain those lines and guide you towards happiness (Jupiter) wealth (Venus) health power and fame (Sun). Call now for information, do not hesitate, your career and your house are your biggest and most important decision and investment you will have to make. Call me for info first - Dr. Turi (602) 265-7667. Work available by mail. World Wide Map, 30 pages of information tailored for you by Dr.Turi.

Children Characterology $150 add $10 S&H

Do not hesitate to invest in your child. You might have given life to a genius or an artist. Find out how and why your child thinks or behaves with you or the world at large.

Find out why your child is the way he/she is. Give him/her the EARLY opportunity to regenerate his/her spirit and get the right direction in life. Let me introduce your star children, as you never knew them before. Do not let the worst of the stars take control over their destiny. In this day and age children need spiritual regeneration more than ever. The sad fact is that over 6000 of them commit suicide every year in the US alone while other children are killing each other in schools. Don't wait until it's too late, understand the dilemma from Astropsychology and let Dr. Turi help your child with this service. Your child's future is worth it! I saved many teenagers from suicidal tendencies, gang activity, drug/alcohol addictions and put them right back on the road of health, success and happiness. Save thousands of dollars on wasteful sessions of traditional psychotherapy and years of guilt and sorrow. Do it for his/her birthday and watch the results.

Click Here To Order Your Cabalistic Healing and Deep Soul Cleansing - $200 per hour

New service ON LOCATION ONLY: Phoenix, Arizona. Call 602-265-7667 for your appointment. Find your health back, your inner peace, lose weight regain self-esteem, love and happiness and clear off all negative energy around you. Let me free your body mind and spirit of all blockages and be born again. On location Phoenix AZ Healing Room - Dr. Turi can help you with: Weight Loss ~ Quit

Smoking ~ Stress ~ Depression ~ Panic Attacks ~ Eating Disorder ~ Anxiety ~ Pain ~ Phobias Stuttering ~ Induce Past Life Regression ~ Extreme Nervousness ~ Anger and Rage Self Improvement ~ Anxiety ~ Creativity ~ Enthusiasm ~ Insomnia ~ Guilt Phobias ~ Relaxation Techniques ~ Pain Management ~ Build Self Confidence ~ Assertiveness ~ Eliminate Substance Abuse ~ Improve Concentration ~ Pain Management ~ Improve Study ability ~ Improve Salesmanship ~ Improve Exercise ~ Sexual Problems ~ Eliminate Depressions ~ Procrastination ~ Nail Biting & Much More... You may call the office at (602) 265- 7667 for more information!

SPECIAL - Healing With Love DVD & a FREE 90 MN Hypnotherapy tape- $50 add $10 S&H

CLINICAL HYPNOTHERAPY ~ THE POWER TO CHANGE YOUR LIFE!

ON LOCATION ONLY: Phoenix, Arizona. Call 602-265-7667 for your appointment. Use form at the bottom of this page for the SPECIAL DEAL - Dr. Turi combines Hypnotherapy and Astropsychology disciplines to heal the body, mind and spirit. This type of service is very sophisticated and deals principally with your relationship to the Universal Mind and your Subconscious' incredible creative forces. Hypnotherapy is safe and the fasters growing discipline practiced today to heal the body, mind and spirit outside of dangerous prescription drugs. Realizing and using your relationship to your Subconscious' remarkable resourceful forces will become a major contribution to reach all your wishes. This 90 MN taped session is designed to hypnotize you and Re-program your subconscious' creative forces.

Science has failed to understand the source of unlimited power we all possess or explain the incredible; such as a 135 pound mother lifting a 2000 pound car to save her child stuck under it...Yes there is so much you can do if you only knew how to access the staggering forces of your own subconscious. Tapes are sent all over the world and SPECIFICALLY TAILORED FOR EACH INDIVIDUAL. The taped session is designed to hypnotize you from distance if you can not make it to Dr. Turi's office physically. Playing this tape will also boost both your self-esteem and your immune system. The goal is to Re-program and UTILIZE your subconscious' immense creative forces to access all your deepest wishes.

Dr. Turi can help you with: Weight Loss ~ Quit Smoking ~ Stress ~ Depression ~ Panic Attacks ~ Eating Disorder ~ Anxiety ~ Pain ~ Phobias Stuttering ~ Induce Past Life Regression ~ Extreme Nervousness ~ Anger and Rage Self Improvement ~ Anxiety ~ Creativity ~ Enthusiasm ~ Insomnia ~ Guilt Phobias ~ Relaxation Techniques ~ Pain Management ~ Build Self Confidence ~ Assertiveness ~ Eliminate Substance Abuse ~ Improve Concentration ~

Pain Management ~ Improve Study ability ~ Improve Salesmanship ~ Improve Exercise ~ Sexual Problems ~ Eliminate Depressions ~ Procrastination ~ Nail Biting & Much More…

You must first call for your appointment at 602-265-7667 or E-Mail

You may also write me a letter about your fears/phobias/needs/aims/desires/wishes etc. and send it to: Dr. Turi ~ Startheme Publications Inc. P.O. Box 45257 Phoenix, Az. 85064-5257

Ordering Courses or Services

Master Nostradamus' rare 16th Century method of Astrology rekindled as Astropsychology by Dr. Louis Turi. These courses are nothing less than mind boggling to those searching for the truth. Help us to set up a course in your city and get it all for free. Check it all up at

If you need more information on the ASTROPSYCHOLOGY course speak directly to Dr. Turi at (602) 265-7667.

PROCESSING INFORMATION

FIRST NAME:______________________ M.I.: ______________________

LAST: ____

GENDER: [M] [F] Circle one

ADDRESS: ____

CITY:____

STATE__________________ZIP:_______________________________

PHONE: (________) _____________________________________

EMAIL:______________________ @ ____________________________

DATE OF BIRTH (Month, day, year):

__________________/__________19__________

(EXAMPLE: FEB. 26, 1950)

TIME OF BIRTH:

_______________AM_____________PM (Circle One)

Note: Time is Needed for Astro-Carto/Graphy Only

PLACE OF BIRTH (City, State, Country):

____

PAYMENT METHOD — PLEASE CHECK ONE

[VISA] [M/C] [DISCOVER] [AMEX] [CHECK] [MONEY ORDER]

CREDIT CARD #:

____

EXP. DATE: __________-__________/____________________

TEL: (_____) ____________________________________

FULL NAME AND ADDRESS OF CARD HOLDER (IF DIFFERENT):

____

____

____

SIGNATURE: ____

DATE: ______ / ______ / ______20____

Mail to:
Dr. Turi Startheme Publications Inc.
4411 N. 23Rd St
Phoenix, AZ 85016
Tel: (602) 265-7667
Fax: (602) 265-8668
E-Mail: Dr.Turi@cox.net

Dear Prospective Star Student;

Often people ask me when I will be in their area to teach them the secret of the stars. Well let's be practical and in the process you will save precious time and a lot of money. There are many good reasons why you should take the course by mail, mostly because you do not need to be present for me to bring forth your cosmic consciousness. Taking the live course means taking off from work and flying to where I will be teaching. This is not only time consuming but very costly and often impossible for many of you. Thus I came up with the simple idea to always record my very last advanced class and make it available to students living far away or outside the US. Many of you may think, but I would rather be present at the class and I am sure I could learn faster and better.

Wrong! Again many of the questions you may have for me have already been asked by some of my smart students. Any student of the stars received my answers and you will learn much more by listening to the twelve ninety minute audio tapes in your own time. For those of you who are visual; the simple but elaborate astrological symbols in the printed material, books and videos are designed to help you to assimilate my teachings to the highest level. Taking the physical course is also much more expensive than the significant deal by mail and time is the essence for all of us. Also, if your natal Mercury (assimilation of information/learning process) is in a slow sign, you will need much more time to assimilate the information and you can always play the tape back as many times as needed. Other advanced students are also there to give you a hand by email if needed. In the physical course, you will be left behind if you can not grasp something right away as time is the essence and mastering the Universal Mind in a few days could be stressing because it is quite a lot of study.

You can do all that in the privacy and security of your home and take all the time you need to learn at your own pace. Your exam questionnaire requires also a specific time and after a few hours that's it; you must remit the paper work for grading. At home you can take all the time you need and no one will rush you, you can also review your tapes if you are not sure of a question. The best part is that; I am constantly learning more and more as the months go by and with your help, you may be able to assist me to come to you. Note also that many of my best students want to keep up with my latest astrological information. Then in time, and with your assistance, I will be teaching in your area and you can still take the course again for a fraction of the price.

Thus you would get the famous two for one deal and you do not waste precious time. If you are serious about mastering the secret of the Universal time you do not want to waste away your inner drive and make a commitment to learn all about the divine as soon as possible. The stars naturally will induce a strong urge to do so and this is when the same stars will assist you to master the secret of the Universal clock. The quicker you start your study, the faster your new life and inner mission will take shape. Be a promoter of the future and help the children of tomorrow to live a more secure and productive life. Your contribution as a light worker will also bring an incredible karma for your next reincarnation. It an honor for me to teach you all that I know about the universal mind and point out the marvel of the stars' impact upon mankind on earth. I will also thank you for electing me to do so and lead the way to your new life and consciousness.

Blessings to all

— Dr. Turi

You may call me personally for more information on any of the courses at (602) 265-7667.

- Live Introductory and Advanced Astropsychology Course:
  $ 1.175.00 (5 days) - Live
- Live Introductory and Advanced Cabalistic Healing Course:
  $ 550.00 (2 days) –Live
- Live Introductory and Advanced Astro -Tarot Course: $250.00
  (1 day) - Live

SPECIAL DEAL for Moon Power readers: BY MAIL ONLY $850.00 Advanced Astropsychology and Introductory Astro-Tarot album course ~ S&H included.

I wish to pay in one full payment of $____________for:

- Astropsychology Course (available also by mail)
- Cabalistic Healing Course (live only)
- Astro-Tarot Course (available live)

Deal of $850 For the album course by mail

I understand that this tuition will provide the full album course package of 12 Audio Tapes, 3 DVD (Cosmic Consciousness / Dragon Prophecies / Astrology and Science) - Internet Files - Exam of 200 questions - 3 Books titled "And God Created The Stars" "The Power Of The Dragon" and "I know All About You" and also a 90 MN tape audio tape titled "Introduction to Hypnotherapy."

A 75% OF GOOD ANSWERS WILL QUALIFY ME AND GRADUATE ME AS AN ASTROPSYCHOLOGIST.

You may start with the discounted basic program for $200. A 10% discount price applies for the complete set of those five professional (cd's/disks) programs which is $ 602.10, or add $180 more for the two new programs if interested. (Total 7 programs 782.10 + $15 S&H) Please note that either Virtual PC or Soft Windows must be installed on your Mac to run these.

Use credit card form AND FAX TO 602- 265-8668 or send a check payable to:

Dr. Turi 4411 N. 23Rd St Phoenix, AZ 85016
E-Mail: <dr.turi@cox.net>

PROCESSING INFORMATION

Credit Card Details— Required credit card information
Total amount $ ___________

Card number:

________-________-________-__________

Expiration Date _______-_______

Customer contact information:

Name: ____

Phone number: ____

Email address; _______________________________________

Billing address:

Street address: ______________________________________

City:___________________ State:____ Zip:_______________

Purchase/product description:

____

____

____

This will be one of the most rewarding experiences in your life!

****

TAKING THE COURSE PHYSICALLY

The celebrated French Astrologer Dr. Turi is offering a 5-day crash course in YOUR CITY. You will enjoy Nostradamus' 16th century Divine Astrology method and become an Astropsychologist in a single week. Master the golden key to the universe and congregate with spiritually advanced people. You will enjoy mental stimulation and meet exceptional new friends. Gain true cosmic consciousness, open your 3rd eye, and develop your celestial affiliation with infinity. Ultimately you will realize your direct relationship with God and the Universe. Start your own career, become financially independent while bringing the light to the children of tomorrow. No complicated math involved and a 98% graduation rate. Certainly the most advanced spiritual experience of your life.

****

GET THE COURSE FOR FREE!

ARE YOU PART OF A NEW AGE GROUP? DO YOU KNOW OR OWN A BOOKSTORE?

IF SO HELP US TO SET UP A LECTURE OR A COURSE IN YOUR AREA

Welcome to the Advanced Course on Astropsychology

Due to the time limit, the personal tuition is much more intense than the home study album course. There is no complicated math involved in Dr. Turi's class and the advanced or beginner students can take this course. In our live class, you will be taught the secrets of the Universal Mind, the Workings of the Subconscious, the Astro-Tarot, Astro-Carto-Graphy, Greek philosophy, Symbolism, Omens, Cabalistic candles rituals, the medical aspect of the stars, how to launch your new business get on the radio and television and so much more. You will assimilate quite a bit of information and slowly build solid cosmic consciousness. You will also refine your psychic powers and subconscious connections through the omens and symbols I will use in the class. For those of you who cannot afford or make the "live" class, you can take the initial introductory Astropsychology Course by mail. Payment options are available. This is an album of quality cassette tapes, books, videos, exams and all material needed to get started. The physical advanced Astropsychology tuition graduation ends up with a Party where other students and friends will also be invited to celebrate and welcome the new members of our star family.

Books, videos, workbook, an exam of 150 questions are part of the advanced Astropsychology courses, while different software are also available upon your request. Those are the Personal Path Natal Interpretations, the Star Match Compatibility Interpretations, the Life Trends Transits interpretations, the Journey Interpretations, and the Career Path Interpretations. Two additional programs added are the Solar Return and child natal reports. You may use those programs immediately to generate an income from your home on your computer as you perfect your knowledge in your Astropsychology practice.

Days: Five days (includes 2 hours examination on the last day).

Examination: 150 questions (2 hours) 75% good answers to graduate.

Graduation: Each student receives an Astropsychology Diploma, 3 Ebooks, and course materials. The taped course is offered to the entire class (optional), but each student must pay for its duplication and shipping charges if they want a copy. Fee for 7 full day live class: $1.175.00 -

TRUE KNOWLEDGE IS PRICELESS

You must call the office at (602) 265-7667 or fax us your information at (602) 265-8668 FOR YOUR SAFE CREDIT CARD TRANSACTION. Graduation upon 75% of good answers.

Software is available and is separate from the class fees

You may start with the discounted basic program for $200. The 10% discount price applies for the complete set of those five professional (cd's/disks) programs which is $ 602.10, or add $180 more for the two new programs if interested. (Total 7 programs 782.10 + $15 s&h) Please note that either Virtual PC or Soft Windows must be installed on your Mac to run these. The children of tomorrow will be able to regenerate and find in your newfound knowledge the golden keys of what it means to be human and attain peace of mind.

If you decide to take the Astropsychology class physically you need to confirm with us ASAP and send your payment to reserve a seat for you. Paid in full - Credit card or check accepted.

Payment options are available: We will work with you and get you started with the DEAL Advanced Astropsychology Course with your fist down payment. Call (602) 265-7667 for information.

Double deal: When two people husband/wife - boyfriend/girlfriend attend the physical Advanced course together the second person's tuition is free. A small fee of $150 is required by the second person for the provided materials or books. Previous students: Those prices do not apply for previous students; if you already took the $850.00 deal course you can take the physical advanced Astropsychology Course for a small fee.

> "Simply magical and extraordinarily rewarding" that's what students said about Dr. Turi's teachings!
>
> Super deal: Bring any new student who pays the full price, and make $100.00 for each. Someone you know may dream of learning the secret of the Universal Mind, bring him/her with you and make some cash.
>
> This will be the experience of your life; you will build a solid cosmic consciousness and congregate with highly spiritual people.
>
> Be there!
>
> — Dr. Turi

Students feedback

UK Student - I found Dr. Turi's course very well presented and easy to understand. Even though I am an astrologer myself, I found the course useful for talking to people from an astrological point of view by just knowing their month of birth.

Cheers,

— Gerald

Do this course and stop wasting your time, energy and money! Dr Turi has created a great, accurate, affordable new experience for any student of astrology whether you are a proficient or novice student of the ancient cosmology school. The course is audio, very clear and revelent. You are placed in the first day of a class where you are learning with those of simular interests, while being in the comfort of your own home, office or other enviornment.

This is discussion of griot teaching, where ASTROLOGY is freely spoken. Dr. Turi a native of France discusses the divine astrology used by ancient seers to counsel the aristocracy and nobility of those times. Nostradamus the great prophet used a particular system of which Dr. Turi is the expert for our times, (he is also a son of Provence, France the birth place of Nostradamus.)

Learning by hearing, remembering, speaking the spiritual science of Divine Astrology, Astro Psychology, and the balance of the mystical path of the major and minor arcane known as tarot, Dr. Turi's students are being eQuipped with all the tools they will need to understand mysteries transformed into useful powers and practice.Sign by sign, house by house, relationship by relationship until the process of life, death and rebirth are well communicated, received and understood. You will find Dr. Turi ripping past the norm and opening your eyes to the reality that once looked only like a possibility.

Reincarnation is discussed and Dr. Louis Turi discusses what progress is all about how the soul journeys and how karmic debt is collected or repaid. Fascinating lectures, additionally speak of the beastly powers of organized crime, government, media, religion, military, education and medicine and what you and I can do to bring enlightenemt, balance and harmony in spite of the chaos so many are living through to our lives.There is follow up by email, newletters, forum that help support your studies. Dr. As you can tell I am a fan of this man and his work. The convincer for me came years ago as his observations and predictions came true as he spoke them for me at a program he did in Arizona back in 1991.

C'est magnifique!

— Dr. Cheryl Golden.

What I liked best about this course is Dr. Turi's eagerness to share his knowledge. He has a generosity of spirit to get this information out into the world. To do that, he has had to develop a method using metaphor and symbolism that would enable ordinary folks to grasp the message quickly so as to be able to apply it accurately in a way to improve life. I suspect this has cost him more than people realize in terms of time, commitment, energy and perhaps even ridicule and danger. For that, I thank him. It's a great course...fun, exciting and very informative. For the rest of my life, I will see things in a new light.

Thank you again,

—Carol Bucklew

Dr. Turi has several books out...that I have found to be very beneficial in understanding His Material & explains...very simply & in depth...how He arrives at His predictions. He is a "straight forward" type of Individual who has...through experience & hardship...been able to bring to light....a form of exact Astrology (from the Stars) termed... Astropsychology. Dr. Turi has been able to calibrate....an understanding of celestial bodies...their energies & effects...closely affiliated with a "Nostradamus" Style of accuracy!

I came across Dr. Turi's Astropsychology...while searching for more information on...Astrology & the planets effects on daily life. In My Life quest...to understand...more of what makes up individuality...I have studied many Sciences... including Graphology (the study of handwriting, doodles& scribbles, etc.) also Psychology & Social Sciences & Behavior modifications....along with Medical effects of medications verses herbal applications & genetics. My study of the "Advance Astropsychology by Dr. Turi" has enhanced My understanding of what makes up individual make up & some good reasons as to why We often do "what We do" in certain situations...due to certain aspects of planetary involvement & the energies that effect...at any given moment in time. His "Gift" of knowledge...transferred to the written word....has simplified... (.a complicated format given in Main Stream Astrology)...with a more precise definition of "cause & effect."

I have always questioned everything that I have come in contact with...in My Life & Dr. Turi's Work ..is no exception! I have pulled apart...bits of information...& have searched on My own. Given My understanding of His work...through His advanced course...I have found His format to be "impeccable" in "accuracy!" The greatest advantage...to becoming a Student...is that this knowledge can be applied...on a day to day basis...not only for Your own personal use...but in every day interaction with the people around You!

I have always had a belief that knowledge forms a protection...which helps in assessing the World around Me. The more informed You are of the dynamics of the people around You...the better the options...of making informed choices in Your Life.

I wish You well in Your search for knowledge.

— Marianne K

From: Mary
To: Dr.Turi@cox.net
Sent: Saturday, August 23, 2003 1:33 PM
Subject: book

Thank you, Dr. Turi.

I was very fortunate in finding your book "The Power of the Dragon"! You have taught me so much, and I just wanted to write to say I am so grateful to you. I have been studying astrology for 18 years and have been toying with the idea of using the solar chart as well as the Placidus system and you confirmed my thoughts that it is correct but to use the zero point instead of the sun degree. I have seen it work with many charts correctly.

I also am thankful for your teachings of the nodes as most astrologers do not really understand them well and some do not even focus on them much going so far as not even putting the south node in the chart which I have never understood. You have given me so much and I am eternally thankful to you.

— Mary Kanz
Cedar Rapids, IA

Hello Dr. Turi,

Hi, this is Veronica (aka january) how are you, and your girls doing??? hope fine, Ihad to write to you, because your class was one of the most intense and exiting experiences I ever had!!! Also, something amazing happened. after graduating, Laurent and I went to a restaurant to have lunch, and to celebrate our accomplishment. And you won't believe what happened. There was a lady talking on the phone (she seemed to know the people who work there, or maybe she was one of the owner's, because she was on the bussiness phone). She was yelling like a crazy woman, and crying. Curiously, Laurent and I were the only two clients there at the time, and couldn't help but to get a bit irritated by that screaming crazy lady. I kept on looking back at her to see what the hell was going on. And suddenly, she was in front of us, calling us names for even doing eye contact. She asked if she could sit and I moved over offering her a seat right next to me. She sat, I could see without a doubt that she was in such pain, it hurt, I could feel it too!!! I was just about to talk to her, when Laurent, who was afraid of her and what she could do, told her to get up and leave us alone. She did. Then Laurent and I guessed she must be a Pisces, and have some strong planets such as Mars and Mercury in her sun sign and first house. After a couple of minutes, she came back, and apologized for being rude. She explained that her husband was filing for divorce, and that he is getting the kids. she loves her kids and that she needed them in her life. I moved over once again and looked at Laurent. He offered her a seat, and we both decided to do her chart to help her out with her situation. Well, I just happened to have my ephemeris with me (we just picked it up after class- before going to the restaurant). So we pulled out her planets, and guess what??? She was a Pisces with Venus and Mercury in her 1st house, in addition to that she had Saturn!!! WOW!! I asked her if her ex-husband was a foreigner (because the tail of her dragon was in Sagittarius) and she said yes. We tried to explain to her that she shouldn't drink (she was soooooooooooooo drunk) because she had Neptune (deception) in her 9th house of foreigneers in Scorpio!!! She also had Libra in her 8th house of life and death!!! She also had Pluto (danger), Mars(agressiveness), and Uranus (unusual way of expressing oneself) in her 7th house of marriage in Virgo. But unfortunately she being drunk, and having Taurus in her 3rd house of the mind didn't help us much because she would interrupt us constantly, and was soooo stuborn about letting go of her relationship, keeping sober, and fighting for her kids. Interesting enough the moon was in Libra (contracts and relationships), the moon will be in Scorpio today, which means her Neptune planet will keep her drinking her problems away, and Sunday the full moon will be in Sagittarius (her tail of the dragon). Laurent and I are completely sure she won't make it past this sunday. She will probably kill herself. What a shame, she was a pretty girl, and looked pretty smart too (when sober). The amazing part is : 1-the universe asked us to get the ephemeris because this was going to happen, 2-we saw her problems as clear as water, 3-this was such a test of our abilities and our passion for helping people and bringing the light. Dr Turi, I am ready to start fullfilling my mission. and it is all thanks to you, Crissy, and Madeline!!!! we are so exited, we can't wait to see what's in store for us!!!

THANKS!!!!!!!!!!!!!!!!

— WITH LOVE
VERONICA (JANUARY)

Hi Veronica,

Dr. Turi sent me your email. I want to add that this is the beauty of his work. It opens the intuitional domain. I have done that many times—guessed some planet in a sign, by the way a person behaved. When you think about how remarkable that is, to know what planet was in which constellation in the sky at the moment of a person's birth, is truely a signal that Astropsychology is absolutely real, and works. When Dr. Turi says this class will "open your third eye" and give you "cosmic consciousness", he is NOT KIDDING!!!
What a great story

— Madeline

Dear Dr. Turi,

I cannot express in enough words how I enjoyed your class. I did not want it to end. I could have gone on another week. I was not ready to leave. I had to leave right after the test to catch my plane at the airport. I looked for you to say good bye, but you had gone. The only thing I regret is that I missed the Jordan Maxwell lecture Friday, because I got lost and could not find the conference hall. I learned more about astrology from your class, than I have learned over the last 35 years. I will never go back to conventional astrology. You are an excellent teacher. You made the class very interesting, with your very witty, and funny personality, and sense of humor. I feel very comfortable around you. Your warm personality made me feel right at home. I feel like I could tell you all my troubles, and you would listen, and give sympathy.

Also, Madeline and the other members of your staff were really great. They were warm, friendly and very helpful. I could listen to your talk all day. Your French accent is very soothing, and a joy to listen too. You'd also make a great hypnotist with your soothing voice. You showed up in my astrocard reading. It was my first reading, therefore, I don't know what it means, but I am happy to know that we will connect sometime again in the future, for whatever reason.

Have a blessed day..

Love,

— Theresa

Dear Dr. Turi,

I liked the mix of students on the tapes, especially Chief Sonne and Claudine!

Dr. Turi you had an excellent program structure, so when you went through the signs, planets and houses you were focused and exceptional in imparting your knowledge.

You are an awesome teacher!

The hidden dragon in ones' chart was the icing on the cake - that really pulled everything together to show the true essence and accuracy of Divine Astrology. Finally, the opening Indian ceremony and closing session were especially memorable and made me feel like part of the class – being there in spirit!

—Eileen

Dear Dr. Turi:

As you know I have been working in the field of Traditional Chinese Medicine for almost thirty years. At the time I was trained there were just the beginnings of schools in this art in this country. Dr. Turi's training reminds me of the roots and traditionalism of my original training. There are no recipes and no short cuts. There is also no dogma or preaching.

Dr. Turi expertly illustrates his teaching from a variety of angles until the facts become an unconscious aspect of the student's life. He is factual and vivid and addresses a current age with traditional concepts.

This is the Astropsychology of today with roots in the past. One of the most outstanding aspects of the course is the many pragmatic uses I can envision. I can already see it's usefulness in business planning, lifestyle decisions and health ramifications.

Dr. Turi has developed a tool for anyone with emotions and a developing lifestyle.

I find the information so practical that I can not compare this course to other astrology philosophies that I am aware of. I have been seeking this information for over thirty years and during the very first tape of Dr. Turi's course I gained more understanding than the other thirty years.

I applaud Dr. Turi for making this fine tool available to those with the vision and understanding to "see" and only hope that I will prove a worthy student.

Please feel comfortable sharing this letter with our teacher and anyone else who can benefit.

Thank you for everything.

Yours truly,

— Tilottama Star, L.Ac.

Dr. Turi:

I wanted to let you know the Astropsychology class in Portland has changed my life! You are an amazing speaker and have incredible POWER. You are too generous to share 30 years of information in 5 days. I am happy you are apart of my life, to help me with my spiritual awareness and to help others learn the stars. Thank you for flying to Portland, and your time. I am forever grateful to you!

Love and Light,

— Lisa

Hello Dr. Turi;

I have just returned from the July Astropsychology class. What a unique and enlightening experience! Besides the valuable knowledge given, Dr. Turi himself makes the class challenging and entertaining. By the end of the week, I could see the reflex action of intuition beginning to form in everyone who was there. I did not think such a thing could be possible. It is a life changing experience, and one can never view the world in quite the same way. When Dr. Turi says, "you will be given the keys to the Universal Mind", he really means it! I encourage anyone who is thinking of attending, to go, as I guarantee they will be raised in spirit. My blessings to all who attend this course in the future.

— Madeline

Dear Dr.Turi,
We are thankful for the profound blessing of enlightenment shared with our July Astropsychology class. With your guidance, we - reunited old souls in the Arizona desert - rededicated ourselves to the vision of sharing Astropsychology with the children of the world, who will carry it forward as the only practical spiritual philosophy of the emerging Aquarian cycle. The highest of spiritual world is now in our hands. Together we are changing the human world into a world of light and awareness. With much love Chief

— Sonne and Claudine

Dear Dr. Turi;

Definitely Divine Astrology for me, I have never been exposed to any Astrology before hearing Dr. Turi on Jeff Rense's national program, but if modern Astrology is littered with mathematical jargon then it is more of a hand down Win for Divine Astrology. The favorite part for me was Dr. Turi's great humor through out the tapes, I of course need to practice the reflex and know it will get more interesting when I receive my computer program and plug in people I know birth dates to practice with the housing system.

Thank you,

— Joyce

To Dr. Turi;

I have just returned from the July Astropsychology class, and it was the greatest class I ever attended. Dr. Turi is the one of the best teacher I have ever known. I have learnt so much from this man. This class is a must for every one. If you want to soar with the eagles and be number one in your field as an astrologer and to help every one that will be in your life take the class. For it is truly enlightenment. Thank you once again Dr. Turi for all that you have taught me.

Love & light

— Alice Brooks

To all prospective Astropsychology students;

It has now been one week since I have completed Dr. Turi's advanced astrology course in Phoenix AZ. It has been about five months since I passed his basic astrology class by mail. I am here to state that I absorbed so much more information and reflex in five days of hands on schooling, than I could ever imagine getting in months of home study. Don't get me wrong, the home course I hold very dearly, and It was an excellent prerequisite, and I highly recommend it, but it only put me on the runway, where as traveling to AZ. to get hands on schooling, placed me in the air. I guess it depends on what you want to do with the knowledge, and how fast you want to do it. Myself I planned to make a career out of it, and I knew that the home course would eventually produce those results. Now having completed the advanced course, I now face that reality. My new career has now sprouted, and I owe it all to one incredible man, Dr. Louis Turi. There are not enough kind words to describe this incredibly gifted, spiritual pioneer. To be taught by him is a great honor, and pure enlightenment. There is no doubt that you will notice that he has a little something different to offer, something you won't find anywhere else. With that I leave it up to you, the prospective student to find that answer.

Thank You,

— Charles

Hi Dr. Turi,

There is a driving force of energy that moves and propels us in our quest for the truth, and the truth does not lie in any one area. This truth that the seeker seeks, lays scattered through out our planet. So we as we seek must be patient and discerning when we come across the path of others speaking the truth. And from my discernment and the trust of my heart, I feel very fortunate and blessed to have crossed paths with Dr. Turi in this time of life. Dr. Turi's wisdom and understanding is a vast as the stars he speaks of. I am thankful that we taped the seminar! Thank You again for sharing your wisdom of the stars! Many Blessings,

— James

Thanks Dr. Turi

You are the greatest. Learning to do astrology the way you do it has made such a difference in my life. I use it all day long every day. My birthday is ///, I have the stars to teach astrology and that is what I want to do, I do it all day long for everyone around me I can't help myself, I see it in the news, the weather, everything everywhere, my cats and dogs, it's wonderful. It is nice to know who you are dealing with, where is Nept? What will you lie about. Where is Pl. what part of your life do you rearrange all of the time. Where is Jupt. What do you want to learn and teach, where will you expand and be lucky. I have Jupt in the 1st house I want to teach. It is all so wonderful. One of these days I am going to call Jeff Rense when you are on the air and ask some general questions, so people can see how powerful it is. Wind heat and fires for the next two years. With the DT in Sag. and Pl. in Sag the list is long for what this will bring. Thank you so much Dr. Turi.

— Barbara

Dear Dr. Turi,

After finishing your Advanced Astropsychology class, my dream state has been enhanced. I've always journeyed my dreams, and I can see a change of consciousness in myself. The Universal Mind has certainly come to new life. It's exciting to meet new people and see the qualities that the stars have influenced in their lives. It helps one to have a more open mind to personality traits that would normally be unpleasant, to understanding what makes people tick. For me, it has made me a more compassionate, understanding person. With the help of your teachings, I've learned the future is the reincarnation of thoughts today. I'm thinking and planning my future with light and love for a beautiful new life. It is just the beginning of great things to come. Thank you for all you've done for me. Thank you for being such a beautiful channel of light in this world.

Your student,

— Kiki

Please help me promote the cosmic consciousness of everyone you care about by contacting me to set up a class in your city and benefit from our deal. You will get the full advanced Astropsychology course for free or you will save $100 per person you bring with you. I need both your spiritual and financial help to build many Astropsychology schools for the children of tomorrow. Understand the importance of my mission and be a part of it in the unfolding world karma. Please help me and invest in the future in promoting the true knowledge of the stars. Your contributions will help me so that I can spend more time on the air, writing, educating and publishing my work to those in need. For centuries many resources have been wasted in discrediting the stars, and for dangerous religious dogmas. Times have changed and the stars above do impose a new consciousness for mankind. Be a promoter of light and invest in the true light. The children of tomorrow need to gain cosmic consciousness and use the stars to live a more productive and safe life. Please communicate my work and help those in need to find guidance, comfort, direction and assistance in the celestial order. You will find the pathway to the stars and the realization of God's ultimate will throughout the Universe.

> "When suffering is on all sides and man hungers for the unmanifested mystery in all phenomenon, He seeks reflection of the Divine. God's higher truths are cloaked in his creation and the message is in the stars."
>
> — Nostradamus

Comments to: Dr. Turi@cox.net

LA Class Summer 2002

U.K. Course April 2005 Class

Phoenix July 2001 Class

U.K. Course April 2005 Class

www.ingramcontent.com/pod-product-compliance
Lightning Source LLC
LaVergne TN
LVHW091027080826
845145LV00002B/384

* 9 7 8 0 9 7 4 5 2 0 9 7 1 *